# DRAFTED!

## MY YEAR IN VIETNAM

## MORGAN MILLER

W. Brand Publishing
NASHVILLE, TENNESSEE

j.brand@wbrandpub.com
W. Brand Publishing
www.wbrandpub.com

Cover design: JuLee Brand / designchik.net
Cover photo: Author's personal collection
Cover photo ripped effect and colorization: Malia Kealaluhi

*Drafted!* / Morgan Miller –1st ed.

Available in Large Print Paperback, Paperback, Kindle, and eBook formats.
Large Print Paperback: 978-1-956906-81-3
Paperback: 978-1-956906-82-0
eBook: 978-1-956906-83-7
Library of Congress Control Number: 2023917021

# CONTENTS

As a helicopter pilot, I had the privilege of returning to base each night, savoring a hot meal and nestling into a cozy, warm bed. In heartfelt tribute, I dedicate this book to the valiant Army and Marine infantrymen who courageously served in the unforgiving jungles of Vietnam. Their nights were arduous, spent in bug-ridden, enemy-infested forests, often enduring relentless downpours.

I reserve a special place in my heart for my dear friend from Borrego Springs, Ric Deichler, who exemplified unwavering valor as a member of the 503rd Airborne Infantry during the harrowing Battle of Dak To in November 1967.

# AUTHOR'S NOTE

This is a work of creative nonfiction. The events in this memoir have been recounted to the best of the author's memory, others may express different memories of the people and events mentioned herein. To avoid repetition and for dramatic effect, some events and missions are a combination of occurrences, not all of which happened concurrently. The author admits to a degree of poetic licence. Some names and identifying features have been changed or combined to protect the identity of certain parties.

The author in no way represents any company, corporation, or brand, mentioned herein. The views expressed in this memoir are solely those of the author.

**Morgan Miller** (2023)

# FOREWORD

I knew very little about the Vietnam war before I met Henry Morgan Miller and helped him with his book. Sure, I knew the background history; Walter Cronkite's intense broadcasts are hard to forget when you are of a certain age. But reading Morgan's manuscript for the first time cut through all the rhetoric and let me see the war from the perspective of a new, raw recruit. Someone who didn't choose to put their life on the line. I was pleasantly surprised that his approach was almost matter-of-fact, taking the reader through the day-to-day life of a draftee who becomes a Cobra helicopter pilot.

Don't misunderstand, there's plenty of drama and excitement; the blood-chilling reality of war is never far from the surface. For instance, I'd never before heard of hunter/killer missions. It's hard to believe there has not been more mainstream coverage of this highly dangerous tactic. During a hunter/killer mission, a pilot navigates a small Scout helicopter low and slow over enemy territory with the explicit intention of drawing fire. It's like, *here I am shoot me down if you dare*! If the helicopter is not fired upon, the aircraft's observer will machine-gun the edge of the jungle to encourage retaliatory fire. Once the enemy engages, a Cobra gunship swoops down with the big guns and wipes out the enemy position.

*Drafted!* tells the story of Henry Morgan Miller's year in Vietnam at the invitation of Lyndon B. Johnson. It is the story of a meat-cutter—wannabe commercial airline pilot—whose life was rudely interrupted by being inducted into a war that he considered someone else's battle for a lost cause. Other than the meat-cutter/commercial pilot bit, that could describe many of the almost 300,000 men drafted in 1968 along with Morgan, or, for that matter, the 1.85

million drafted between 1964-73. It is the story of your brother, your son, your friend—some who came home safe and sound, and others who perished, or were no longer whole.

In his book, Morgan also exposes a major mechanical issue with Vietnam-era Cobra helicopters; so serious that had they been Ford cars they would have been subject to a major recall. He suggests that Cobra helicopter pilots were guinea-pigs for aircraft plagued with serious, not to mention deadly, hydraulic problems.

*Drafted*! is for readers who want to experience what it was like, on a day-to-day basis, to go through basic training, learn to fly gunships, and then be shipped out to the Vietnam warzone. What it's like to be shot at and shot down. To serve your country honorably, while fighting a war you don't believe in, only to return and be ostracized by a misguided faction of the general public.

The original title of Morgan's book was *A Life Interrupted*, but the book is more than that, it's about a young man doing what he has to do to survive. It's about stepping up and doing the right thing, serving his country. *Drafted*! provides readers with a "lived" experience. If you've ever wondered what it was like to suffer the indignities of learning to be a soldier or flying into battle in a mechanically dubious Cobra gunship, then read on.

**Mike Wicks** (*Wall Street Journal* Bestselling Author)

# CHAPTER 1

# DRAFTED

Sunday, June 28, 1968, was perfect until it wasn't. The temperature reached eighty-one degrees; the sky was clear and the wind light—ideal conditions for our flight home from Big Bear Airport in the San Bernardino Mountains, about 106 miles almost due north of San Diego. I was flying a Cessna 172 Skyhawk; back then, you could rent the plane for $20 per flying hour. Today, it's around $200.

My girlfriend, Marcheta, and I were returning from a long weekend away at Big Bear Resort. As I started my descent over Palomar Mountain thirty miles north of Gillespie Field and thirty-seven miles northeast of downtown San Diego, Marcheta reached out, squeezed my hand lightly and smiled warmly. We'd just had a fantastic weekend at a first-class resort. *Life was good.* I was a lucky, proud man. Marcheta was 5'4", confident, intelligent, athletic and, back in those less-than-politically-correct-times, other guys would turn their heads whenever she walked into a room— with or without me.

I'd gotten my private pilot's license just over four years earlier. It was my dad who introduced me to flying. He correctly sensed that academia wasn't for me and asked his friend Stan Dehart to take me up in his airplane. I think my father thought that if I became interested in flying, I might make it as an airline pilot. He was right. I quickly became enthralled with flying. By the time of the Big Bear trip, I was only thirty hours short of being able to apply for my commercial pilot's check ride, where an FAA flight examiner would test my aeronautical knowledge, risk management, and flight proficiency. Getting my commercial pilot certificate was the first step toward getting paid to fly. As you will see, part of my dream came true, only in a nightmare sort of way.

• • • • •

Marcheta and I met during our first year in college. We took several classes together, became friends, and a few years later broke off our high-school relationships to go steady with one another. Neither of us graduated, so she went to work full-time for her father. He owned Cottonwood Golf Club, nestled in the hills of Rancho San Diego, just five miles from El Cajon.

I was less fortunate. My father and I struck a deal that if I went to college for two years to get an associate degree, I could live at home rent-free. He would buy all my textbooks and give me $20 a week for gas, which left me a little spending money. The catch was that I had to earn "C" grades or better, or the deal was off. All the time I was at college, I'd told him I was doing fine, but the truth caught up with me. I'd received three "D" grades in mandatory classes and failed to graduate.

His look of disappointment was difficult to take, and I had no doubt what was coming. Dad was a man of his word, and his patience ran out. He kicked me out of the house and told me I had to find a place to live. My father was a lieutenant colonel in the army reserve, so I was no stranger to his discipline.

When I was seventeen, I received three traffic violations in as many weeks. My dad and I were summoned to appear before a juvenile court judge. The judge read the citations and then turned to my father and asked him what he felt would be a fair punishment. Without hesitation, he said, "Suspend his license for six months."

The judge looked at my father and smiled slightly, "I agree; here's his license, give it back to him on June 15th."

When I flunked out of college, my dad didn't let me off with a warning like he did when I, at the tender age of nine, sassed my mom, and she told him to discipline me. He grabbed his Sigma Kai paddle and dragged me to my bedroom. Once the door was closed, he lowered his voice, looked at me sternly, and said, "Son, this sassing back to your mother needs to stop right now! Got it?" I nodded as tears stung my eyes. "Now, I'm going to hit your bed with this paddle four or five times. Each time I do it, you need to yell out. Okay?" I did as I was told and had a newfound respect for my father. Dad repeated this performance on several occasions before my mother became suspicious and quietly walked in on the scene. She said, "I should have known better," shook her head and left. Dad and I smiled sheepishly at each other.

Tough love often has a way of helping you mature. I moved in with Bill James, my high school buddy. I'd worked at the local Food Basket grocery store through college, so I had some savings and was still earning a modest wage; I could afford to pay half the rent with a bit of belt-tightening. In January 1964, shortly after I moved in with Bill, Food Basket had an opening for an apprentice meat cutter. I applied and was accepted as a State of California Meat Cutter Apprentice. Six months later, Marcheta and I moved in together.

• • • • •

Traveling back from the airport to our second-floor, two-bedroom apartment in El Cajon, sixteen miles east of San Diego, *Mrs. Robinson* played on the radio. We'd seen Dustin Hoffman playing Benjamin Braddock in *The Graduate* the previous December, and the character's uncertainty about what he wanted to do with his life resonated with us. Still, we both felt we were beginning to get on the right track.

El Cajon translates to "the box" in Spanish and refers to the shape of the valley where the city sits; it also gives the city its nickname. Our apartment was fifteen minutes from the golf course where Marcheta worked. Life was playing out nicely. We had well-paying jobs and were saving diligently to buy a place of our own. As a meat cutter apprentice, my starting pay was $3.10 an hour, with good benefits. This was a good wage at the time and helped make flight training a possibility.

It was approaching ninety degrees when we arrived home. As I carried our bags upstairs, sweat dripped from my forehead; Marcheta went to pick up the mail. I joked that there would only be bills. I'd no sooner dropped the bags in the bedroom than Marcheta appeared at the door, tears streaming down her face. In the few minutes since arriving home, her manner changed from relaxed and carefree to mournful. I thought someone must have died. I moved toward her, my arms outstretched to embrace her and to make things better. But she stepped back and, with two hands, her arms outstretched, held up a beige envelope marked with the words "Selective Service – Official Business."

Neither of us spoke for the several seconds it took us to absorb the reality that our lives were about to take a dramatic turn, and not for the better. My hands trembled as I tore open the envelope and read "Order To Report For Induction." I looked at the order: The President of the United States, to Henry Morgan Miller, Greetings. The incongruity of the word "greetings" made me smile, but only for a second. I had thirty days to report for duty.

I'd avoided the draft for two years by attending college. I then extended my 2S deferment by getting into a state-approved apprenticeship program. In truth, I'd been trying to age out and thought by now I was too old to attract Uncle Sam's attention.

In 1968, all men between eighteen and twenty-six were eligible for the draft, with those between eighteen-and-a-half and twenty-five most vulnerable. To say that receiving the draft notice was unexpected is an understatement. My first thought was, *why me?*

As I read the warning in bold, red ink, "Failure to comply with this induction notice is a federal offense," my dream of becoming an airline pilot began to fade. Marcheta looked forlorn; her shoulders slumped, and she no longer looked like the confident young woman of a few minutes ago. I looked at her and said softly, "I guess I'll be heading to Vietnam." She stared at the draft notice in my hand as if it was a death sentence. It might as well have been.

Over the next few days, a sense of inevitability mixed with doom crept over us. We hadn't spoken much about the letter, which silently taunted us from the hallway table. We each processed the news in our own ways. In hindsight, getting our thoughts out in the open would have been healthier. I suggested a night out. Marcheta stood silent with her arms folded defensively. She looked at me for a second, then forced a weak smile, shrugged, and almost imperceptibly pursed her lips, lifting her chin in agreement.

She mentioned that Kenny Rogers and The First Edition were playing at our go-to restaurant, the Red Coat Inn. We agreed that the distraction would help ease the tension and the feeling of dread that overcame us. During the drive to the restaurant, the mood was gloomy and distant.

The Red Coat Inn had a large dance floor with a disco ball hanging from the ceiling. It was a popular hangout because it also housed a bowling alley that offered midnight bowling. When we arrived, the band was singing "Things Can't Be So Sad." As we waited for our hamburgers to come, The First Edition launched into "Rainbows on a Cloudy Day"—the universe was trying to tell me something. So was Marcheta, but it wasn't something I wanted to hear.

I pulled myself away from the music and tuned into what she was saying. She looked at me squarely and said, "I think we should fast-track our wedding." I felt cornered, like a rat in a drainpipe. Marriage was the *last* thing on my mind. I turned my attention back to the band and listened for a minute or two. I could feel Marcheta waiting for me to say something. I thought of the Animals' song,

"I Gotta Get Out of this Place," which at the time was resonating with American troops in Vietnam. The song became an anthem; a band couldn't perform at an Armed Forces Club without the audience demanding that song.

After pushing food around my plate for a few seconds, I said, "I think we should revisit marriage after I've completed basic training." I was still thunderstruck by the news. My life was about to be turned upside down; my goals and dreams evaporated. It felt like I was about to jump out of a plane without a parachute. The last thing I wanted to think about was getting married.

She nodded, but her eyes showed she vehemently disagreed with me. Marcheta was generally calm and composed, but she could also be determined and competitive. She was one of the most beautiful women in the El Cajon valley. Her fearless spirit was apparent whenever we played football at the beach with friends. She'd play quarterback and outrun the defensive guys. One time at the beach, a friend, who was a wide receiver in high school, took me aside; he said, "Morgan, that girl of yours plays like a guy." He was right; she could throw huge distances and straight as an arrow. She was almost always quiet and reserved, and I'd never seen her lose her temper, so the look in her eyes as the mirror ball flickered cubes of light over her face drove stakes into my heart.

As planned, after dinner, we went to the bowling alley, where we ran into one of my old high school football teammates. Skip Newman was 6'2" and weighed 180 pounds. He'd played right defensive end at school, and though he was a little light for the position, he possessed the speed, agility, and stopping power of someone far bigger. He was tough and determined, traits I would eventually witness firsthand.

The last time I'd seen him was when he was leaving for the army almost two years earlier. He'd filled out; he looked toned and tough. He smiled and introduced us to his girlfriend, Judy. "I'm on leave from Fort Bragg," he said, "I just completed Special Forces Training."

Inadequately, all I could utter was, "Wow!"

I was impressed. No wonder Skip looked super fit and every inch a professional soldier; he'd just survived some of the most brutal military training in the world. He went on to tell us that his next posting was to South Korea for further training before heading to Vietnam. When they left to go and eat, Marcheta and I talked about the war for a while and then we bowled; I scored a 200—I'd always had a good eye. Over the next few weeks, my thoughts rarely strayed far from the Vietnam War.

• • • • •

I'd been a fan of Walter Cronkite for years and followed him on *CBS Evening News.* Cronkite was a unifying figure in American culture. His steadfast, professional boots-on-the-ground reporting was balanced with true grit and genuine heart. Cronkite's stern, yet comforting delivery was legendary, but I remember he showed his true humanity when he displayed a momentary loss of composure to report that President John F. Kennedy was felled by a successful assassination attempt in 1963. Cronkite was like America's grandfather, always there to uphold the tenets that made democracy great. He was also there to educate, support, and comfort his viewers in challenging times and celebrate with them in wondrous, happy times. Walter Cronkite was the most trusted voice in U.S. media. His sign-off line, *And that's the way it is,* rang true in my current situation. Watching Cronkite anchoring the news was my weeknight ritual throughout the 1960s—6:00 p.m. on the dot. Everything I knew about the war came from listening to Mr. Cronkite. In those days after my call to duty arrived, I recalled what I knew about the war and our involvement.

South Vietnam was a capitalist republic, and the American government's foreign policy was to contain the spread of communism; therefore, supporting South Vietnam was crucial. In the 1950s, President Eisenhower sent several hundred military personnel, military aid, and funding to South Vietnam. In 1961, President Kennedy sent 500 special forces troops and military advisers to shore up support. A year later, there were more than 10,000 advisers in the country.

The South Vietnamese government fell on November 1, 1963, and President Ngo Dinh Diem was assassinated the following day. Fewer than three weeks later, Lee Harvey Oswald assassinated President Kennedy.

The Gulf of Tonkin Incident was the catalyst for America to become embroiled in the war. On August 2, 1964, the destroyer USS Maddox was attacked by three North Vietnamese torpedo boats and reportedly again two days later—although there is doubt whether the second attack occurred. Another destroyer, the USS Turner Joy, went to assist during the first incident and was itself attacked. As a result of these attacks, the Gulf of Tonkin Resolution was put before the U.S. Congress. Once passed, it gave President Johnson the wide-ranging constitutional authority to escalate American military involvement in the Vietnam War. The attack on the Maddox and the ensuing media coverage had been enough to encourage some of my high school friends to enlist.

February 1965 saw Cronkite reporting on troops arriving in South Vietnam. Among the first on the ground were Marines sent to protect U.S. Air Force bases. In March, Cronkite reported that the 173rd Airborne Brigade—consisting of 3,500 men—was sent to Vietnam. Over 10,000 troops from the 1st Cavalry Division and marine and army combat units joined them a few months later.

The Battle of la Drang was fought between November 14-18, 1965, and it resulted in the deaths of more than 300 Americans. It was the first significant American engagement of the war[1].

Just before Christmas 1967, Cronkite announced that, to date, 16,250 U.S. military personnel had been killed in action. Several of my close friends served their time and returned from Vietnam.

---

1. https://www.vvmf.org/topics/Ia-Drang/

Luckily, most completed their tours without ever running into the enemy. My friend Dennis Weaver was not so lucky. Wounded in action, he spoke very little about his time in Vietnam. The less he said, the greater the impact on me.

I kept hoping Cronkite would report that the war would end soon. Instead, his reports centered on our increasing military involvement in this faraway land. Then, on January 31, 1968, the North Vietnamese attacked over 100 locations in South Vietnam, including U.S. military bases. The Tet Offensive coincided with the Tet holiday, Vietnam's new year celebration. The American public had been led to believe the North Vietnamese were almost defeated and incapable of such audacious attacks. On February 27, 1968, Cronkite went to South Vietnam to witness the battle for the city of Hue, where, he said, the communists had come closer to seizing the city than anywhere else.[2]

Less than a week later, he declared that the only reasonable conclusion given the circumstances was that "we" were mired in stalemate. He said, *"It is increasingly clear to this reporter that the only rational way out of Vietnam will be to negotiate, not as victors, but as an honorable people who lived up to their pledge to defend democracy and did the best they could."*[3]

Two weeks after the North Vietnamese attacks, casualties exceeded 3,000, most of whom were South Vietnamese soldiers. The death toll brought the conflict front and center for all American citizens, who began demanding that the U.S. government stop interfering in the politics of other countries and immediately get our boys out of danger and back to the safety of U.S. soil. Support for America's involvement in Vietnam plummeted from eighty percent to forty-six percent, and anti-war protests became increasingly common nationwide.

• • • • •

2. https://youtu.be/wJnJfYBA0es
3. *CBS Evening News*, February 27, 1968

I called my parents the morning after we went bowling. Mom answered, and I told her that I'd been drafted. Without saying a word to me, she screamed out. "Bing! Morgan's been drafted." I could hear my father say something in the background, and Mom told me that Dad would call me back. Hearing Mom refer to Dad by his nickname made me smile. My father was an excellent singer, and his friends always said he sounded like Bing Crosby, so he was forever called Bing. I hung up and said to Marcheta, "I can't believe it; he didn't even come to the phone, just said he'd call back."

An hour later, there was a knock on the door; it was my father. "You didn't need to drive over, Dad," I said.

"Are you kidding me? Of course, I did. You're my only son, and this is big. Get me a coffee, and let me see that draft notice." Once he had his coffee, we sat in the kitchen, "You know you can request a thirty-day extension, don't you?"

"No, I didn't, but why the heck would I want to do that? It only postpones the inevitable. I wish I could leave tomorrow and get the damned thing over with."

He looked across the table and said, "Well, son, I agree with you."

It was a peacetime draft; America had not declared war, nor would it. I was to join thousands of other young Americans fighting someone else's battle for a lost cause. I felt like I was no longer in charge of my own life. Overnight I'd gone from a budding commercial pilot to a name and number on a dog tag.

CHAPTER 2

# SAYING GOODBYE

The huevos rancheros at the Pancake House in El Cajon were
good; hot and spicy, just the way I liked them. It was Sunday, July 28, a month to the day since I received the letter
from the president inviting me to join his war. Technically, of
course, it wasn't a war; it was a conflict. But, potato, po-*tah*-to, I
wished I could just call the whole thing off.

Had it been later in the day, I would have considered this my
last supper, but it was 6:30 a.m. and the day was already heating
up. After breakfast, Dad drove Marcheta and me, along with our
Moms, to the Greyhound bus terminal in downtown San Diego.

As we pulled into the bus station, I noticed other recruits with
their families milling about. Everyone looked tense and awkward,
and many were crying. We parked and found a spot closer to where
my bus would leave. Buses arrived and departed, leaving behind a
thick odor of diesel fumes and wafts of hot, stale air in their wakes.
I was hoping that we'd manage to say our goodbyes quickly, and
I could leave, but there was a loud crackle, like someone rustling
parchment paper. A tinny voice announced, "The charter bus to
Fort Ord has a minor mechanical problem and will leave one hour
later than scheduled."

Mom and Dad were not coping well with my imminent departure, which made saying goodbye more difficult. Their faces were
strained, and Mom's face was streaked with tears. I was their only

*11*

son and could imagine the scenarios they feared and visualized during the last month. A knock on the door. Two somber officers standing there as they handed my parents my dog tags. The last things I ever wore. The last items to touch my skin. Two pieces of stainless steel that represented me. When I was alive and when I was dead. I stood silently and tried to wish the time away, and eventually, the bus driver called us to board, and a well-choreographed mass "hug-a-thon" took place. The emotional quotient in the air ratcheted up, the tears flowed, and all I wanted to do was get on the bus. I hugged my mom and dad, and held Marcheta close for as long as I could. Despite my wish to just get on the bus already, there was part of me that never wanted to let her go, that perhaps, if I embraced her long enough, this would all go away and we would just go back home and make lunch and carry on as if this was all just a bad dream.

The bus was hot and dusty, even with the windows cracked open. There was an empty window seat next to a young Black kid, so I asked him if the seat was taken. He looked up and said, "No, help yourself, sir."

*Sir.*

My eyes swept the bus, and I realized I was probably the oldest person on board except for the timeworn driver with his salt and pepper beard and long grey hair. I smiled, offered my hand, and said, "My name's Morgan; what's yours?"

"Merritt," he replied.

Across the aisle, some of the other recruits were talking animatedly about something happening outside on their side of the bus. Merritt stood up to see what was going on. I said, "What's all the fuss about, Merritt?"

He looked back and said, "There's an older gentleman, standing at attention saluting our bus." I stood to look, but the bus had already pulled out of the terminal. I was sad I missed such a heartfelt sign of respect.

As we headed up the I-5 freeway, the bus was quiet; everyone was wrapped up in their own thoughts. I asked Merritt what high school he attended.

"Lincoln High, in San Diego."

"Ah," I replied, "I know that school; I went to El Capitan High in east San Diego County, and our football team scrimmaged Lincoln when I was a senior back in 1960. You about eighteen?"

Merritt looked at me, smiling, "Nah, I just turned seventeen."

I'd thought he looked very young. "That means your parents had to sign off on you joining up?"

"Yep, it wasn't hard. My new stepdad wanted me out of the house, so he made my mom sign the papers."

"That's rough."

"Not really. I didn't get along with him. It was better for everyone that I left."

He looked out the window, and I wondered how much he was hurting inside. I was certain the stoic approach was just a front. Much like the "Silent Generation" that my parents came from, the Baby Boomer generation was pretty stoic; except for the hippies, of course. They talked about everything. Sometimes too much. But those of us who weren't hippies stayed away from talking about our feelings too much, and many ended up needing therapy later in their lives. When it came to war, the generation of WWII and Korean War soldiers did their duty and carried on with life afterward, never to speak of the war experience again. When Vietnam came, though, everything was different. The reasons for this war were different. Gone were the days where young men followed directions without pushing back. With Vietnam, not only were there still silent types—like Merritt seemed to be—but now there were also throngs of young men who were vehemently against the war and showed their disdain by becoming draft dodgers, peace activists, and protesters at home and abroad. Despite this new, vocal faction, many came back from Vietnam in need of major therapy, no matter how much they denied it. Soldiers needed and wanted help, but in those days, you'd be ostracized by society if you went to support groups or therapy. It wasn't a common thing amongst regular society like it is nowadays.

"What military occupational specialty did you sign up for Merritt?"

"Artillery."

"You should be safer there than where I'll be heading. I'm going into the infantry."

He looked out the window for a few seconds, his head touching the glass.

"You get drafted?

"Yeah, I thought I was too old at twenty-five, but Uncle Sam ferreted me out."

"I've heard that a lot of grunts are getting killed over in 'Nam."

I changed the subject and said, "Hey, Merritt, you have the army jargon down pretty good."

He turned and smiled, "A lot of the older guys from the neighborhood have been signing up since I was a freshman. Vietnam is all they talk about when they get back."

I nodded and looked out the window, wondering when I would see home—and Marcheta—again. The bus remained quiet, and as the freeway passed the Marine Corps Training Center at Camp Pendleton, I began remembering my childhood.

My father, as an ROTC graduate from the University of Kentucky, was training recruits at Fort Benning, Georgia, when Japan attacked Pearl Harbor on December 7, 1941. In the fall of 1942, Dad got his orders to the Pacific Theater. Mom was pregnant with me, moved to Lakeside, California, about twenty miles northeast of San Diego, and moved in with her brother, Trigg Stewart, and his wife, Doris. Trigg was a physicist and worked for the Naval Undersea Warfare Center, Point Loma. His team was responsible for improving the capabilities of underwater sonar detection and radar systems for the Navy.

When my uncle's father died, his mother came to live with him. Then, when my aunt announced she was pregnant, my mother felt the house was getting too crowded and began her search for a new home. Shortly after I was born, Mom put down a deposit on a small Pennsylvania Dutch-style house. It sat on the top of a hill and offered fantastic panoramic views of the surrounding mountains. I had fond memories of that house. It only had one bedroom, but as soon as I was old enough to climb the ladder to the loft, that became my bedroom.

Uncle Trigg was very much a part of my childhood. He eventually sold his house and bought a new one on five acres of land adjacent to our house. I remembered my black Labrador named Gummy, and my two cats, Sir Anna and Big Kitty. My trip down memory lane left me smiling, but was interrupted as the bus slowed to a stop at a Jack-in-the-Box. Merritt and I walked into the restaurant together, but after ordering, he left to sit with some other guys. I took my Bonus Jack, fries, and Coke outside and enjoyed the solitude and fresh air for thirty minutes before the driver called us back to the bus.

As I got back on the bus, Merritt was sitting with his new friends, so I decided to sit next to a long-haired hippie with a sullen face and wearing sandals. I asked, "Mind if I sit here?"

"Yeah, go for it," he said without making eye contact. Remember what I said about hippies talking too much? I must've just met the only one who didn't. He never said another word for the next five hours as we headed up the 101 freeway to Monterey. I wondered what his story was, and whether he'd been torn away from friends and family just like me.

Right before sunset, the bus slowed down to catch the exit for Fort Ord. I looked out over misty fields and thought about my family and Marcheta and how lucky I was to have them. Their moral support would surely help me get through this ordeal. Suddenly, hippie-guy asked, "Do you think the base commander will be there to welcome us?"

I confidently said with a grin, "I'm sure he will be." His naivety was little comfort. A growing sense of unease crept through my body and made my skin prickle. *What the devil had Uncle Sam gotten me into?*

# CHAPTER 3

# WELCOME TO BASIC TRAINING

D rill instructors screamed at us as we filed off the bus, their spit flying wildly in the evening air. The soldier at the foot of the stairs shouted, "Grab a formation, privates." We haphazardly shuffled into some sort of "formation," which wasn't what he wanted, so we were pushed and shoved into four ten-man squads. Standing in rows, we soon learned that if we didn't look straight ahead, a drill sergeant would stride toward us and shriek, "Eyes straight ahead, Private!" It was natural to want to look at the person talking, but that brought a world of grief, "Don't eyeball me, Private! Are you deaf? Get down now and give me fifty push-ups!" There were bodies scattered all over, face down, huffing and puffing, banging out push-ups, most collapsing before they even reached twenty.

The torture continued. Who knew the act of standing at attention could be so challenging? Drill sergeants walked up and down, poking men in the stomach, "Chest out! Stomach in, Private! Put a curve in that lower back, Private!" By now, it was dark, and the heavy mist had turned to a cold, penetrating fog. I stood at attention for what seemed like an eternity while waiting for four more buses to arrive. We watched as the same welcoming committee greeted the incoming recruits. Those of us who had arrived first were fidgeting, trying to stretch our backs, or flex our legs without catching the attention of one of the drill sergeants.

The newly arrived recruits were short, tall, thin, fat, muscular, athletic, geeky, and everything in between. More than a fair share of them suffered severely from acne; war has always been a young person's game. The majority were several years younger than me, but I was surprised to see a few older faces dotted here and there, including one I recognized. Don Wakefield, a high school buddy. Once we were told to fall out, I went over and shook hands. I said, "Man, you haven't changed a bit." He returned the compliment and slapped me on the shoulder. He'd been on the Los Angeles bus.

However, before we could catch up, our drill instructor said, "No talking!" and we followed him to the mess hall.

Over dinner, Don and I sat together, reminisced about school days, and caught up with our lives since graduation. Back at the barracks, we hung together and managed to share bunk beds, me on top, him on the bottom. Sharing my first night in the army with an old friend—what were the odds?

I was woken by a drill sergeant banging trash cans, my watch said 5:00 a.m., if I wanted to eat, I needed to be in the mess hall in thirty minutes. Breakfast was scrambled eggs, bacon, and toast. After breakfast, we were forced into two groups; volunteers and draftees. Volunteers went to pick up their army gear and headed straight to basic training. Don and I, along with other draftees, spent the next two days taking a series of tests to assess our mental aptitude and intelligence level. Because I was a qualified pilot, I also took the Warrant Officer Candidate Flight Aptitude Tests. The days dragged on and taking army tests got boring fast. As we began to wrap up testing, I caught the eye of one of the civilian administrators. I translated the look he gave me as, "You poor bastard, you're on your way to Vietnam!"

My reunion with Don was short-lived; he was ordered to join another group of draftees. My group were mostly from Utah. They were almost all in their mid-twenties and looked majorly ticked off.

Later I discovered that many of them had left behind successful careers. One guy, Dan Majeres, was a thirty-two-year-old lawyer with a family of five. He was a guest of the army because although he got a 2-S deferment while studying law, which had taken him to the age of twenty-six, the age at which you become draft-exempt, there was a catch. Deferment meant precisely that; instead of being draft-exempt at twenty-six, in Dan's case, it became thirty-two. Uncle Sam grabbed him just as he was about to time out.

Five days after arriving at Fort Ord, we assembled next to the trucks that would take us to our first day of basic training. The company commander was there and gave us a briefing, "Privates, just a quick heads-up. To help you identify the personnel you are about to meet, the commanding officer has two silver bars on his collar and is the captain in charge. His XO, or executive officer, has one silver bar. The sergeant in charge of all enlisted men and drill sergeants, has three stripes up and two down. This indicates he is a Sergeant E-7.

During the ride up to "The Hill" for basic training, we were all quiet; punctuated only by the sound of the truck's engine. It was eight in the morning, and my scalp itched; it had been unceremoniously shaved—I was bald. I wondered how Marcheta felt about bald men. Earlier, I had stuffed my military-authorized clothes and shaving kit into my army green duffel bag and was now heading off for what everyone said would be a hellish eight weeks.

Our trucks, holding many guys in each one, approached the basic training billets. The road was wide enough for trucks to travel in either direction around a quadrangle, with the three-story concrete buildings across the road. In the center, there was additional parking and picnic-style seating.

We drove up the right side, and I noticed that each building had its own separate asphalt paved entrance with a grassed area on either side between the pathway and billets. Our truck reached the top of the road, turned, and started down the other side of the quadrangle, eventually grinding to a halt between the second and third buildings coming back down the hill.

Once the trucks stopped, we could see and hear the yelling, Smoky Bear hatted, drill sergeants as we got off and ran up the paved driveway lugging our duffel bags. They were immediately in our faces, barking orders, pushing people, pointing, and getting us to line up by last name in alphabetical order. We were told, repeatedly, to form four 50-man platoons. I ended up in the third platoon, in the middle of the third row.

In a moment of peace, while the drill instructors created the fourth platoon, I looked over at three figures standing on the elevated barracks entrance with hands on hips. Thanks to the briefing earlier, I recognized they were the captain, his executive officer and the first sergeant. The morning was cool, but I was sweating.

I noticed that every drill instructor and the captain's team wore the three-inch Combat Infantry Badge. It featured a rifle on a blue background, surrounded by a silver crest. I was impressed that they had all seen combat. The chaos gradually turned to silence, save for some shuffling of feet; the captain told his drill sergeants to inspect their platoons. I felt conspicuous, uncomfortable, and uneasy. I fought an urge to step away and tell them this was all a mistake. Out of the corner of my eye, I could see a burly sergeant, about 5' 8" with red hair and a short red mustache starting to inspect our platoon. He looked mean. I could hear him complaining and making derogatory remarks as he walked along the front row, down the second, and past me to the end of the third row. I would have let out a sigh of relief if I hadn't been scared he'd hear it and come back and rail on me. At the end of my row, he kicked it up a notch when he walked up to a member of our platoon who was a national guard trainee. Regular army personnel were not impressed with Guardsmen because they were only required to serve six months of active duty followed by five and a half years in the reserves. As a result, most of them were never sent to Vietnam. I later learned that our drill sergeant had been trying to ferret out conscientious objectors, known as COs.

A CO is given a wooden rifle during basic training. From there, they are sent to Fort Sam Houston and trained as medics. It's a tough assignment; their first stop is Vietnam, where they join an infantry unit to hump the jungle with only their medical supply bag for protection. Infantrymen have massive respect for these courageous medics.

Our drill sergeant had reached the last row; he was directly behind me. "What the hell do you have in your mouth, Private?"

Silence.

"Don't eyeball me, Private! What is in your mouth?"

Silence.

My heart was racing. I could feel the tension.

"Are you deaf, or dumb, or don't you understand English?"

The private said nothing.

Our drill sergeant continued berating him in an attempt to solicit a reaction. He then said something about the private's family, and I heard a sickening thud. The drill sergeant bounced off my back and hit the asphalt like a sack of potatoes. I turned around; he was face down and out for the count. A stunned silence, and then every platoon member talked at once. A few seconds later, the company commander ran up to us to see what had happened. We snapped to attention but quickly stepped aside when he said, "Make way!" Once the commanding officer had assessed the situation and saw his drill sergeant was out cold, he summoned his executive officer and first sergeant to attend to the man and then told the remaining drill sergeants to send their platoons to the barracks. He then strode off toward the mess hall.

The executive officer was on his knees attending to his sergeant, who was now beginning to stir, groaning a bit. The first sergeant pointed to me, two other men, and the nonverbal private. He told the four of us to stay where we were and dismissed the rest of the platoon. The company commander returned with a cook from the mess hall, and they helped the still wobbly drill sergeant to his feet. The CO looked at me and said, "You, follow me." As I walked away, I could hear the XO and the first sergeant questioning the other two witnesses.

The captain was around my age, tall, and lean. Away from the rest of the platoon, he said, "What happened back there, Miller?"

"Sir, all I can say is that the drill instructor was trying his darndest to get that man to react. He was tearing the guy down big time. When he started insulting the guy's family, I heard a sickening thud and the sergeant's body bounced off the right side of my back. As I turned, I saw him land face down, hard."

"Did Private Paulson say anything?"

"No, sir. He did not."

He looked grim and stared at me for a second, assessing what I had just told him.

"Okay. You are not to discuss this with anyone. Get your duffel bag and head for the barracks."

As I headed toward the barracks, I saw the CO walking back to where they were questioning Paulson. The other two witnesses caught up to me, and even though we'd all been told not to discuss what had happened, we couldn't resist reliving the drama. As soon as we entered our platoon's room upstairs, everyone gathered around to hear the story.

A few minutes later, Paulson entered the room, came over to me, eyebrows raised, and whispered, "I think I broke his jaw." At that moment, one of the eavesdroppers bumped into Paulson who turned around quickly, startling the men. They lurched back, causing one of them to fall to the floor. Paulson reached out and helped the young man to his feet, asking, "Hey, buddy, you okay?"

"I'm fine," the private replied, looking relieved.

One thing was sure; no one ever messed with Paulson after that day.

At the end of my first week of training, I received a letter from my mother. Receiving mail is a massive morale booster, and this letter made me smile. She asked whether I had seen my dad standing at attention and holding a salute as the bus had left the terminal in San Diego. I was sorry I'd missed seeing him, but it didn't surprise me that the guy Merritt saw saluting was my dad.

CHAPTER 4

# A TEMPORARY BAND
# OF BROTHERS

After all the excitement, we eventually got around to
unpacking our duffel bags. However, we had only just
started when the first sergeant arrived and told us to
fall out for lunch. The four of us at the center of the drama stuck
together through the chow line and then went and sat at a table.
This was the first time I had an opportunity to fully appraise
Paulson and the two other witnesses. Private Oakley said, "Perhaps we should introduce ourselves; after all, we seem to have
been thrown together in this little drama," he said with a grin.
He looked at Paulson, "Of course, I know you're Paulson. No
one is ever going to forget you."

Paulson smiled. "Yes, I am Brad."

As I was sitting next to Paulson, I said, "I'm Morgan Miller."

The guy to my right waved and said, "I'm Aaron Ault."

Private Oakley nodded and said, "I'm Don. Don Oakley."

It felt good to have something in common, and we went around
the table talking a little about ourselves and our backgrounds. We
were all in our mid-twenties, and, of course, we were all draftees.
As we were about to chow down, Paulson pulled a Skoal can out of
his hip pocket, took the infamous piece of chew out of his mouth,
and placed it carefully in the tin. I couldn't take my eyes off this

cowboy. He was tall and lean, and his face was weathered to the point it looked like it was made out of barbed wire and rawhide. Tough.

"I'm from Big Piney, Wyoming. I've been a professional cowboy since I graduated from high school. This here military stuff is all new to me, as you might have gathered. Things are very different on the ranch. There's more respect."

· · · · ·

Before we had the chance to hear everyone's stories, we were ordered back to our billet to finish unpacking and make up our beds. The new army fatigues went into our wall locker; underwear, socks, and personal items went into our foot lockers.

First Sergeant Woods came into the room and walked over to Paulson. "Come with me, Private." Woods was an imposing figure. At 6'2" he carried around 230 pounds of pure muscle. His very presence demanded respect. Everyone in the room stopped what they were doing and watched them leave.

When Brad returned, he said, "The sergeant took me to the captain, who drove me to the brigade commander's office. The colonel asked me what happened, and I told him. That was it; he sent me on my way without another word. Before I left, I asked the captain what would happen, but he told me to go back to my room." The following day, our drill sergeant had been replaced by an older DI and we never saw "red" again.

The most challenging adjustment for me was the strict daily routine. Our day started at 5:00 a.m. with a company formation on the asphalt out front, followed by a thirty-minute run around the quadrangle. Only then did we get to enjoy breakfast. After our meal, we went back to our platoon room to shave, shower, make our beds, and prepare for inspection.

The first order of the day was marching practice. Our new drill sergeant said, "Marching is the method the army uses to move large groups of men from one place to another." Duh! It was then time to attend classes, but first we were expected to move into our company formation before marching to our first class. Before lunch we studied army history, traditions, and tactics. After lunch we picked up our M14 semi-automatic rifle to take with us to gun safety class, where we began learning how to assemble and disassemble it. Even now, I feel I could do it blindfolded. The army loves repetition.

At the end of each day, when all we wanted to do was rest, we had physical conditioning exercises to build our body strength. After those routines, we were taught the correct way to run, the army way, through an obstacle course. I struggled a lot with traversing the twenty-foot horizontal ladder which was high enough that even the tallest recruit hanging from it couldn't touch the ground. It took everything I had to work my way along it hand-over-hand. I was sweating, exhausted, and my hands burned by the time I successfully got across.

The forty-foot low crawl was another obstacle I hated. We lined up shoulder to shoulder, down on our bellies, ready to race. A drill sergeant would yell, "Ready . . . go!" and we'd race along the dirt lanes to a marker, and then turn around and race back again. Any private who didn't keep his hips on the ground or failed to use only their knees and arms to progress—or heaven forbid, came in last—was yelled at. After we survived the obstacle course, we marched in formation back to our barracks to shower and change our uniforms before our evening meal.

As the weeks progressed, things got more interesting. Because of the Monterey Peninsula misty fog, we learned our gun safety and practiced how to assemble and disassemble our rifles in an empty basketball gym. We were also trained in the proper firing positions, standing, kneeling, and laying on the floor.

The following week knowing every part of our M14 intimately, we marched several miles to the rifle range, which was close to Monterey Bay. There, the company commander looked down at us from the conning tower, microphone in hand. "Privates,

assume a prone firing position and raise your hand when ready."
Our drill sergeants ensured we were all lined up correctly with
our individual targets 100 yards away, and gave a thumbs-up to
the captain; they continued to stand directly behind us. A few
seconds later, the captain's voice crackled over the loudspeaker,
"Privates, load the magazine into your rifle," followed shortly
after by, "fire at will."

I enjoyed shooting. It was the first time I, or for that matter, any
of us, had obtained any formal training with firearms. It was a hot
topic of conversation when we got back to the barracks.

We were a mixed bunch of guys from various backgrounds,
so the drill instructor's job was to teach us how to function as a
squad and a platoon. This involved going back to the basics, such
as proper dress and grooming. Other "niceties" included what we
had already learned through recent experience: never make eye
contact with a drill instructor, and always answer any question
with, "Yes, drill sergeant," or "No, drill sergeant." Once the platoon mastered the instructors' rules and expectations, life got a
little more tolerable.

When we reached the sixth week of basic training, I asked
my drill instructor if I could apply for helicopter flight school.
He wasn't hopeful, but said he would see what he could do. Two
days later, I met First Sergeant Woods in his office and asked the
same thing. He said, "Sorry, Private, it's too late. You should have
signed up before getting drafted. Your orders have already come
down from the Department of the Army stating that your port-of-
call date at Travis Air Force Base is January 9th." I was crestfallen;
this was my one hope of avoiding being an infantryman.

That night, after waiting for an age to use the pay phone, I
called my dad and told him what the first sergeant said. He asked
if I had taken and passed the Warrant Officer Candidate Flight
Aptitude Tests. "Yes," I replied.

After a momentary pause, he said, "I'll see what I can do," and
he ended the call. My father was a man of few words. He was an

old-school military man; he'd been a captain and executive officer of an infantry company in the Pacific during World War II, and had stayed in the reserves.

A few days later, I was on the rifle range and heard my name over the loudspeaker, "Private Henry Miller, report to the conning tower." I double-timed over, reported at attention, and saluted the major standing next to my captain. The major said, "Get in my Jeep." As we took off, I asked where we were headed.

"To the base hospital to get you a physical for flight school," was his reply.

I was ecstatic. At the hospital, the major gave a nurse the necessary paperwork and then went to wait while I spent the next several hours taking the Class-1 flight physical. On the drive back to the company area, the major told me it would take about two months for my orders to get changed, but the good news was, I would be going to flight school!

He told me this was all very unusual and to be sure to thank the colonel. I discovered later that Dad had called the Department of the Army at the Pentagon. Dad explained that his son was in basic training and that he possessed a civilian private pilot license with 170 hours of flight time. He also told them that I passed the Warrant Officer Candidate Flight Aptitude Tests and that he would like me to go to flight school. Obviously, it worked.

After I graduated from basic training, I was put in a holding company to await my orders for flight school. It was frustrating; along with twenty others, I cleaned empty buildings, painted, trimmed trees, pulled weeds, and did many other menial tasks. After two days, I'd had enough, and asked the captain in charge if I could rejoin my friends in advanced infantry training.

"Are you nuts, Private? Why would you want to do that?" he said.

I explained my rationale: if I got shot down in Vietnam, the infantry training might save my life. I wasn't learning anything here painting, cleaning, and gardening. He shook his head, looked at me for several seconds, and said, "Stand right where you are, Private, while I make a call."

A few minutes later, he handed me a transfer document and told me to get my stuff and meet him at his Jeep. He dropped me at the advanced infantry training company, and after signing in, I sought out Oakley, Ault, and Paulson who were stunned that I was back, and man, oh man, did they give me some heat over my decision to come back and do another eight weeks of hell-on-earth training.

CHAPTER 5

# ADVANCED INFANTRY TRAINING

From 1965 to 1967, the GI casualty rate in Vietnam was high, and the blame fell on inadequate training and inexperienced sergeants who lacked combat training.

When you think about it, it's no surprise. Guys were drafted into the war when they were barely out of their teens. Of course, there was a lack of training. It was older boys "training" younger boys, and everyone was scared shitless, no matter how brave they pretended to be. You never ever admitted fear, weakness, exhaustion, or anything other than a "SIR, YES, SIR" while keeping what the British call a "stiff upper lip." Well, let me tell you, those stiff upper lips hid a lot of fear. A LOT. Imagine having to live every second of every day wondering if it would be your last? And for many of us, we'd just started our lives with our girlfriends or new wives or new jobs, and even new and young families. Ault was a police officer and Oakley worked on his family's farm. We feared we wouldn't get back to our careers or see our families again.

These days, boys in their late teens and twenties complain about how hard "adulting" is while they still live rent-free in their parents' homes. Some don't even know how to drive or make decisions about their wardrobes without their parents or an online app. It was a totally different time.

Paulson, Ault, Oakley, and I were in Advanced Infantry Training (AIT) together, where our new platoon sergeants greeted us.
By the time we attended AIT, the army had begun posting platoon
sergeants to Vietnam with the recruits they had trained.

Our platoon sergeant, Sergeant Burrington, completed AIT
and then underwent thirteen weeks of intensive leadership and
combat training at the Fort Benning NCO Academy. His job was
to prepare our platoon so we could all go to Vietnam together as a
well-oiled unit. I liked Sergeant Burrington; he was younger than
me, maybe twenty-two or twenty-three, about 5'10" tall, and thick-
set. He looked as if he'd already experienced some challenging
things in his young life and came across as older than he looked;
my assessment was not incorrect, as I discovered sometime later.

Our permanent party instructors were all combat veterans who
had fought in Vietnam and survived action in places like Khe
Sanh, Dak To, Cu Chi, Tây Ninh, Quần Lợi, and Camp Hollo-
way in Pleiku. Sergeant Laffer, the non-commissioned officer in
charge, had gone into the Ia Drang Valley, at LZ X-Ray, with the
7th Cavalry of the 1st Cavalry Division in 1965.

The new training system meant platoon sergeants assisted the
specialist trainers at the camp. The experts taught us to handle the
various weapons we would come across in Vietnam, including the
M16, which had come into service late in 1964. Although initially,
the gun had a poor reputation, by the time I got to use it, the manufacturer had ironed out its operating kinks. I found it superior to
the M14 we used in basic training. It was lighter, more accurate
than the M14, and fired more rounds per minute. The M16 was a
high-velocity rifle with less recoil and was quick to reload. Its flat
trajectory and long-range accuracy allowed the shooter to take out
the enemy even when only a small part of their body was visible.

While some might think these descriptions clinical, it's what
I—and other soldiers—had to do to keep ourselves sane. Think of
how you would react if you were ripped from everything you held
dear and ordered to kill an enemy in a war you never should have

been in to begin with? All we were told was that Vietnam was the enemy, and the mantra was "kill or be killed." It was as simple as that. And so, the only way you can even hope to justify your actions is to compartmentalize them; to keep everything emotionless and logical, like Mr. Spock always did in *Star Trek*. For me, focusing on the technical components of weapons helped me do just that.

For example, learning to throw grenades was a scary experience. We weren't allowed to handle live grenades at first, but throwing the dummy ones still felt deadly serious. When it came time to handle a live grenade, I sweated bullets—literally—because they seemed unpredictable. At the explosives range, when it was our turn, we stood on a concrete mound ten feet wide, with a narrow ten-foot-deep moat surrounding it. I asked what the ditch was for, and the instructor said, "Son, if you pull the pin and drop the grenade instead of throwing it, it will hopefully roll down into the moat. If that happens, duck!"

When it came to my turn, I followed the routine we'd practiced to the letter. I held the live grenade in my dominant hand, carefully keeping steady pressure on the safety lever. Honestly, I might have been pressing a little harder than necessary! The grenade was about the size of a large lemon, and looking down at it was mesmerizing. Early grenades were shaped like small pomegranates and could be slippery in your hands. Later versions had perfectly aligned, carved rectangles or squares around the grenade body to provide a better grip for the user. These versions were also shaped like footballs with flat ends, so the overall visual effect earned the nickname "pineapple grenade."

I planted my feet solidly so I was balanced, bent my knees slightly, pulled the pin, took a step forward, and hurled it with all my might, just like a deadly baseball. No one needed to tell me to duck! I instantly threw myself down to the concrete. A few seconds later, there was an explosion. I'd braced myself for a thunderous, ear-splitting explosion but soon realized the real-life detonation wasn't as bad as I feared. I felt relieved. Good, but relieved. We didn't get to handle many live grenades during training—it was too dangerous.

In training, everything feels slightly removed from reality, but as I handled these deadly weapons, the horror of war began to sink in. One of the scariest weapons I learned to set up was the Claymore antipersonnel mine. It was a curved green plastic box of pure destruction. A little over eight inches by five, it used almost a pound and a half of C-4 explosive to fire 700 ball bearings in a 60-degree arc, approximately fifty yards toward the enemy. "Front Toward Enemy" was stamped on the front of the box. There was no need to tell me twice.

My tour of deadly weapons continued with the 60mm M2 Mortar. It is a smoothbore, muzzle-loading, high-angle of fire mortar used for infantry support. It could fire high explosive shells, parachute flare shells, and white smoke grenades to provide cover. Getting up close and personal with these weapons was morbidly fascinating, but we all knew they could one day, in the not-so-distant future, save our lives. At one point, I saw Paulson grinning from ear to ear while firing the M72 light anti-tank weapon, otherwise known as *the LAWS rocket*. The M72 was a lightweight, one-use, 66mm rocket launcher that fired from the shoulder like a bazooka. It effectively penetrated concrete bunkers and heavy armor.

Using the M60 machine gun was exhilarating, especially when I got to simulate a live situation by walking along and shooting at pop-up targets. You had to react quickly to the "threat" before the target disappeared. Later we got to fire the big-boy .50 caliber machine guns at moving targets 500 yards away, ride in an armored personnel carrier and watch an M60 tank demonstration. These practice sessions were the video games of the day, and many of us became immune to the real reason for their existence. We were just a bunch of young guys from all over the country getting to play shoot-'em-up with fake targets and real guns. I'll bet if you asked any one of us if we fully understood their purpose and eventual harm and destruction to human life, the answer would have been "no." Aiming at a plywood target or empty vehicle is a massively different scenario than coming face-to-face with Charlie in the jungle, even if he was my enemy. First and foremost, he's a human being. And the ever-present question—why are we here?

At the end of the final class, our instructor asked if we had any questions. One of the guys asked, "How long should we expect to be in the jungle?"

The instructor, Sergeant Laffer, a combat veteran, smiled, and I sensed he was about to tell us a story. "My experience, gentlemen, was that after each four to six weeks' stint in the bush, we'd head back to base camp for up to two weeks. On the first day back from the jungle, I always told my guys their first job was to clean and check their weapons, fill their ammo belts, and repack their rucksacks with clean underwear, and five pairs of socks. They needed to be ready to return to the bush at any time. After inspection, I told them they were free to relax. Some indulged in heavy drinking, others smoked pot, and others visited the indigenous ladies off base. Myself, I always relaxed with some stiff drinks during my first few days back from the bush. No, let's be honest, I didn't draw a sober breath for at least two days. On one occasion, we had only been back three days when orders came down to pack up and get on the arriving helicopters. We flew into a fire support base, at night, to provide backup support. Luckily, I was sober by then."

Everyone laughed. Sergeant Laffer looked pleased that his story had been well received and said, "Good luck. And remember, the best way to come back alive is to stay healthy, use a condom, and always be prepared for the unexpected."

As I walked away from the class, I asked myself, "How in the heck does someone prepare himself for an unnatural act like war?"

During my final week of AIT, we took part in a simulation. Paulson, Ault, and Oakley had been building it up for several days, and now it was here; my adrenalin was pumping. Our platoon and one other were transported to a staging area about ten miles east of Fort Ord. To make the re-enactment as authentic as possible, they'd built a Vietnamese village where we were to stage an air assault. The XO briefed us on how we got on the helicopter, where to sit, what to hold onto, and how to exit the aircraft at the landing zone by jumping and rolling. He warned us that the helicopter wouldn't land; it would still be moving as we jumped out, so remembering to roll was important. At that point, we were to keep down until the Huey pulled away and we could assess whether anyone was shooting at us. I was excited; this was as close to the real thing as I would get before being posted to Vietnam; however, it was still kind of an unrealistic obstacle course. You knew no one was going to get killed, and it was safe to say that none of us really understood the ramifications of our actions, even in a simulation. The excitement would turn to horror soon enough. If only I knew then what I know now.

Then we heard, in the distance, *whap, whap, whap*, and then saw them: seven Huey helicopters in perfect formation bearing down on us. It was a fantastic sight. A few minutes later, I joined half of our squad and our squad leader, Sergeant Burrington, as we climbed into the helicopter. Once in the air, he told us to be prepared to jump out on his command when we were about three feet from the ground. Fifteen minutes later, my heart was racing as I could feel the aircraft slowing down and beginning its descent. Sergeant Burrington already had his feet hanging out of the door, and I could see him squirming his butt toward the edge. I was close to him and couldn't believe it when he jumped, *shit, we're too high*! I felt the private next to me ready to follow the sergeant, so I grabbed his arm and calmed everyone down. The pilot took over responsibility for telling us when to jump, and at three feet, we got the signal, jumped, rolled, and all landed safely. Sergeant Burrington, however, was lying on the ground with a broken leg. His rash decision to jump early stemmed from his desire to avoid having the rest of us land on top of him. The best-laid plans, right?

A medic from the final helicopter tended to him, and they flew him to the hospital, and that was the last we saw of him. Well, that's what I thought at the time. As it turned out, he and I were destined to have much more excitement together. And he would be the best man at my wedding.

Other than that mishap, the rest of the attack simulation went as planned, and I felt things were beginning to get very real. I wasn't sure whether I was more excited or scared shitless. However, before I could indulge in any serious analysis, we all had to overcome the final hurdle before graduation—the twenty-five-mile quick-time hike, carrying sixty-pound rucksacks, 200 rounds of ammunition, and our M16 rifles. On the Friday of our eighth week at camp, our company XO lead our company, followed by our flagman, with our drill sergeants leading their respective platoons out to the road. The XO gave the order, "Forward march!" A few seconds later, he called, "Quick – march!" I glanced at my watch; it was 7:30 a.m. I figured that, at three miles an hour, it would take over eight hours to complete the march. My heart sank a little, but I heard the XO begin a cadence call to the "Johnny Comes Marching Home" tune, and my spirits lifted.

*They issued me an M16 hurrah.*
*They issued me an M16 hurrah, hurrah.*
*They issued me an M16 and turned me into a killing machine.*
*And we will be dead by December of '69.*
*Hup, two, three.*
*They issued me an American Flag, hurrah, hurrah.*
*They issued me an American flag hurrah, hurrah.*
*They issued me an American Flag and shipped me home in a*
    *body bag.*
*And we will all be dead by December of '69.*

The XO and drill sergeants took turns repeating the cadence calling every fifteen minutes or so, which took our minds off the long day ahead. For the first hour, the terrain was familiar because we had double-timed over it many times. But then we turned east onto a new road and continued repeating our cadence call. Time lost all meaning for a while; the calling became the center of everything. Sometime later, I looked at my watch, and it was 11:30; four hours had passed. Unbelievable. The road started to go downhill and led to a small valley with a stand of oak trees. The XO came alive, "Prepare to march! March!" Followed by, "Halt! Privates, this is your thirty-minute lunch break. Fall out!"

Oakley, Ault, Paulson, and I found a grassy spot under a tree and sat down. Sergeant Burrington's replacement came over to tell us we were ahead of schedule. Oakley commented that he was pleasantly surprised the forced march was not nearly as bad as he had anticipated. We all agreed it wasn't as bad as our drill instructors led us to believe. Thirty minutes later, we were back marching to the XOs cadence call. After two hours, our surroundings became familiar, and we stopped for a ten-minute water break. I was in good spirits and ready for the final leg of the march. Soon, we could see the company area, and the XO shouted, "Prepare to march. March!" I took another look at my watch; it was 4:45 p.m. Our company commander and his first sergeant greeted us, grinning and applauding as we marched up the asphalt road. When the XO shouted, "Halt! Left face! At ease!" The captain, still smiling broadly, said, "Congratulations, gentlemen. Job well done. Back to your rooms and get cleaned up for dinner." As we walked past them, heading to the barracks, they both shook our hands to signal a job well done.

I was amazed that I had just managed to do a quick-time, twenty-five-mile hike and still felt refreshed. I was beginning to feel like a soldier. At dinner, the conversation focused on how happy we all were that advanced infantry training was over and that, despite the dread we all felt, what we had learned over the previous eight weeks would be invaluable.

# CHAPTER 6

# DRAMA AT HOME

The days after graduating were anti-climactic. The previous eight weeks had been intense. Every day was a challenge, and the extreme growth I experienced was an adrenaline rush like no other. Going from a working-class civilian to a honed soldier in just a few months was an achievement I never expected to reach. I knew how to shoot rifles, guns, and pistols. I could handle a live grenade and target human enemies as well as take out armed tanks and other vehicles. My stamina had increased ten-fold. If I thought I was fit before, now I was like Superman. I could march twenty-five miles with a heavy backpack and weapons on my back without stopping.

I was ready to go.

My flight orders had not arrived, so I was back in my holding company, twiddling my thumbs and riding on pent-up adrenalin. Three weeks later, on December 18, the orders finally arrived. My commanding officer authorized leave until January 15, when I would be at Fort Wolters, Texas, in my thirty-eight-week warrant officer candidate course. I couldn't believe it; I was going to be home for Christmas.

Back in El Cajon, I surprised Marcheta at our apartment a few days before Christmas. When she saw me at the front door, she was all smiles, excitement, hugs, and kisses. I melted as soon as I saw her and held her in my arms, her perfume an instant reminder of everything I'd missed over the last months. As soon as I stepped over the threshold, she pushed me back and said, "Wow! Look at those muscles! You're in great shape."

I smiled, "I sure am. Would you like to jog over to my parents' house and surprise them?"

She looked at me with a grin and said, "Later, I can think of something much more exciting I'd like to do right now," and she led me into the bedroom.

It was wonderful to be home, and I told Marcheta how happy I was that infantry training was finally behind me. She asked me about training, and I told her about Paulson, Ault, Oakley, and Sergeant Burrington. She couldn't believe everything we'd been through in such a short amount of time and looked at me in shock and disbelief at some of the stories I shared. I found out later that she was terrified of losing me, but did her best to hide her fear and support me.

Thinking back, if I'd been a little more mature, I would have recognized the depth of Marcheta's feelings about my involvement in the war and not dismissed them. At the time, I was in my own head and focused solely on my needs.

I wondered if my basic-training buddies were experiencing the same challenges with their wives and girlfriends. Then I thought about the youngest recruits, those who might not have had a chance to form romantic relationships yet. The military gave them a purpose to live, goals to strive for, and much-needed fellowship and camaraderie that they might never have experienced had they not been drafted or voluntarily enlisted. The downside was that I was discovering how all-encompassing military life was and how quickly it could distance you from those you love.

Later that afternoon, we drove over to see Mom and Dad, and I discovered that the three of them had seen each other regularly while I was away. They watched the nightly news with Walter Cronkite and were more up-to-date with what was happening in Southeast Asia than I was.

After the initial excitement at seeing me, my mom became unusually quiet. Over dinner, I talked about the army, what I'd learned, the friends I'd made—all the usual stuff. Over a dessert of homemade apple pie, she looked at me sadly and said, "Morgan, you're heading into a nightmare situation. Our boys are being massacred. And for what?"

I reached out and put my hand on hers, "I know, Mom, that's why Dad helped me get into flight school, where I'll have better control of my destiny. Plus, it will postpone my deployment to Vietnam for another nine months; by then, the war could be over."

She glanced at my dad, as if she was doubtful and shouldn't say anything, but finally said, "Have you heard about what happened at LZ X-Ray and Albany in 1965?" I shook my head. "Well, I did. There was an article in the *San Diego Union* a couple of weeks ago about the LZ. Morgan, in just four days, two hundred and thirty-four of our young men died, and 250 were wounded, some by friendly fire." Her face was red, and she was tearing up. Dad tried to put his arm around her, but she shook it off and left the room. Marcheta followed her.

I looked at my father, "Dad, what does she want me to do, escape to Canada? I didn't enlist; I was drafted. I don't have a choice."

He stood up and started pacing, "Mom worries about you, and she's frustrated. She doesn't understand why the United States got involved in Vietnam's political problems in the first place. Why couldn't they have kept out of it instead of sending young men off to be killed? It's hard on her knowing that you will be heading into the thick of the fighting."

My dad, being a military man, had been following the Vietnam stats, and when I'd asked him after my mom had left, what the casualty figures were for the year, he told me the truth, "Well, son, we're getting close to 17,000 young Americans killed and over 87,000 wounded." I gasped; I'd had no idea the numbers were that high. No wonder Mom was worried.

When we returned to our apartment, Marcheta sighed and said, "We need to talk. You said we'd get married after basic training, and that's done with, so . . . what's next?"

She caught me off guard. I was still thinking about how upset Mom was, and it brought into focus what I "hadn't" signed up for—this war was killing a heck of a lot of my generation.

Marcheta was still staring at me, "Hello, Morgan? Earth to Morgan." I shook my head to clear away the vision of so many dead young bodies. "Marcheta, I'm sorry, but right now I need to put all my energy into the Warrant Officer course, which starts in a few weeks.

There was a long pause after I'd said my piece. I looked down, inspecting the linoleum; I couldn't look at her face. As I lifted my head, Marcheta had folded her arms and adopted an unforgiving stance as if readying herself for battle. "I love you, Morgan! I don't want to wait. I want to be with you while you're in flight school and support you when you go overseas."

Her outpouring of love, affection, and support made me feel uncomfortable now. Superman had left the building. I realized, of course, that her feelings should have made me want to embrace her. Instead, I said, "Honey, can we talk about this later? This conversation adds to the pressure I'm already feeling, and I'd just like to relax, for now, okay? For heaven's sake, I've only been back a few hours!"

"The pressure *you're* feeling?" she snapped. "What about *my* feelings? I don't want you to go through this alone! I want to be there to support my husband and his parents, not my boyfriend. It seems you don't want to make the emotional commitment. Do you really love me, Morgan—do you?"

I didn't have an answer, so I left the room. Lying in bed later, I mentally re-read the loving letters Marcheta sent me during the exciting—but lonely—days of training. The message was clear; marriage was the only option in her eyes. It was an inevitability. Thinking it over, I realized that I wasn't ready to navigate a marriage while trying to maneuver my way through flight school. Before I drifted off to sleep, my last thought was that if I loved her enough, none of that would matter.

The following day, over a bowl of Cheerios, a cold front was blowing in from across the breakfast table. "What's the problem?" I asked.

Marcheta stood up, put her hands on her hips, and said, "We're done, Morgan; it's over."

With my spoon halfway between the bowl and my mouth, I said, "What the hell does that mean?"

"You're a smart guy; I'm sure you'll figure it out."

I put the spoon down, splashing milk on the table, "Hold on a minute!"

Now she was angry. "Get your stuff and leave—now! And don't expect me to write to you in flight school; you're on your own. Which seems to be what you want!"

I was dumbfounded. I put my spoon down, went to the bedroom, packed my stuff, and headed to my parent's house, my tail firmly between my legs.

Christmas came and went, and I wasn't sure how I felt about the breakup. I knew I should have been heartbroken or more upset, but I couldn't seem to dredge those emotions to the surface. One evening I went out for a beer with my long-time friend, Bill James, and told him that Marcheta and I had broken up. I must have looked sad because he said, "Just give her a few days. We both know she loves you."

I looked down into my beer, "Well, Bill, I'm not sure I want to get back with her. Marriage is too much pressure right now, and if she doesn't understand that, tough." It was the first time I'd admitted to myself that she wasn't the most important thing in my life at that moment. Letting her go was surprisingly easy. Too easy. Perhaps I had just dodged my first bullet.

Back at Bill's place, we ran into one of his neighbors, Ginger Palmer. She invited us to a New Year's Eve party, and we accepted.

I said to Bill, "This is just what I need to take my mind off Marcheta." Boy, was I right. At the party, I bumped into several old friends from school and college, but most of the night, I danced with Ginger. She was a registered nurse, and I learned about her interests, hobbies, and what she liked and didn't like. The connection was immediate, and for the first time, I realized that there had always been something missing in my relationship with Marcheta; I felt that Ginger and I were on the same wavelength. I hoped it wasn't the beer talking, but I asked if I could write to her while I was at flight school, and she agreed. She gave me her address, wished me good luck, and we parted company.

# CHAPTER 7

# ON THE ROAD
# REMINISCING

My leave was over way too fast, and on Wednesday, January 8, 1969, I loaded my army gear into the trunk of my Marina Blue '66 Impala, hugged Mom and Dad, and set off for the 1,200-mile drive to Fort Wolters. I left early so I could get as many miles under my belt on the first day as I could manage; it was dull, drizzly, hazy, and cool. I'd estimated the journey would take three days; the highway would be long and straight, and the scenery flat and boring. But, as they were my last few days of freedom as a civilian, I was going to do my best to enjoy the drive and be comfortable with my own company.

It was always hard to say goodbye to my parents, but this time was a little different. Deep down inside—and this is hard to admit—I felt a little bit of relief that I was leaving. I hated to see my loving and devoted mother so upset that I was preparing to go off to war. Knowing it was because of me—albeit indirectly—was hard to take, and seeing her cry made my stomach churn. What else could I do? I had to consider Dad, with his military background . . . how could I have dodged the draft without insulting him? Without bringing shame on all that he had achieved in his life? It was an inescapable position for me, and all I could do was make the best of it.

For the first few miles, all I could think of was the Warrant Officer Training course and how crucial it was that I do well. The thought of going to Vietnam as a grunt—a nickname for infantrymen and an observation of their status in the army—was too much to bear. One thing I knew for sure was that I didn't want to spend my time in Vietnam leaping out of helicopters and facing enemy fire. I'd prefer to be the guy flying the aircraft. As the day wore on, I listened to the radio, and sang along to "Sugar, Sugar" by The Archies, "Aquarius" by The Fifth Dimension, "I Can't Get Next to You" by The Temptations, and one of my favorites, "Honky Tonk Woman" by The Rolling Stones.

I thought about Ginger and the impression she made on me. What was it that she had that Marcheta lacked? I'd thought I was in love with Marcheta, but within a matter of days, I was intrigued by another woman. Maybe a lot more than intrigued.

Even though I stopped for gas in Phoenix, I'd been driving for more than nine hours and needed a break, so I stopped at Lucky Wishbone, on Sixth Street in Tucson for some fried chicken and fries. They were good, the chicken was crispy and juicy, and who doesn't like fries? It was good to rest for a while and down a few coffees. Walking to my car and feeling sleepy I decided to look for a motel for the night. Pulling out of the Lucky Wishbone, I saw the Sahara Motel and pulled in. It wasn't much, but all I needed was a bed for the night—hopefully a clean one. It had a small fridge, so I put the six-pack of beers I'd bought in Tucson in the refrigerator and drank one immediately. I said "cheers" to myself and celebrated the first third of my journey—only another 800 miles or so to go. The following morning, I woke early and headed off to look for breakfast. I soon discovered the Horseshoe Café; pulled in, parked, and sat down for a meal of corned beef hash topped with two fried eggs.

Set up for the day, with a sandwich boxed to go and fresh ice for my cooler I hit the road. It was a beautiful morning as the sun was brightening the day. On the outskirts of town, I had to swerve to avoid running over a skunk. I thought, "Man, that was a close call; it would be just my luck to have hit it and have it spray my car. The stench would have been with me all the way to Fort Wolters."

The near miss made me smile. A wave of nostalgia washed over me—even though the critter hadn't sprayed, I could swear I could smell skunk. I was transported back to fifth grade when Dave DeNure, Mike Hill, and I decided to take a skunk to school for show-and-tell. It sounds crazy, but the skunk was sort of a pet. We used to have a small pool in our front yard in Lakeside, California, and each year as summer turned to fall, my dad would drain it. One morning, Mom discovered a baby skunk trapped in the pool. The sides were too steep for the tiny critter to climb out. Mom built it a small shelter, and she'd feed it some greens mixed with a raw egg every day. It wasn't long before the skunk bonded with her—he probably thought she was his mother. As the months went by, the skunk grew but never showed any aggression or tendency to spray us; we just hung out every day, and he became as tame as a house cat.

All would have been good if Mr. Granjean, our teacher, hadn't asked us all to bring in something interesting to share with the class. I ask you, what could be more interesting than a tame skunk? Mike, Dave, and I decided that Pepé Le Pew—my nickname for him—was just what our classmates needed to see. We were sure Mr. Granjean would love him. By this time, I could handle Pepé with no problem, and he never led me to believe he might spray me. Early one morning, I went to his shelter. He immediately came out to greet me, and I picked him up and placed him gently in a large cardboard box. Mike and Dave hung back until he was safely in the box.

We had commandeered my father's old army stretcher and placed the box in the center so Pepé would have a comfortable trip to school. I took one end and Mike the other and began walking carefully down the hill. Dave was out front as our scout, warning us of any obstacles. Halfway down the hill, I tripped, jerked the stretcher, and Pepé unceremoniously bounced off. The box opened, and the skunk panicked and ran for his life; Mike was immediately in hot pursuit and quickly caught the runaway. Unfortunately, the skunk didn't know Mike well and resented being manhandled, so he did what any skunk would do in the same situation; he sprayed Mike with everything he had. I was only a few paces behind and got some of Pepé's perfume, but I managed to calm him down and get him back into the box.

I looked at Mike; he was hunched over, throwing up as if his life depended on it. Before I had the chance to smile, my breakfast made an unexpected and forceful reappearance. Dave, who had witnessed all this from a distance, and had just got a whiff of skunk and vomit, called out, "I'll tell Mr. Granjean you're going to be late." That was helpful, I thought, as I saw him hightailing it away from us as fast as his legs would carry him.

Mike and I weren't quitters. We decided to complete our mission; after all, Pepé must have run out of juice by now. Twenty minutes later, we proudly walked into our classroom, and there was an immediate uproar. The whole class held their noses and yelled, "Ewww, you guys stink!" Mr. Granjean looked incredulous and horrified at the same time. He raised his arm, pointed to the door, and shouted, "Take that animal and stretcher outside now! And, then report to the principal's office." He hadn't thought through his final instruction because when we arrived at the principal's office, he was also horrified, and we were again ordered out of the building.

The principal's secretary called my mother. We could hear her through the open window, "Yes, he smells like skunk. Yes, he had a skunk!" Mike and I sat outside, ostracized from the rest of the school. It wasn't long before Mom turned up in her car. As she approached, we got up and started to walk toward her, but she raised her arm, "Stop! Stop right there, do not come any closer. Stay right where you are." She was carrying a bucket of water and a large jug of tomato juice. She poured the tomato juice into the bucket of water and, at arm's length, slowly poured the contents over our heads. The school nurse and the principal's secretary came over to help. We had to remove our t-shirts and shoes and place them in the empty bucket. Mom told us to get the skunk, which didn't surprise me—she was very fond of the little fellow. After all, none of this was his fault.

Mike and I retrieved our pungent friend and put him in the trunk of Mom's car. It was a quiet ride home, or at least it was until we dropped Mike off at home. That changed as soon as we were alone. I saw Mom's shoulders shaking as she tried to suppress her laughter at our show-and-smell, but she managed to control herself long enough to dress me down for being so stupid. I asked her if Pepé would be okay and was relieved when she said he'd be just fine. And he was; he remained our stinky pet for several years.

I learned later that Mom had laid into the principal about his policy of asking kids to show-and-tell anything they liked with no guidance regarding what was inappropriate. That made me smile, and with a jolt, like coming out of a hypnotic trance, I returned to the present moment. When I realized I'd daydreamed through several small towns and a few hundred miles, I was glad that the road was straight, flat, and boring. The rest of the journey was uneventful, but the closer I got to Fort Wolters, the greater my anticipation began to keep me awake.

# HELL MONTH

T hree days after leaving El Cajon, I drove into Mineral Wells, Texas on the afternoon of January 10, 1969, and stayed at the Travel Lodge Motel. I double-checked my flight school orders and with no time to report on them I went out for dinner and slept late. Around noon I drove under the orange archway that announced the U.S. Army Primary Helicopter Center, which was about fifty miles west of Fort Worth. This grand entrance was flanked by two classic helicopters, a Hiller OH-23 and a Hughes TH-55. Stopping at the post entrance gate, I presented my ID to a Military Police Officer (MP) who directed me to the 10th Warrant Officer Candidate Company. Once in the headquarters building, I handed the clerk my papers. He looked at them and said, "You're a day late, Private."

My heart skipped a beat for a second, but then I suggested that he recheck the date on my orders. "Wow! You're correct; someone made a mistake." Shrugging this off, I signed the papers that made me an official member of the 10th WOC Company and got directions to my barracks. I gave the clerk his pen, and he said, "Your platoon is having lunch in the mess hall. I suggest you get out of your civvies, change into your fatigues, and get yourself some lunch. After lunch, return here, and I'll have your parking permit. I can park your car for you and keep the keys on the board behind me with the other guys if you like."

I changed and walked over to the mess hall, and as I entered, it felt as if all eyes were on me. I felt like the new kid in school—which, of course, I was—and just wasn't prepared for the scrutiny now wholly focused on me at that moment. I half-smiled and gave a quick "Hey" to the nearest diners, then looked around to find the lunch line. Thank God, a distraction. Just go get some grub, and everyone will go back to their lunches. An officer walked over and introduced himself.

"Well, well, well, candidate Miller, you finally arrived. I'm Chief Warrant Officer Boren."

"Yes, sir." I handed him my orders. Thankfully, the clerk had circled the incorrect date in red pen. After scrutinizing the document, CW2 Boren said, "Okay, Candidate Miller, no problem. Go ahead and get your lunch." I had the feeling that I'd just dodged my first bullet. However, inside I felt like this was a whole new world, a world of secret code words and unspoken understandings between students and ranking officers. I had no idea how to infiltrate this world or how to act. Maybe they knew that my dad pulled some strings to get me in. If they did, how did that make me look? Like some pasty-faced, entitled kid with connected parents and entitlement out the wazoo? How would they react once they met me and discovered I was none of those things, that I was just a regular guy from a traditional family who just wanted to be a helicopter pilot? Would they always assume that I was "acting" regularly just to fit in? This was worse than the cliques in high school, and I hadn't even met anyone other than CW2 Boren and the clerk.

I'd barely gone through the chow line and sat down when CW2 Boren ordered everyone to stand and form in a platoon outside. I looked down at my food with yearning and regret. I was starving, and the thought of abandoning a trayful of chow was kind of maddening. This was not a good start. Luckily, his assistant, Super Senior Johnson, came over and told me to finish my lunch. He sat down and brought me up to speed. There were 250 candidates in the 10th Warrant Officer Company, one of ten warrant officer candidate companies at Fort Wolters. Each Company was at a different stage of training. I was surprised to learn that Fort Wolters graduated 250 phase-1 pilots every two weeks. I asked him what a super senior was and he told me that grads who showed superior leadership skills were asked to help provide orientation to the new cohorts.

I was grateful for the overview. Johnson told me that all I'd missed the previous day was the company orientation delivered by the company commander followed by a tedious check-in process. CW2 Boren and his team checked that each candidate had everything the army issued in basic training and reviewed health records and immunization status.

Johnson walked me back to the company area after I finished my lunch and offered to show me my bunk. I was only in my cubical a few seconds before someone walked in; my jaw dropped. "Sergeant Burrington! Holy shit, Jere, how's your leg?" Before he could answer, I reached out and shook his hand, "It's so good to see you, but how did you know I was here?"

"Easy! This morning, at roll call, they called your name. I let them know you'd be here a day late. You're not the only one whose orders had the wrong date."

I was so pleased to see Jere; I'd connected well with him during advanced infantry training. "Hold on, when did you take the test for flight school, Jere?

With a big grin, he said, "When I was in the hospital at Fort Ord getting my leg fixed, I noticed an announcement about the test on the bulletin board and thought, 'what the heck?' I took the test and passed. I had to get my cast off before I could take the physical, but here I am, raring to go."

His enthusiasm was contagious, but I couldn't resist reminding him that we were now equal in rank. All candidates who qualified for this program were promoted to E-5 upon signing into their Warrant Officer Company.

My pay grade had gone from E-2 to E-5. As a sergeant, Jere was already at E-5, and entering flight school didn't change that. He looked a little peeved for a moment but quickly got over it.

The following day, "Hell Month" commenced, where our platoon Training, Advising and Counseling (TAC) officer, Mr. Boren, and his super senior assistant Johnson actively worked on weeding out "substandard" individuals. Teaching us to fly helicopters was expensive, and the army doesn't like to waste time or money on men with weak character. The army may be stuck with you, but it only wants the best people in its officer candidate schools. Weeding out weak characters was undertaken with a great deal of conviction. I was determined not to be substandard and end up as cannon fodder.

During Hell Month, reveille was at 5:00 a.m. Our five platoons, consisting of fifty men each, were given fifteen minutes to be dressed and in formation in front of our barracks, ready for inspection. This may not appear too difficult until you consider that we had to be clean-shaven, wearing a clean, starched uniform with spit-shined boots, and have all brass insignia shiny and in their proper places. The biggest challenge was shaving because the up and downstairs bathrooms could only accommodate ten guys simultaneously in front of the long mirror. Our candidate platoon leader told the younger guys with almost non-existent beards to shave at night, freeing up space for us "older" guys. Rome wasn't built in a day, and it took many candidates up to three weeks to master the journey from bed to inspection consistently on time.

In our platoon, Jere was the best at military life's spit-and-polish and general demands. His thirteen weeks of non-commissioned officer (NCO) school before arriving at Fort Ord gave him a considerable advantage. Jere might have been the better soldier, but the fact that I was already a pilot meant a lot when it came to heliport operation, so we leaned on each other a lot during our time at Fort Wolters and became the best of friends.

Pre-flight instruction involved hour after hour of listening to our instructors explain the function of the OH-23 helicopters controls. The collective flight control that changed engine power and gave the OH-23 the ability to go up or down. The cyclic flight control that changed the tilt of the main rotor for direction changes and the two separate pedal controls that changed the pitch of tail rotor to compensate for the engine and main rotor torque.

To help us follow the correct OH-23 pre-flight procedures we were given a laminated pre-flight card checklist, with a picture of the OH-23 and a black dot of where to start your pre-flight check, followed by a black line with arrows indicating direction and what to check next. The most important was the visual of gas in the gas tank and making sure the cap was on tight. On the back was the OH-23's starting and shut down procedures.

Next we spent many hours learning how a helicopter manages to become airborne. Of course, as a pilot, I knew the basics of flight and how an airfoil creates lift. The only thing I had to understand was that a helicopter's main rotor is nothing more than a rotating airfoil. Helicopters are far more challenging to maneuver than an airplane because when you change the direction of flight or move a helicopter from a static position to hovering three feet above the ground, you have to increase engine power. At the same time, you have to move both floor pedals to compensate for the power change and torque that is created. The airfoil concept was difficult for most candidates to comprehend and caused Jere to continually scratch his head in confusion.

Jere and I were sitting one evening chatting about the army, the training, our lives, and how the U.S. had landed in this mess in the first place when I turned to him and asked him why he'd enlisted. "Ah," he said, "there's a story, my friend. Well, I didn't have much choice in the matter. In January 1967, I was hauled before a judge in Downey, California, on my second DWI in six months. He read the police report, looked at my record, and offered me two choices."

He paused for dramatic effect. I decided to play along, "And, they were?"

"I could spend thirty days in jail effective immediately, or I could return to him within thirty days with a signed enlistment agreement with any branch of the military, and he would drop the charges."

Not for the first time, my jaw dropped. "That was a harsh punishment."

Jere shook his head and smiled. "Depends how you look at it. The police officer had noted on my latest DWI ticket that when he told me to sign the notice to appear, I'd asked him if he could hold my beer."

I laughed so hard that my ribs hurt. "Yep, now I get it."

Hell Month continued, and the pressure to remove weaklings continued.

During the second week of pre-flight when we returned from classes, we saw Dave Bonello's bunk stripped of its bedding, which was now piled in the middle of the floor with all his clothes from his footlocker piled on top, along with a sprinkling of Tide soap.

Mr. Boren must have thought he might be close to Dave's breaking point and was ratcheting it up a notch. Sometimes the infractions were minor; the following week Boren gave Dave a written warning for having an unauthorized copper penny in his footlocker and for the fact it was not shiny. Dave fought back by filing Lincoln's beard off the coin and then shining it with Brasso. That got him written up again, this time for defacing government property.

One of CW2 Boren's favorite ways to harass us was to wake us in the middle of the night to ensure we were all wearing our olive drab, army shorts, dog tags, and white T-shirts with our last names stenciled six inches below the neckline. If one guy out of the fifty in our platoon missed something, we all had to fall out for inspection.

The outside temperature hovered around eight degrees, and it wasn't long before many of us were shivering. CW2 Boren's solution to our dilemma was to take us on a run around the company area. When we eventually returned to the barracks, we were warm but now also wide awake. I remember it taking an age to get to sleep only to wake moments later to the sound of reveille.

Oh, the army life. And, I still had to survive another few days of Hell Month.

CHAPTER 9

# SOLO SUCCESS

I survived Hell Month as I knew I would. There was no other option. Dave Bonello also survived, but two of our platoon members couldn't cope with the constant harassment, or bullshit as they called it, and dropped the course on request. In army lingo, this meant that they DOR'd. I thought a ninety-six percent survival rate was pretty good.

Those who survived were given their first Sunday to visit their wives and to rest; it felt good to have some time to myself. I called Mom and Dad to let them know I had survived and asked about Marcheta. Mom had lunch with her shortly after I left for Fort Wolters but said she hadn't heard from her since. I had mixed feelings. On one hand, I realized that I still had feelings for her—which wasn't surprising, seeing how we had been in a serious relationship for three years—but on the other, I was going to stick to my decision not to reconnect with her.

On the following Monday, we began primary flight training. The whole platoon was excited and looking forward to the next several weeks flying helicopters. Although the brutal persecution by our TAC officer ended, everything else stayed the same. We were still expected to be bright-eyed and bushy-tailed at 5:30 a.m., day in, day out.

Our morning classes covered the academic and technical side of flying a helicopter. After lunch, they bussed us to the flight line, where we took turns flying a Hiller OH-23D. It looked like a dragonfly, but it was reliable and predictable and, as such, was a fantastic training helicopter. Our laminated checklist was incredibly useful and made our pre-flight checks and cockpit procedures easier.

As far as I knew, I was the only FAA qualified pilot in our platoon and thought I was at an advantage. That turned out to be accurate as far as standard flight operations were concerned, but the controls on a helicopter were way different, and I had a lot of difficulty handling the aircraft. Korean war helicopters are like old cars; the controls are purely mechanical and have a lot of play. They take a lot of concentration if you hope to get them to obey your commands.

After three or four flights, my civilian instructor realized I'd flown airplanes because my rudder control was awful; practically nonexistent. Once on the ground, he turned to me and said, "Miller, if you can't control the rudder on a copter, you could be dead meat in a matter of seconds. Tomorrow, I'll demonstrate simulated engine failures, otherwise known as auto-rotations. In these exercises, I'll use the full right pedal to compensate for the engine and main rotor loss of torque the instant I cut the engine power to idle. When that happens, I have to instantly lower the collective and enter autorotation all the way to its intended landing spot. You better watch carefully because you'll be doing it after me."

I nodded and he continued, "To save wear and tear, and the potential destruction of training helicopters, we will simulate engine failure recovery with power, a few feet above the runway. In order to do that you will slowly increase engine power, while slowly raising the collective and adding left peddle."

I must have looked confused.

"Okay, Miller. The pedals move from full right slowly back to near full left as you increase power and raise the collective to stop your descent three feet above the runway."

"Yes sir, I think I've got it."

Understanding the interrelationship between the collective control, anti-torque tail rotor pedals, and the cyclic stick is vital to keeping a helicopter safely airborne. Hovering meant learning to finesse the harmonious integration of these controls with both feet and both hands. It was the most difficult skill I had to master.

That evening, I was able to call Ginger and she asked me to explain how helicopter controls work in layman's terms. I told her, "The collective lever (left hand) makes the helicopter go up and down by changing the angle of pitch of the main rotor blades while adding or decreasing engine power with the twistgrip throttle control integrated into the collective lever. The cyclic stick (on the right hand) between the pilot's legs, controls the helicopter's movement forward, backward, or laterally. The anti-torque foot pedals change the angle of pitch of the tail rotor blades to counteract the increase or decrease of the engine and main rotor torque. When hovering, you are constantly making minute adjustments to all these controls. None of these adjustments can be done in isolation, you need to constantly adjust each of them to maintain a hover.

"Morgan, that sounds impossible. It makes that old party trick of rubbing one's tummy while patting one's head sound easy."

"Yes, this a whole new level of difficulty. What really makes hovering so difficult is that as soon as you attempt to gain height in a helicopter, the aircraft wants to face to the right and continue rotating in the opposite direction of the main rotor rotation, so you have to push down on the left pedal to compensate. The same happens in reverse, if you are too high you have to use the collective lever to lose height, while slowly adding right pedal. If you are not using your pedals and collective in harmony, you will find yourself spinning and hurtling toward the ground. While all this is happening you have to be in control of the cyclic stick which moves the helicopter forward, backwards, or sideways."

I heard Ginger sigh, and instantly regretted the "*you will find yourself spinning and hurtling toward the ground*" comment.

"It's okay Ginger, I'm beginning to get it. Basically, I have three sets of controls which I use simultaneously to hover—that is, maintain control of the helicopter while several feet off the ground neither going up nor down, yawing left or right, and not traveling forward, backward, or sideways. Easy!"

Silence. Ginger obviously didn't think it would be easy, then, "Morgan, if anyone can do it, you can. I have complete faith in you, honey."

What I learned at Fort Wolters was that helicopters are fundamentally unstable; they don't want to fly, and unlike an airplane they won't glide. I soon came to the realization that the only thing keeping a helicopter in the air was a pilot balancing the forces of machine against gravity, which was determined to pull the aircraft to the ground like a stone. In many ways, helicopters are ludicrous machines, but I grew to love them and trust them with my life.

Over the next few days, I studied hard and spent many hours in the dragonfly. By the end of my second week, I could fly the crazy bug around a traffic pattern without help from my instructor. By the following Monday, I made three successful trips around the traffic pattern and gained a ton of confidence. But then my instructor scared the life out of me. He told me to land so he could get out. "Miller, it's time for you to go solo; I want you to make three trips around the traffic pattern and then come pick me up." I'm sorry, WHAT? Flying solo after just two weeks?

He closed the door. I took a deep breath as I prepared for departure. If you are ever seen as weak in the armed services, you will never live it down. You could be THE T-800 Terminator—the perfect, logical killing machine—but express fear, sadness, or vulnerability, and your life might as well be over.

Once I was airborne, I began to worry more about a mechanical failure than my ability to fly this ancient aircraft. All I could think about was that helicopters could not glide. When they fail, they simply fall out of the sky like a rock dropping off a cliff.

After completing the third trip, I was confident that I'd conquered the rudimentary skills to operate a helicopter. I knew I had a long way to go, but it was a good start—I'd soloed! On the way back to the barracks at the end of the day, our bus driver stopped at the Mineral Wells' Holiday Inn where the management team greeted us warmly. My platoon members ushered me and the others who had soloed, from the bus to the hotel swimming pool, and in keeping with long-standing army tradition, grabbed me by my hands and feet, swung me back and forth several times at the edge of the pool before hurling me, fully-clothed, into the pool, while the hotel guests watched and laughed.

Talking to some hotel employees, I learned that some candidates performed crazy antics as they flew through the air to the water. I was too stunned to do anything but wave my arms and land face down. It was a rite of passage, and I wouldn't have changed it for the world. I'd passed the first big hurdle of flight school—I was on my way. Actually, I was on my way to find some dry clothes.

Later that week, Jere told me he struggled to control the helicopter. It was the first time I'd seen him under pressure. He said, "Morgan, I need to solo, and soon." I went to speak to my TAC officer, and after explaining the situation and what I had in mind, I asked permission to go to a hardware store and purchase two toilet plungers. A few days later, I sat Burrington in a chair with his back to our cubicle wall. I stuck one plunger between his legs to act as the directional control and attached the other to the wall on his left, just below his hip, to represent the up and down control. I'd already told him to wear socks so he could slide his heels back and forth to mimic using the anti-torque pedals on the helicopter floor, which need to move in concert with the other two controls.

Having built an extremely sophisticated flight simulator, I sat him in the "flight simulator" every evening before lights-out and talked him through the various flight maneuvers. My aim was to instill some muscle memory in him, so that handling the controls became second nature. Less than a week later, he told me that his helicopter control coordination had improved to the point that he felt more confident about soloing. A week later I watched Jere get thrown into the pool. My toilet plunger "flight simulator" became popular with other platoon members, who reported that it also helped improve their flying skills. By the end of the four-week solo syllabus, every member of our platoon had been for a swim.

The other four platoons didn't enjoy the same success rate, but the army was aware people learn at different rates, and it made allowances for them. If an instructor felt a student needed more time, they would arrange for the student to retake the last two weeks of the syllabus. In the end, very few people who survived Hell Month failed to solo.

*Warrant Officer Candidate bringing his OH-23 on final approach to a hover*

# CHAPTER 10

# TIME TO CELEBRATE

Soloing was a significant milestone in flight school, and the army recognized it by hosting a party for all Warrant Officer Candidates. On Saturday, there was to be a formal dinner dance. We were encouraged to invite our wives or sweethearts. Our TAC officer, Mr. Boren, informed our platoon that if anyone didn't have a guest for the party, a student from the Texas Woman's University, north of Dallas, would be happy to join them. It was a casual blind date where everyone could celebrate graduating, have a dance partner, and enjoy a fun evening.

I was excited; this would allow me to have another date with Ginger. We'd been corresponding for several weeks by then. Letters flew from Texas to California in double-quick time, and it felt very comfortable and intimate. When I called her and told her about the dance, she enthusiastically accepted my invitation. I suggested she fly in the day before so we could spend some time together. She asked whether she could bring her friend Shirley, so she didn't have to travel alone. I thought that was a good idea and told her that my good friend Jere would be happy to escort Shirley to the event. The next time I spoke to Ginger, she said they were excited about the trip and that all their co-workers were green with envy and bombarding them with questions. I liked that she was excited.

Midday on Saturday, after the company inspection, our platoon was dismissed so we could prepare for the dance. Jere and I had to pick up Ginger and Shirley, who were staying at the Hilton in Dallas about an hour's drive away. Before we left the base, we stopped off and got a pint of Canadian Club and some 7-Up so we could have pre-dinner drinks in their room. A few miles along the road, I turned to Jere and said, "Hey, I just thought, what if they don't like CC?"

Jere turned his head, grinning, "Then, I suppose we'll have to drink it!" Anything to please the ladies!

We found them waiting for us at the Hilton in the lobby. They invited us to their suite, where Ginger had thoughtfully arranged for room service to deliver a tray of cheese, crackers, and sliced meats. It was just what two hungry soldiers needed before dinner. I was impressed.

The inevitable comparisons between Marcheta and Ginger grew almost daily, even though I tried to fight them off. Marcheta was a great woman, and I did care about her a lot, but there were also many times when I had to hold my tongue to prevent an argument. One bone of contention between us was that her mother was at the apartment at least three times a week. When I came home from work at 7:00 pm, after a nine-hour shift, I just wanted to relax. With her mom there, I couldn't completely be myself.

Jere made the drinks, and I grazed on the platter while our dates donned their evening gowns and put the finishing touches to their hair and makeup.

Sitting there nursing my cocktail, I thought about Ginger and how she carried herself. She had confidence, grace, and intelligence, which showed in her deportment. Her presence belied that she was only five foot four because when she walked into a room, you noticed her.

Ginger and Shirley didn't keep us waiting long; even if they had, it would have been worth the wait; they looked amazing. Ginger wore a navy blue, knee-length dress, which accented her figure, and Shirley wore a similar dress in dark purple with a high collar. Once they finished their drinks, we headed back to Fort Wolters in my trusty Impala. Once there, we gave the girls a quick tour of our living conditions. It's fair to say that they were less than impressed. However, that all changed when they saw us in our dress uniforms. Ginger couldn't take her eyes off me; apparently, she also liked how I carried myself. I felt something stir in the pit of my stomach, and it wasn't the hors d'oeuvres or the drink.

We entered the Service Club ballroom and joined the line waiting to be received by our commanding officer and his wife. Also, his executive officer and five TAC officers were in the receiving line with their wives. Officer training prepared us for these events, and we knew the correct protocol. However, I sensed our dates were nervous, but they personified class and grace. I was proud to have Ginger on my arm. And there was that flutter in my stomach; perhaps I did need some Rolaids.

Once the formalities were over, we found four seats at one of the round tables next to two guys from our platoon sitting with their wives. Now that some other women were around, Ginger and Shirley relaxed and talked about the size of the ballroom, the decorations, the beautiful table settings, and the fashionably dressed guests.

Ginger leaned across and asked me, "Are all these men going to be flying helicopters in Vietnam?"

"Yes, Fort Wolters graduates about 250 pilots every two weeks."

She looked surprised, "Geez! That's a lot!"

We had a choice of prime rib or sea bass for dinner, with a tossed green salad, either baked potato or rice, and peas. I tucked into the prime rib, and Ginger opted for the sea bass, which somehow fit her gentile manner. After dinner, our commanding officer gave a speech recognizing our achievement of learning to fly solo in a matter of a few weeks and for completing this phase of our training.

Once he sat down, the band began to play "Tighten Up" by Archie Bell, and almost immediately, the dance floor grew crowded. I took Ginger's hand and led her onto the dance floor to try a modified swing. We danced for several songs, talking, laughing, and learning more about each other. Being with her was becoming increasingly comfortable; it felt so good, so right; so . . . normal. I told her how happy I was at this moment, not only because I had completed the first phase of my training and could see graduation as a reality, but more importantly, that she was there to share it with me.

Later, while dancing to "In the Still of the Night" by The Five Satins, I couldn't resist kissing her gently on the lips. Her response was warm and tender, it was the first time we'd kissed, and I prayed it wouldn't be the last.

As the evening wound down, I looked around the room. Everyone looked happy and relaxed, thoughts of war far from their minds. I wished it didn't have to end. I was broken out of my reverie by a band member shouting, "Last call!" We had one last dance, gathered our belongings, and prepared to leave. The four of us walked over to the commanding officer's table and thanked him and his officers for a fantastic evening.

When we got back to the car, Jere and Shirley got in the back seat, and Ginger sat next to me in the front. We drove slowly through the base, talking about our fabulous evening. Once on the interstate, everyone became lost in their thoughts, with only the road noise filling the silence. Ginger snuggled close. I sensed that the memories of an exciting evening were slowly turning into far more romantic thoughts for all of us.

About fifteen minutes later, I looked in the rear-view mirror to discover that Jere and Shirley had disappeared from view. Good for them. Ginger's head was on my shoulder, and I could smell her perfume. There was that flutter again.

On arrival at the Hilton, we escorted the girls to their room and were invited inside for a nightcap. I wasn't exactly sure what to infer, but in keeping with proper army conduct, we kissed the ladies goodnight and told them we'd booked a room at the hotel and would be back in the morning to take them to breakfast and the airport. The following day during breakfast, Ginger smiled and reached out to touch my hand. It's incredible how much is conveyed in a simple touch, how much electricity can pass between two people, and how even strangers passing the table can see that you are in love, even if you don't know it yet. It was hard to say goodbye; I already missed her, and she hadn't even left. And any thoughts or memories of Marcheta were quickly becoming hazy in my mind and my heart.

# CHAPTER 11

# LOVE IS IN THE AIR

After breakfast a few weeks ago, when Ginger reached out to touch my hand before I took her to the airport, our relationship stepped up a gear. We were now firmly a couple. We exchanged letters frequently, and I called her every Sunday. Our talks were so easy, so natural. I was talking to someone whom I knew was not judging me, not demanding that I be anyone other than who I was. Ginger was very different than Marcheta. My thoughts of Marcheta receded even further in my memory. One Sunday evening, after much hesitation, I finally took the plunge.

"Ginger, I think I'm falling in love with you."

Her instant reply was, "You only think?"

I stuttered, "Well, no, you, you, know what I mean."

She laughed and whispered, "I feel the same way, Morgan; I have for a while."

I was glad she couldn't see my face. I wasn't sure what I felt, but it felt good.

A few nights later, I told Jere, "I'm thinking of asking Ginger to marry me."

He looked up from polishing his boots and said, "Whoa there, buddy! Ginger's a super nice lady, but what's the rush? You were all about delaying it with that previous girl of yours."

"I know, Jere, but this feels different. For the first time, I feel confident I'll go to Vietnam as a helicopter pilot, not an infantryman. That changes things."

He looked up again from his boots, "Come on, how does it change things?"

I felt he wasn't being as supportive as I'd hoped, but later I saw that he was testing me, making me think things through. He was a good friend.

"Look, I know I could wait until after I graduate in September, but if we got married, we'd be able to live off base when we go to Fort Rucker. I really like . . . I *love* this girl. All this, of course, depends on whether she'll have me."

Jere had put his boots down to give me his full attention. I looked at them, one shiny one dull; I hoped I wasn't the dull one in Ginger's eyes. "Oh, don't be so dense, Morgan; a blind man could see that she adores you. She'll say yes."

"The other thing is that I'd like to have a life together before I go overseas. I want to enjoy spending time with her, I want to be with her . . . in case . . ."

Jere smiled, "Well, it looks like you've made up your mind. Good luck; you have my support, my friend. If she says yes, you will be one lucky man."

I remembered, when I was a kid, asking my mom what love was.

"Oh honey, you're a little too young for that."

"But Mom, I really wanna know! Do you and Dad love each other?"

"Well of course we do, Morgan."

I had noticed that when I mentioned Dad, she immediately smiled, and the corners of her eyes wrinkled. Also, her expression changed. Her eyes sparkled and she seemed to glow.

"One day, you'll fall in love, and you'll know when it's right. I can't really explain it. But you'll know."

Fast forward twenty years later and sure enough, Mom was right. *I knew.*

Not one to rush into things, though, I thought about proposing for a month, and then, one Sunday, I called Ginger and popped the question. I'd played the call out in my head a dozen times, and in all scenarios, the question hung in the air, silence at the other end of the phone. A silence that lasted for varying lengths of time; the longer the silence, the greater the embarrassment. I needn't have worried; Jere was right. She immediately and enthusiastically shouted, "Yes, yes, Morgan, I would love to marry you!"

My aunt owned an antique store in San Diego, so I called and asked if she could send me some photographs of any stunning engagement rings she had in stock. I chose an 18-karat gold Edwardian ring with a one-carat diamond in the iconic Tiffany setting, where the diamond is held by six platinum prongs allowing it to float above the gold band and so attract more light. It was stunning.

My cousin delivered the ring to Ginger at the hospital a week later. Thank goodness she loved it. I was sad I didn't get the opportunity to place it on her finger, but under the circumstances, it was as romantic as the Vietnam War and the U.S. Army would allow.

The following few calls were all about wedding plans. It wasn't going to be straightforward and would need precise planning. Setting a date was going to be difficult. I was due to graduate on May 31, and then I . . . we . . . would head straight to Fort Rucker, in Alabama, for the advanced phase of my pilot training. As I had been the men's platoon candidate leader for the previous two months, many of them wanted to attend the wedding. Time and circumstances were not our friends.

However, fate stepped in to relieve a little of the pressure. I was talking to my TAC officer about the wedding, and he said, "How about you stay behind for two weeks after graduation and be my super-senior and help me get my incoming class get squared away?"

Without hesitation, I said, "Sure! That will give Ginger and me time to adjust to marriage before we drive to Fort Rucker for my final eighteen weeks of training."

The following Sunday, I called Ginger and said, "How about we get married the day after Saturday's graduation? Our families can be here for my graduation and our wedding. Also, members of my platoon will be able to attend because they don't have to leave for Fort Rucker until the following day."

There was a momentary hesitation, and then, "Wow, Morgan, that's perfect. We don't have much time, but I can make it work on my end. But hold on, that means we'll be heading off to Alabama the day after our wedding. How the heck is that going to work?"

"Oh, sorry, Ginger, I left out an important part. My TAC officer has asked me to be his new super-senior for two weeks after graduation. That will delay Fort Rucker long enough that we get some breathing space. We can get used to being married. It won't be a honeymoon, but it's the next best thing."

I was silent for a few seconds as the reality of it all sank in; I was going to be a married man—and very soon. Ginger interrupted my thoughts, "I'm going to ask Shirley to be my maid of honor." I said that was great, as I wanted Jere to be my best man, and I knew he would be delighted to see Shirley again.

The next couple of months dragged on; navigation classes in the morning, two hours a day of flight training in the afternoon. I learned to land on steep slopes and rounded pinnacles high above the surrounding terrain. After dark, I partnered with another candidate and practiced night flying, a scary procedure. Looking down into the inky blackness, our thoughts went to how, in an emergency, we would put the helicopter down when we couldn't see the ground. Hard, I imagined. Very hard.

Graduation day crept closer, and Jere and I went to the airport the day before the big event to greet our guests and, of course, the bride-to-be. At the airport, there was a flurry of introductions. The Miller family met the Palmers, and everyone met Jere. My parents and soon-to-be in-laws rented a car, and Jere and I drove Ginger and Shirley to the Holiday Inn in Mineral Wells and helped them settle in. That night we all had dinner at the hotel. It was my first time meeting Ginger's parents, so I was nervous and keen to make a positive first impression. During the meal, questions shot back and forth as we all got to know each other better. I was pleased that our parents seemed to get on well and that Ginger's parents seemed to recognize that I was a man of integrity who loved their daughter and was about to serve my country.

The graduation ceremony the next day was held on base. The major spoke first, commenting on the training we had just received and the importance of our phase one flight training in preparing us for heading to Fort Rucker, where our training would reach a new level of intensity. Following the ceremony, there was a reception at the Holiday Inn. It was a happy event for graduates and for those families who could attend, punctuated by hearty pats on the back, hugs, and ear-to-ear grins.

The celebrations continued the following day when we got married with the support of our parents, friends, and platoon members. Ginger wore a figure-hugging, full-length, light blue dress with spaghetti straps. Shirley looked very chic in a light blue suit. Jere and I both looked debonair in our dark blue dress uniforms.

It was, of course, the highlight of the weekend. The ceremony took place in Fort Wolters chapel, a long, white, two-story, clapboard building with a steeple. The building dates back to 1921, when the base first opened as a National Guard Training Center. It had a high coffered ceiling, and balconies ran along each side featuring leaded glass arched windows. Ancient, dark, burnished wood pews ran the length of the church. The altar at the far end was under a dome framed by a massive arch. There was a sense of grandeur and peace about the place. As I stood at the altar waiting for Ginger, I could hear the wooden pews creak and squeak as our guests fidgeted. I resisted the urge to turn and look down the aisle. I knew that I would be spending the rest of my life with her, so I waited until, at last, she was by my side. She was beautiful. The ceremony itself was short and straightforward and delivered by the camp chaplain. Neither of us had written vows; we knew what we meant to each other. We looked into each other's eyes as we said, "I do," and when the pastor said, "You may now kiss the bride," it was the happiest moment of my life. Even better than flying solo for the first time.

After the ceremony, everyone made their way to the Holiday Inn; for the second time in two days, we enjoyed typical hotel banquet food, shrimp cocktail to start, and a choice of chicken and roast beef for the main. The hotel manager did us proud by decorating the tables with light blue tablecloths and dark blue napkins. In a touching gesture of support, the centerpiece was a model Huey helicopter. That made me smile.

Jere and Shirley picked up where they left off in January and looked like a lovely couple. They would continue to write to each other for quite some time, but by the time Jere headed home to Los Angeles after his stint in Vietnam, the fire had gone out, and Shirley had found someone else.

It was a unique time in history; it was an unpopular war that divided the country. Regardless of whether America should have become involved or not, patriotism and support for the military ran deep. When my father-in-law went to settle the catering bill, the manager said, "Mr. Palmer, the bill has been paid in full."

Shocked, he asked, "But, who the heck paid it?"

The manager smiled and said, "Mr. Palmer, I am not at liberty to divulge the person's name, but he is a local rancher who, it seems, wanted to help your daughter and her new husband before the young man heads overseas."

Honeymoons in times of war are a luxury. I was at work the following day by 5:00 a.m., helping my TAC officer prepare for the incoming cohort.

# CHAPTER 12

# OFF TO FORT RUCKER WITH MY BRIDE

Within days, I questioned my decision to stay behind and take on super senior duties at Fort Wolters. I'd rented a furnished mobile home just outside the base, and before dawn, I'd creep out of bed so as to not disturb Ginger and head to the base, returning sometime after 5:00 p.m. It was only two weeks, but twelve hours a day, six days a week, when your new wife was waiting at home for you, was not a great start to married life. After two days, I told Ginger, "This was a mistake; we should have gone straight to Fort Rucker."

"It's not a problem, Morgan; how were you to know it would be this tough? We both thought it was a good plan, and we're in this together, and it's only for two weeks. Don't worry about me; I can sleep in late and figure out what I want to take with me to Rucker and what I want to toss. And besides, I can relax a little and dream about this wonderful adventure we've just begun."

It was an adventure, alright, but whether ending up flying helicopters in a war zone was going to be wonderful was another question. When I opened the front door every evening, the wonderful smell of home cooking greeted me. Ginger was a great cook; I'd come home to chicken fried steak with fresh vegetables and a green salad. She also did a mean tuna casserole with noodles.

After dinner, I'd shower, and shortly after, we'd head to bed and begin a delightful exploration of each other's bodies. I'd fall asleep a happy man. On one occasion, I remember awakening and realizing that Ginger was no longer beside me. I got up and walked into the living room to find her reading a book. She turned to me, "Sorry, I hope I didn't disturb you; I couldn't sleep. Our lovemaking is so new, so exciting, so . . . exhilarating; I need a little time to settle myself down. Otherwise, I'll never sleep." I kissed the top of her head and went back to bed. Being married to Ginger was going to be just fine.

Ginger was correct; the two weeks went by quickly, and orienting new warrant officer candidates was rewarding. It allowed me to prepare them for the boot camp they were just about to endure, but I was so glad I wasn't in their boots, though!

We loaded a small U-Haul trailer with all our earthly possessions, hooked it to the back of my Impala, and set off for Fort Rucker, almost 800 miles east. We thought about taking the more scenic route through Baton Rouge and Mobile but elected instead to stay on the I-20 and spend the night in Jackson, Mississippi. It was a long first day. The reward was that by leaving the motel at eight a.m. the following morning, we arrived at Fort Rucker by early afternoon. Several of my Fort Wolters classmates—who arrived two weeks earlier—were there to greet us and help us unload the trailer. I'd rented a furnished mobile home close to Rucker, so we were settled in no time. I'd heard some less than charitable descriptions of some of the many trailer parks and homes in the area, so we were pleasantly surprised that our trailer, at Hidden Springs Mobile Estates, was clean and well-furnished. A communal swimming pool and barbecue area served as a gathering place for people in the trailer park. These get-togethers gave our wives a chance to connect and were especially important because some women's husbands were serving overseas.

It was not uncommon for army officers to turn up with news that someone's husband had been killed in action, so the camaraderie between military wives was strong. The trailer park wasn't peaceful; the constant sound of helicopters overhead, night and day, was a reminder of why we were all there.

• • • • •

Every morning throughout my training, Ginger would go on a five-mile run into Daleville and back. I was very proud of her; she was fit, followed a healthy diet, and made the other guys' heads turn.

In Primary I flight training, we had civilian pilot instructors, mainly from Southern Airways; and at Fort Rucker, our instructors had recently returned from Vietnam. It was good to know that these men had been flying helicopters in war zones and were ready to impart their first-hand experience to us. It's one thing to understand how to take off, hover, and land a helicopter, but I knew doing it in enemy territory would be completely different.

Everything was more intense and immediate at Fort Rucker; it felt like Vietnam was much closer than ever before. We flew in and out of Hanchey Army Airfield, which was the largest in the free world. Hanchey was huge; imagine more than fifty-two football fields, and you will have some idea of how vast an area it covered. Approximately 600 helicopters were active on any given day, and there were more take-offs and landings daily than at all three New York airports combined. To say it was busy would be an understatement. The slap, slap, slap sounds of hundreds of rotor blades—sounds caused by each blade striking the wake of air caused by the previous blade—was breathtaking and, at the same time, immensely powerful and reassuring. On my first day at Rucker, I watched dozens of take-offs and landings, in awe of the pilots' skills and anxious to take my turn.

My first fifty hours of flying were in a TH-13T Bell helicopter, specially equipped for instrument training. Learning to fly an aircraft on instruments alone is hard enough, but the army had a way of fast-tracking the learning curve. My instructor explained, "Mr. Miller, the hardest thing about flying solely by instruments is to trust them. We tend to believe what our senses tell us, but our senses are not always correct. At night, or in fog, you may feel like you are flying upside down, even though your instruments dispute that belief."

Many years later, I recalled my instrument training vividly. It was when President John F. Kennedy's son, John Jr., and his wife Carolyn Bessette-Kennedy, took off on a short plane flight from Fairfield, New Jersey for a wedding in Hyannis Port, Massachusetts. Although Kennedy was a licensed pilot, he experienced a phenomenon called "spatial disorientation" as he flew over the coast of Massachusetts on that summer night when conditions were described as dark and hazy. Sadly, Kennedy was a non-instrument trained pilot, which meant that he relied solely on his flying skills and not the plane's instruments, a fact that proved fatal to him, his wife, and sister-in-law.

My instructor handed me a face shield to attach to my flight helmet. The "hood" had a top and two sides and prevented me from seeing anything outside the aircraft. I felt like a racehorse with blinders. All I could see was the instrument panel. I felt like I was walking along the edge of a cliff blindfolded.

We took off, and it was the weirdest feeling. I knew our exact altitude and speed, but it all felt wrong. My instructor told me to climb, descend, turn, and do many other maneuvers. I flew from point to point by homing in on radio beacons and carried out a ground-controlled approach. This involved coming in for a landing using only instruments and the guidance of a person on the ground tracking me by radar. I knew I was approaching the ground; it felt like it was getting menacingly close and getting closer. Not being able to see it or whether there were trees in the way was unnerving.

Over four weeks, with only one hour of flying time per day, I gradually learned to trust my instruments, no matter what my senses tried to tell me was reality. It wouldn't be long before I put my newfound skill to the test. Torrential downpours, fog, thick smoke, and nighttime missions were on the horizon; I just couldn't see them yet. At the end of my training, I received my Tactical Instrument Card—one more step in my journey to Vietnam.

After completing the instrument phase of my training, I was introduced to the UH-1B Huey helicopter, which I would fly for the following sixteen weeks. Unlike the Bell, the Huey was not a training aircraft; it was a veteran helicopter used for reconnaissance, cargo transport, search and rescue, medical evacuations, and airborne assault. It could also be a gun platform carrying rockets, grenade launchers, and machine guns.

The Huey was impressive, unlike the other helicopters I'd flown to that point. It was a smooth ride, simple to fly, handled well, and very stable. I loved its responsiveness and power; more importantly, its renowned reliability was comforting as I thought about flying over a jungle packed with enemy combatants.

At Fort Rucker, we built on all that we learned at Fort Wolters, but the graduation from small training helicopters to the Huey made a big difference. In Vietnam, our roles would be to deliver our infantrymen into suspected enemy locations, evacuate casualties, perform armed reconnaissance, and resupply American and ARVN units on the ground. Our training Hueys were often loaded with Jerry cans filled with sand to replicate the weight of troops. A laden helicopter handles very differently from an empty one, especially when the wind is howling, it's pitch black, and the enemy is shooting at you.

It became second nature to take off and land in small clearings, and from pinnacles and slopes, often between towering trees. As did low-level, high-speed approaches to a target site—the idea was to get in and get out fast or be shot down. I negotiated close combat formations until my head hurt. Plus, landing without power was a skill that could save your life if it didn't give you a heart attack first. As our skills improved, our instructor left us to practice formation flying day and night with a fellow trainee.

The intensity was such that, unlike at my previous two camps, I didn't develop strong friendships with fellow trainees. Part of this was because, as a married man, I was allowed to live off base. After twelve hours of training, all I wanted to do was get home, eat, and sleep. Although we got Saturday afternoon and all day Sunday off, the only people we'd socialize with were the other trailer park residents. The strange thing is that I never once saw Jere while I was there; it was only weeks later I discovered that his class went to flight school at Fort Stewart and Hunter Army Airfield, near Savannah, Georgia.

My eighteen weeks at Rucker were intense, nerve-wracking, exciting, and ultimately rewarding. I no longer had any doubts about graduating from flight school. Once the end was in sight, our platoon was shipped off to Florida to undergo a five-day escape and evasion training course. We reached Camp Rudder, located at the Eglin Air Force Base, feeling apprehensive after hearing stories of a scary, final-day simulation. Throughout the week, we learned survival skills that included building shelters and skinning and cooking whatever animals we could catch. Evasion was next, including how to evade the enemy if trapped behind enemy lines and how to escape if the chance arose. In real life, almost no one ever escaped a North Vietnamese Army Camp, but a few did manage to extricate themselves from jungle camps. I can attest to this, but that part of my story comes later.

The rangers told us that we should expect imprisonment, torture, starvation, and more if caught. It was a tough week, during which I ate things that would make a billy goat puke and tromped around the hot, humid, forested swamp.

It all turned very real on our last day, just when we were preparing to go home. It was 6:00 p.m., and we were waiting in formation outside the barracks with our rucksacks packed and on our backs. An army ranger brought us to attention, "Okay, men, I hope you took the training you received this week seriously because today you will put it to test in a very realistic simulation."

We looked at each other, and I could almost hear the entire platoon suppressing groans of resistance.

"Here are maps and coordinates to safe pick-up locations. If you make it, helicopters will be waiting to take you back to Fort Rucker. Easy, yes? Well, maybe not. Between here and the helicopters, there is a lot of swamp to navigate. Oh, and just to make it interesting and even more realistic, we've released a bunch of experienced rangers whose sole job is to prevent you from escaping."

I looked around, and many of the men were smiling as if it was a game of hide-and-seek. The ranger continued, "If captured, you will be brought back here, imprisoned and tortured. I am being deadly serious. If you are caught, under no circumstances will you give the "enemy" what they want."

I'd heard that the North Vietnamese were less interested in military movement information and tortured prisoners into giving statements that could be recorded and used as propaganda.

The ranger looked from man to man and said, "This will not be a pleasant experience, and I guarantee if my men catch you, they will torture you. And, I promise, you will crack—eventually."

By the look on his face, he was enjoying his job.

The smiles disappeared, and you could have cut the tension with a knife. I'd heard rumors they used waterboarding—maybe it was true. Waterboarding was where captors strapped a hostage to a sloping board or table with his head and face completely covered with cloth or a hood and positioning his body so that his head was lower than his feet. The captors would then pour water over his face—an action that simulated drowning and could cause enough physical and psychological trauma to force the hostage to "break" and divulge secret information. I didn't want to find out, not only because I wanted to get home to see Ginger but because I didn't like the idea of being tortured by my own side. I planned to take this exercise seriously. It could be a life-and-death situation in a few months if I had to put down behind enemy lines. Reports from Vietnam told of prisoners suffering extreme torture, solitary confinement, and life-threatening malnutrition. That is, if the enemy didn't kill them first.

Before we set off, my group of five agreed that there would be no talking and we'd make as little sound as possible. We quickly got off the trail and disappeared into deep cover. There, we found a different kind of enemy—relentless bugs. The Florida swamps have biting midges or no-see-ums; they and mosquitoes gathered in clouds. What they lacked in size, they made up for in numbers. It was difficult not to inhale them. We'd learned that snakes were less of a problem because they scattered if they heard you coming, which would have been comforting if not for the fact we were trying to be silent. The more significant threat was spiders, the brown recluse and the brown and black widows. I'd read that there were also scorpions but took comfort in my sturdy army boots and pants tucked into my socks.

Most of the time, we walked in ankle-deep water. The biggest threat was the "enemy," I did *not* want them to catch me. The thought of torture was one of the scariest things I could imagine. I became super-vigilant and raised my hand to silence the group whenever I heard voices, however distant, even though no one was making a sound. We'd stop to see if the voices got closer or faded away. I suppose the bad guys would have been silent, so we probably heard the voices of other poor saps like us. I'd never felt as uncomfortable in my life.

A previous student had advised me, before we left Rucker, to pack candy bars to supplement the terrible food we had to eat during our time in Camp Rudder. It was a long, wet night, and they'd given us no food, but those candy bars saved the day. I'm not sure how far we hiked, the going was slow, and we stopped every few yards to listen for anything that might indicate we were walking into a trap. We walked all night, navigating with our senses more than anything, as we didn't have flashlights and couldn't have used them even if we had. We tried to keep the road in sight wherever possible as we could see from the map that it led to the safe area. Later, we heard that some of our platoon members had left the forest cover for the easier road. They were captured almost immediately. In the army, there are no shortcuts.

As the first rays of daylight broke the darkness, we came to the clearing where we were to meet the helicopters. We kept low and hidden in the trees at the edge of the open space. We didn't trust that the "enemy" wasn't lying in wait for us. We rested there for about forty-five minutes until we heard the familiar, sweet sound of a Huey—*thwap, thwap, thwap*. Once it landed, we ran to it and climbed aboard as if our lives depended on it; I think by then, we'd convinced ourselves that it did. The smell that greeted us was mind-blowing. Knowing we'd be cold, wet, and starving, the crew had brought us hamburgers and fries from a local fast-food joint. Nothing ever tasted as good.

Later, we heard what our captured colleagues had suffered. The stories were unsettling. Some had spent the night in cages without food; others had electrodes attached to their nipples and given shocks. It may not have been waterboarding, but it certainly wasn't fun.

That night, I slept in my own bed, snuggled up to Ginger, and thought about Vietnam and whether I'd need what I learned that week at Camp Rudder. I hoped not.

A week later, on October 18, 1969, I graduated from flight school. I got my Warrant Officer bars the day before and wore them to the ceremony. Ginger attended and proudly watched as I accepted my certificate and shook hands with a receiving line consisting of instructors, officers, and the camp commandant. I was now officially a Warrant Officer and had earned my wings. Next stop, Vietnam or . . .

CHAPTER 13

# VIETNAM DELAYED

S hortly before we graduated from Fort Rucker, I learned that not all of our remaining class of nearly 200 pilots were going directly to Vietnam. Now that President Richard Nixon was at the helm, he reassessed America's role in Vietnam. South Vietnamese troops began to assume more responsibility for ground combat, and, in late June 1969, the U.S. gradually began to withdraw its forces. During this period, troops' morale in Vietnam was low, and public opinion back home was ramping up as anti-war protesters became increasingly vocal. In October, just six days before I graduated, thousands of protesters stormed Fort Dix Army Post in New Jersey. The Secretary of Defense, Melvin Laird, announced that between six and seven thousand troops would remain in Vietnam after hostilities ceased.

In Vietnam, after the TET offensive, discipline among U.S. forces started to break down as ground troops lost faith in their leaders as fast as a tsunami hitting a village and wiping it out. Many soldiers began questioning what they were fighting for and why they were even in Vietnam. There were a few stories of embedded military personnel (often addicted to drugs) killing their senior officers and unit leaders with fragmentation hand grenades because they thought they were inept and directly endangering the lives of soldiers under their command and care. This blatant disregard for human life became known as "fragging."

However, the war continued, so I wasn't out of the woods yet. But a reprieve is a reprieve, and I gladly accepted my new posting. My fellow platoon members were sent to army bases across the United States; I drew Fort Riley in Kansas. After learning my fate, I asked Ginger, "Where the heck is Fort Riley?" We unfolded a map on the kitchen table and discovered that we'd be moving to Junction City, one thousand miles away.

I was due at Fort Riley on October 21, so housing was a priority. We found a Junction City newspaper at the local library and were relieved to see, in the classifieds section, *Downstairs Apartment for Rent, $400 per month.* Given that we were in panic mode, we called the number, talked to a pleasant man, and rented the place sight unseen. It was that or a far more expensive hotel.

A few days later, I reported to Fort Riley, and then Ginger and I went in search of our new "home." When we pulled up at the house, we were pleased to see that it was a picture-postcard, single-family home on a large city lot. Our hopes were high; we knocked on the door, and a smiling, middle-aged couple greeted us. The man held out his hand and announced, "We're the Millers." I shook his huge, meaty hand, grinned, and said, "So are we. I mean, we're the Millers too." Everybody laughed, and they invited us in.

Mr. Miller was still laughing as he led us into the living room, "Well, welcome, have a seat. Would you like something to drink?"

We were tired, so I said, "No, thanks, we'd really just like to see the apartment please."

"Okay, follow me, it's in the basement."

We looked at each other and nodded; *this might be perfect.* Our optimism quickly died, though, as we descended the stairs into a family room occupied by four children stretched out on the floor playing a game. Our new landlord led us to the rear of the basement where they had erected a flimsy partition, with a door to section off the "apartment." Ginger gripped my hand so tight I thought she was in pain. We entered what was going to be our new home, at least for a while. There was a musty smell and no natural light. I couldn't believe it; there were no windows—no windows meant no daylight and no fresh air. It was a cramped living space, with a tiny bathroom and kitchen. I knew Ginger could not cook great meals in this limited space, which the owner laughably called a kitchen. We later discovered that even making a grilled cheese sandwich might catch the room on fire! I wasn't sure what concerned me most, the space itself, the lack of light and ventilation, or as a young married couple, the complete lack of privacy. With only the uninsulated wall separating the family room from our "apartment," we could hear the children playing on the other side of the paneling, even though their parents had obviously told them to be quiet. If we could hear them even being quiet, that meant we could never do *anything* that generated any kind of noise without them hearing us. It was worse than being in front of a live studio audience.

I turned to Mr. Miller, "Sir, you have to be joking; we were expecting a lot more for $400 a month." I couldn't figure out if his smile conveyed a snarky *You sucker*, or a resigned *Sorry, pal, it is what it is!*

"Well, Mr. Miller, I'm not sure we're going to take it, but we're tired and hungry, so we'll sleep on it and get back to you."

He smiled again, which was already more than annoying. "Do you want the keys to our front door and the door to your apartment?" he asked.

I thought about it and decided not to burn any bridges. "Okay, considering you have our deposit and first month's rent, I'll take the keys." He handed them over, and I told him I'd be in touch.

We stayed at the Junction City Holiday Inn for several nights. It was frustrating to pay twice for accommodation, but neither of us could bear the thought of our namesake's basement. We searched for somewhere better but struck out, so I eventually called the Millers and said we'd move in that Saturday.

We learned after a few weeks that Fort Riley had a strong connection to Vietnam. The 9th division had been deployed to

Vietnam in January 1967 and had returned the previous August, which was why Ginger and I were having so much difficulty finding a place to live.

It was a stroke of luck that I was assigned to the 9th Division Command Aviation unit, with the only two operational helicopters on the base, a Sikorsky CH-34 and a Hiller 23D. The 9th Division in Vietnam didn't have its own aviation unit, it relied on the army's 1st Aviation Brigade for helicopter gunship support, troop movement and medivac.

The Command Aviation unit, to which I was assigned, was responsible for the base's airport, control tower, and 24/7 security. Fort Riley's commanding general's pilot, Major Spencer was on call to fly the general or staff member wherever they needed to go in the base's six-passenger, twin-engine Beechcraft airplane. As I was airplane-rated, I was lucky enough to be one of his co-pilots and had the opportunity to fly the Beechcraft at least once a week.

Six pilots were in the unit, and we were on duty Monday through Friday from 7:00 a.m. to 4:00 p.m. Weekends rotated, so I only had to work one in five. After a week at Fort Riley, I realized my life was going to be very different. I was an officer and a professional pilot and respected as such. It was more like having a job than being a soldier.

Ginger quickly secured a position as a nurse at the Memorial Hospital in Manhattan, Kansas, only twenty-five minutes from Junction City. Getting a job was huge for Ginger, because it meant she could escape our apartment during the day. She would have gone insane, trapped in that windowless dungeon. Her job doubled our income, which allowed us to enjoy an active social life. We joined my fellow pilots and their wives at the officer's club every Friday night for cocktails, dinner, and dancing. It was very civilized and polar opposite to my life during army training. Life felt good; we went to the movies and attended cultural events at Kansas State College in Manhattan.

My commanding officer encouraged me to join the Post's Flying Club and finish the necessary training to pass my commercial airplane check ride. I was impressed; he had checked my records and seen that I'd taken and passed the FAA written examination and had my FAA commercial helicopter rating. Going for my airplane check ride was a massive step in the right direction; my long-term goal was still to be a commercial airline pilot. The club's president, who possessed an FAA flight instructor's certificate, prepared me for my commercial airplane flight test, and several weeks later, I took and passed that flight check.

Being a member of the club as well as friends with the president had several advantages, none more so than being allowed to use the club's Cessna 172 during the weekends. Ginger and I were excited to explore Kansas from the air but, coming from California, a land of mountains, lakes, and an ocean, it looked like a home without furniture. We were always looking for something exciting to do, and the club's president suggested we fly to the abandoned Schillings Air Force Base in Salina to watch the new Boeing 747's test flights. It turned out to be a fantastic day. We taxied to within 100 yards of the main runway, sat in the shade on folding chairs under the Cessna's wing, and watched as the massive aircraft was put through its paces by Boeing's test pilots.

I turned to Ginger and said, "Honey, not to bore you but did you know the 747 will be the first aircraft with two aisles? The economy cabin will have ten seats across, ten! And, it will have a first-class lounge upstairs, can you believe that! It'll carry 366 passengers—amazing! It can fly over 4,500 nautical miles with a cruising speed of over 550 miles per hour."

Ginger smiled.

I watched, enthralled, as the pilots flew the giant aircraft around the traffic pattern, repeatedly taking off and landing. Maybe one day . . .

Back to reality, we could stand the apartment no longer. Maybe things would have been different if an actual wall had separated

us from the rambunctious, eavesdropping kids, but knowing they
were still close would still have made for an awkward, impossible
existence. This was no way to live. With no idea how long we
would be at Fort Riley, we visited a mobile home dealer close to
Ginger's job and looked at a new 12' x 60' two-bedroom Marlette
unit. Inside, we stepped up from the sunken living room into a
large kitchen featuring modern appliances, including a dishwasher
and trash compactor. There was a laundry room with a washer and
dryer that separated the two bedrooms. Back in the living room,
I could see Ginger looking at the large windows on either side of
the unit. I said, "How about that? Light and ventilation, what a
novelty!"

She playfully punched my arm, held onto it, and asked, "Can
we afford it?"

We decided to buy it, but there was a problem. We had to have
somewhere to put it, and all the local trailer parks were full. In the
end, we told the dealer that we'd buy it, but only if he could find
us a pad to put it on. With this incentive, he went to work on finding a home for our new home. Several days later, he called to say
he had found us a spot at a local KOA campground immediately
outside Fort Riley's front gate. We went to investigate. It wasn't
perfect by a long shot; there were no trees, and the neighboring
trailers were close. We thought about it for thirty seconds; it was
a million times better than living with the Millers. The dealer was
lucky that we were so desperate to have our own space and privacy.

Again, we rented a U-Haul trailer. I was beginning to think we
should buy shares in the company! Our next month's rent was due
at the Millers, so we moved out and went back to the Holiday Inn
while they put the finishing touches on the Marlette and moved it
to the park. It wasn't long before we moved into our first real home,
and Ginger quickly put her stamp on it. Once she got it up to her
homey comfortable standards, we had a housewarming party and
invited my colleagues and their wives from Command Aviation.

Standing outside with a beer before everyone arrived, I thought back over the past sixteen months of training. I'd come so far from:

"Grab a formation, privates."

"Eyes straight ahead, Private!"

"Don't eyeball me, Private! Are you deaf? Get down now and give me fifty push-ups!"

I was now an officer, a qualified pilot, a married man, and had a flying "job."

Despite Vietnam hovering in the background, I felt, at that moment, my life was remarkably better than the one I'd left behind in Lakeside, California, fewer than two years ago.

# CHAPTER 14

# VIETNAM LOOMING

A little less than five months after arriving at Fort Riley, my orders came through and posted me to Vietnam. I'll never forget the date: It was March 10, 1970, and my heart sank. We'd just settled into our new home; I enjoyed my "job" and I absolutely loved being married to Ginger. Life up until that point was pretty damned perfect. However, upheaval is a way of life in the army, so I expected it but was hoping it would be several months later than it was.

The army gave me a thirty-day leave and was generous enough to pay a trucking company to move our trailer to Lakeside, California—my old hometown—and where my parents still lived. A new mobile home park recently opened in Lakeside, and my dad had managed to get us a site for our trailer. Once again, we rented a U-Haul trailer to transport our possessions back to California.

We decided to turn the 1,500-mile trip into a 3,000-mile journey and visit Carlsbad Caverns and the Grand Canyon. This was the honeymoon that we'd never managed to take. There are 119 caverns beneath the Chihuahuan Desert, and we decided to take a guided tour to see some of the most impressive. Some of the guided tours were extreme and required crawling through small, wet, muddy tunnels. For some visitors, the experience was overwhelming, and not in a good way. According to the guides, there were always one or two visitors who experienced panic attacks because of the sudden realization that the caves could, well, cave in. Some even freaked out when they approached smaller and smaller cave entrances and the tour group had to stop while these poor souls backed up into the more open areas and stayed put while the group explored and then rejoined them to exit the caverns. Hearing this, we opted to do the mile or so Big Room Trail. The Big Room is the biggest cave in North America and has spectacular cave formations with descriptive names such as "Chinese Theater," which had formations shaped like Asian pagodas; "Temple of the Sun," featured spooky-looking outcroppings that looked like giant upside-down animal tusks; and "Longfellow's Bathtub," which is a cave pool that lies beneath a frozen waterfall. Ginger's favorite was "Doll's Theater." It had hundreds of soda straw stalactites and columns, which looked like string cheese dripping from the cave roof. I was especially in awe of the Rock of Ages, so-called because an ex-superintendent of Carlsbad Caverns—Colonel Boles—used to sing "Rock of Ages" to visitors, who would join him in singing the hymn. The voices echoing across the cavern were, by all accounts, awe-inspiring. That tradition died out in the mid-1940s, and the guides told us to keep our voices low so visitors could experience the silence of being deep underground. At the Rock of Ages viewing spot, I found myself quietly humming the tune; Ginger gave me a nudge to quiet me. The lookout, set on top of a hill, enjoyed a view across the 4,000-foot long and over 600-foot-wide chamber to other stunning formations. It was a far cry from the hot and humid jungles I would soon be experiencing.

A few days later, we visited the Grand Canyon; it was as if we needed to see more of God's grandeur before I put myself in his hands in that far-off, war-torn country. We did lots of sightseeing and learned a lot about the geology and history of the canyon. We were both stunned that the canyon was forged six million years ago by the waters of the Colorado River. The trip's highlight was a mule ride halfway down the canyon. The mule wranglers introduced us to our steeds for the trip; mine was named Gypsy, and Ginger's was named Buttercup. The wrangler told us that the mules had been specially trained and were incredibly sure-footed—that was comforting. It was hot and dusty, and it was only March; I couldn't imagine what it would be like in June and July when I heard the highs regularly hit the mid-eighties. At times, the mules took us along narrow, steep cliffsides; I was so glad I wasn't scared of heights. My other preoccupation was watching out for rattlesnakes; I'd heard they could spook the mules and mountain sheep above that could dislodge rocks. The ride wasn't for the faint-hearted. After a one-hour lunch break, we headed back up the trail. Saddle sore doesn't begin to describe how we felt; it took us six hours to get back to the rim.

We stayed at the historic El Tovar hotel, which first opened in 1905. It had been designed by the architect of the Atchison, Topeka and Santa Fe Railway, Charles Whittlesey. It was a little rustic, but clean and well maintained. Dinner was a flavorful, "cowboy-grilled" ribeye steak with baked potatoes, green beans, baked beans, and a salad in the dining room. It was the trip of a lifetime.

After stopping for a night at the Desert Inn, in Las Vegas, our five-day honeymoon came to an end, all too quickly. But it felt good to be back in Lakeside. We stayed in my childhood home with my parents while we waited for our trailer to arrive. As a married man, it was odd sleeping in my old bedroom, a tiny loft overlooking the kitchen. Again, privacy eluded us. The clock was ticking, and I would be on my way to war in three weeks.

At last, the trailer arrived, and Ginger and I unpacked the U-Haul. It was good to have our home back. I would at least be able to visualize Ginger at home whenever we managed to speak by phone or when I read her letters. It was ironic that just as we managed to get ourselves a permanent home, I was leaving for an unknown amount of time and facing an uncertain future.

I surrounded myself with family and friends and embraced being home, even if it was just a fleeting visit. However, three weeks passed quickly, and discussions soon centered on the logistics of my departure. I was due to fly out of Travis Air Force Base in Northern California on the morning of April 10, so Ginger's and my last night together would have to be somewhere closer to the airport. We decided to fly from San Diego to San Jose the day before and book into the Holiday Inn north of the city. We would take a cab to the base to say our goodbyes. Poor Ginger would then take a taxi back to San Jose airport for the lonely flight home.

On the morning we left, Mom cooked a big breakfast. Ginger's parents joined us, and we all tried to be as upbeat as we could. Mom's face was strained; she'd been crying. I knew that it was tough for her. Dad said she was reliving the time he left for the Pacific Theater during WWII. Everyone came to San Diego to see us off; it was heart-wrenching to see my mother so upset. After many tears, Ginger and I waved goodbye and made our way to the gate.

The flight to San Jose was uneventful; we were both lost in our own thoughts and barely spoke. There was so much to be said and yet so little. Vietnam had been front and center for so long that we'd learned to shove it to the back of our minds and no longer talked about the eventuality. However, we both knew one day it would be upon us, and now was that day. We took a cab to the hotel, and once we got to our standard commercial grade hotel room, Ginger made dinner reservations at an upscale restaurant nearby. We wanted our last evening together to be memorable. The restaurant served excellent steak, but we both decided on the catch of the day: white sea bass. The chef cooked the fish perfectly, the skin was crisp, and the flesh, which was slightly opaque, glistened and flaked satisfyingly away with the merest touch of my fork. This and Ginger's glass of wine and my rum and coke should have put us in an excellent state of mind, but the cloud hanging over us was darkening.

I took a shower back at the hotel, and Ginger arranged for a cab to pick us up at six in the morning. The atmosphere between us was tense; there was too much pressure. We both wanted intimacy, but it would be the last time for who knew how long? We lay on the bed, neither wanting to make the first move. I suggested we go down to the pool. With our robes tightly wrapped around us, we made our way through the lobby and the courtyard to the pool deck, which was dark. No one was there, and Ginger suggested we get into the Jacuzzi. I arranged a few chairs between us and the lobby and hung towels over them. Dropping our robes, we slipped naked into the warm water. I put my arm around Ginger, and she put her head on my shoulder. After a few minutes, she stood up and sat on my lap facing me, her head in the crook of my neck. All I could say was, "I'm glad I suggested this; it's just what we needed."

"Babe," she whispered, "I know how difficult it must be for you thinking about Vietnam and what might happen. But know this, I am so happy to be here right now with you as your wife. And I'll be at home waiting for you when you return."

A wave of emotion swept over me, and I realized that we should quickly remove ourselves from the public place we were occupying because things were heating up fast. Back in the room, nothing could have stopped the passionate coming together of two lovers, save for a nuclear explosion, and even then, we would have died happy.

The alarm woke us the following day, and we packed quickly and checked out. The cab was waiting, and we headed off to Travis AFB for my 8:00 a.m. departure. As we arrived, hundreds of protesters held signs bearing anti-war slogans. I looked at them; they were scruffy and disheveled with long, unkempt hair. They were cursing and yelling at soldiers entering the base and attempted to block traffic. One guy rushed the cab in front of us and banged on the window; with lightning speed, someone in the cab grabbed him and dragged him through the window. The cab inched forward, and after about twenty seconds, the protester was hurled out of the cab on the other side like a sack of potatoes. He looked even more disheveled than before. Turning, I could see another protester helping him to his feet.

Outside the terminal, when we retrieved our bags, I asked our cab driver if what we had witnessed was common. He turned and said, "That was a first for me, but I have heard from other cabbies about similar incidents."

When I paid him, he said, "My son is over there with the Marines. Good luck, Sir."

In contrast to the near riot outside, the terminal was relatively calm, and the check-in process went smoothly. The waiting area was packed with wives, kids, moms, and dads, all saying their goodbyes. I held Ginger's hand until the last moment. At exactly 7:35 a.m., the announcement was made to board the aircraft. Ginger and I got up and headed to the boarding gate. Many wives were crying, but Ginger was steadfast as we walked along with our hands gripped tightly. Finally, at the separation point, we kissed and hugged, and with tears in her eyes, she said, "I will be sending you my love and prayers every night, and I'll see you in Hawaii for your R&R."

With that, I turned and boarded the aircraft to whatever destiny awaited me.

# CHAPTER 15

# TWENTY-THREE HOURS WITH HENRY

I walked out of the terminal into the sunlight and turned to look for Ginger, but the windows just reflected the sky and the gray airport apron. I was on my own. I looked again when I got to the top of the stairs. Even though I knew I wouldn't see her, I waved, hoping she could see me. Sighing, I ducked slightly, entered the aircraft, and started walking down the long aisle of the Douglas DC-8. The DC-8 is a narrow-bodied, long-range plane that came into service in 1959; it was tried and true, and that felt as comforting as anything could when you looked at my circumstances. Seating was six abreast; I looked for a vacant aisle seat. I wanted to have the freedom to stretch my long legs during the twenty-three-hour journey.

Halfway down the aircraft, I found the ideal seat and hoisted my bag into the overhead compartment. In the middle seat was a young man. A teenager. Man, he looked young, just a kid. I don't think he'd even shaved yet. An army staff sergeant occupied the window seat and looked out toward the terminal. I wondered who he had left behind. His face was as devoid of emotion as a plate of steel. I recognized the Combat Infantry Badge on his left chest and several rows of ribbons. *He'd seen action.* I sat down and tried to catch his attention, my hand stretched out to shake his and introduce myself. He was either lost in thought or ignoring me. I withdrew my hand and turned my attention to the kid.

"Hi, I'm Morgan."

We shook hands. He had a firm grip, his hand calloused; he was used to hard work.

"Hi, I'm Henry," he said with a sheepish grin.

I smiled, "My first name is Henry too, but I go by my middle name Morgan."

I settled into my seat and looked again at the inscrutable man in the window seat. On closer inspection, his medals were impressive. He had a Bronze Star with a "V" and two oak leaf clusters and a Purple Heart with one oak leaf cluster. The Bronze Star is awarded for distinguished or heroic service in a combat zone. The two oak leaf clusters indicated he had been awarded the medal three times. The Purple Heart is award-ed, in the name of the president, to people wounded or killed in battle. It indicates great sacrifice, and this sergeant won the medal twice. It was then I noticed, gripped in his left hand was a green beret. The Green Berets were special forces soldiers who specialized in guerilla warfare; they were one of the most elite fighting forces on earth. This guy was a bona fide American hero.

He must have sensed that I was staring at him because he turned and looked straight through me with a blank stare that sent chills up my spine. He said nothing and resumed his scrutiny of the terminal and its traffic. I recalled something my AIT instruc-tor had told us trainees, during machine gun training, "You will run into combat veterans who have what's called the 1,000-yard stare. When you see it, you'll never forget it." I was never sure what he meant until now. I couldn't—or more importantly, didn't want to—imagine what this man had been through to earn all those commendations and that 1,000-yard stare.

Next to me, Henry fidgeted; he had seen the stare and was clearly nervous. In an attempt to fill the silence, questions came tumbling out of him nonstop. "Where are you from? Are you married? What is your military occupation specialty?" After answering this initial barrage, I told him that I was going to relax for a few minutes as we waited for the plane to take off.

We pushed back from the terminal and began a long, slow taxi to the active runway. The huge rubber wheels bumped over the cracks in the tarmac in a rhythmic, hypnotizing dance. Eventually, we stopped at the top of the runway, and I could imagine the pilot and co-pilot checking their instruments as they waited for the final all-clear from the tower. Then, the familiar high-pitched whine of the jet engines as the DC-8 accelerated down the runway pushing me back in my seat as the aircraft quickly gained speed. I loved that feeling. I still do. Soon after the plane left the ground, I could hear the landing gear retracting into the aircraft's undercarriage with a satisfying clunk.

I watched as we passed over San Francisco and headed out to sea. I sat back, reclined my seat, closed my eyes, and thought of Ginger. Her new husband was heading to a volatile combat zone, and she was flying home alone. That made me feel sad. I thought about how much had changed in her life over the past ten months and all the sacrifices she had made for us. I couldn't believe the depth of my love for her.

Henry broke into my thoughts with another deluge of questions. I had a flash of impatience and was about to brush him off, but when I looked at him, I saw that he was scared to death. Talking was his way of not thinking about the dangers that lay ahead. Somewhere over the Pacific Ocean, the plane became progressively quieter, the cabin crew dimmed the lights, and we fell asleep.

Stress is exhausting, and it was five hours later the captain's voice woke us. "Gentlemen, fasten your seat belts. We will be landing at Hickam Air Force Base in Hawaii in about twenty minutes."

I told Henry, "This is our first of three refueling stops."

"Okay, gentleman." It was the captain again. "We ask that you all deplane and get some refreshments. We'll be on the ground for about an hour."

Henry and I walked into the terminal together and sat down for lunch. As we ate, he bombarded me with even more questions. I didn't have answers to many of them; even though I was older, I was just as green as he was when it came to anything related to Vietnam.

It was the first time I'd been able to see him face to face. He was young, he had peach fuzz below his sideburns and on his upper lip—a dog could have licked it off. He was solid, though; he reminded me of the drill sergeant Paulson decked in basic training. The memory made me smile. It felt so long ago.

I was warming to the kid; he was obviously in need of a big brother figure, and I needed a distraction. After lunch, we wandered over to the newsstand, and I picked up a copy of the book *Instant Replay: The Green Bay Diary of Jerry Kramer*, which had received good reviews when it was published in 1968.

The hour went by quickly, and we were soon back on board for the next leg of the interminable flight. I intermittently read my book and listened to Henry. He was nineteen and from a small town in Wyoming. His family owned a cattle ranch, and he grew up doing chores and working on the farm after school and during holidays. I could see how he had earned those rough, workman's hands. After high school, he enrolled in a few classes at community college, but was at a loss as to what to do with his life. His grandfather fought in WWI and his dad was part of the Normandy Invasion, landing on Utah Beach with 21,000 members of the 4th Infantry Division. He thought he'd like to carry on the family tradition, so he enlisted in the army. What surprised me was that it was a spur-of-the-moment decision, and he hadn't discussed it with his parents. I shook my head; it sounded very much like me at his age: ungrounded, naive, and needing direction. Henry was no more than a child who would soon be forced to make life-and-death decisions in split seconds in a combat environment. I prayed that he would quickly grow up and learn to make wise choices.

And that he—and I—would survive to tell those tales to our children and grandchildren.

I looked out the window and saw that we were at cruising altitude heading over the open ocean on our way to our next layover in Guam. Talking to this young man made me think about my childhood, mainly as a preteen in Lakeside. In Lakeside, where every dad was your dad; it was a close-knit community. I was thinking back to when I was ten, and I went to the movies with my best pals, Dave and Mike, of taking-the-skunk-to-school fame. After the movie, we waited outside for Mike's dad to pick us up. Dave looked at his watch and announced we had time to cross the street and get a candy bar from Graeme's Market. We walked over, but after checking our pockets, we discovered we didn't have a dime between us. I started to walk away, and Dave said, "Let's steal a candy bar!"

Mike and I looked at him, our eyes wide as if he'd just cursed out loud in church. But Dave looked defiant, "Me and Mike will go in and distract Mrs. Graeme—we'll go to the magazine rack, that's sure to get her attention. Then, Morgan, you come in and grab a candy bar. Easy."

Dave repeated the plan, and we all shook hands to seal the pact. We went back to the store, and Dave and Mike went in; I was to count to 100 and then wander into the store. I was so absorbed in counting and nervous about my part in this grand theft that I didn't see Mr. Walt Hartung come up behind me. He put a hand on my shoulder, and I nearly jumped out of my skin. Mr. Hartung was in his early forties, 6'2" tall and 240 lbs. He rode Brahma bulls in the annual Lakeside Days rodeo and was hired by our County Sherriff whenever he needed "muscle." Walt was known around town by troublemakers for his patented warning. He'd look down at a miscreant and say, "You don't want me to come back."

"What are you boys up to?"

He'd seen us planning and shaking hands. I lowered my head and said, "Dave and Mike went to get a magazine."

"*Hmm*, that sounds fishy to me. You stay right where you are—don't move." I was rooted to the spot, no one messed with Mr. Hartung. He went into the market and came right back out, holding Dave and Mike by the scruff of their necks. He lined us up against the wall outside the store and said, "Let me see your money."

We looked at each other and hung our heads. I said, "We don't have any money, Mr. Hartung."

"Okay, now we're getting somewhere, we're all going to go back inside, and each of you will apologize to Mrs. Graeme for planning to steal from her store."

We trooped into the market without another word, Walt close behind. When we got to the counter, we turned and looked at Walt. His look was thunderous, "Go ahead, gentlemen."

I started by apologizing for planning to steal a candy bar and further explained that Dave and Mike were just the decoys. Dave and Mike said they were sorry and admitted that we were all in it together. Mrs. Graeme said nothing. She just looked at us with no expression on her face. I felt guilty and sad. She looked disappointed.

Walt said, "Now, you kids, get out of here."

"Wait a minute, boys," Mrs. Graeme said, "for your honesty, I want to give each of you a candy bar." We couldn't believe our luck. But Walt held up his hand.

"No, Ma'am! We are not going to reward bad behavior here."

Then he looked at us, pointed to the door, and boomed, "Get out!"

That was the first and last time I tried to steal anything.

I'd been so deep in memories that I hadn't noticed Henry talking to the staff sergeant. I was surprised. I leaned forward to let them know I was back from my daydream and ready to join in the conversation. Henry was asking all the questions I hadn't known the answers to and was getting a wealth of information from the veteran. So was I.

I stood up to stretch, wondering why the sergeant had changed from taciturn to talkative. All I could think was that it had been emotionally challenging for him to get on the plane back to Vietnam, where I was sure he had been wounded on more than one occasion. Now, beyond the point of no return, he had accepted his fate and had re-entered army mode.

A few hours later, the captain came on the intercom and told us to fasten our seat belts. He said we would be landing on the island of Guam for fuel, and once again, everyone would have to deplane. Henry and I walked together to the terminal and were pleasantly surprised to see the staff sergeant catch up to us and offer to buy us a beer. It looked like Henry might have two big brothers. Since talking to Henry, I got the feeling that the hardened veteran had softened and perhaps remembered his first time heading to Vietnam. I noticed that the sergeant was taller than me; he must have been at least 6'2", and you could see solid muscle under his T-shirt. There were three empty seats at the bar, and he took the middle one.

"What'll you have?" he asked.

Henry said he'd like Coke, and I said I'd have the same.

The sergeant ordered a beer, and I noticed his name tag, *Forbes*. He was about my age, but he was more worldly. The things he'd seen and experienced were etched into his face, and his eyes reflected a deep sadness. I reintroduced myself and discovered his first name was Bill, and he was heading back for his second tour. On hearing this, young Henry started with the questions again; he seemed to have an endless supply. Bill patiently answered as many as he could. Henry hung on his every word as if something he learned from Bill might one day save his life.

When, at last, Henry could think of nothing else to ask, I asked Bill why he thought the previous three American presidents—including current President Richard M. Nixon—thought it a worthwhile sacrifice of more than 40,000 American lives in Vietnam to try and stop the spread of communism. The question flew out of my mouth before I could filter myself. I immediately panicked, wondering whether the question would upset him or otherwise set him off in a previously unleashed spate of frustration and fury. But you can't un-ring a bell. I just had to hope he wouldn't lash out at me in any way. He was unpredictable, that's for sure. The transformation from a hardened, stiff-upper-lip soldier to bar buddy was unnerving, at best, so who knew how he'd react to this line of questioning? Bill paused for a while before answering. I didn't know which way it would go. But in the end, I realized he'd had his answer prepared long beforehand and was just waiting for someone—anyone—to pose the question.

Instead, Bill softened as he answered. Part of his answer sprang from the time he was a student at Rutgers University in New Jersey. It was during those years that he recalled learning how President Franklin Delano Roosevelt, Harry S. Truman, and Dwight D. Eisenhower felt about Russia and its then-totalitarian way of government. Generals in the United States were tasked with putting an end to communist aggression and applied their knowledge of domestic guerilla tactics, as well as those of the North Vietnamese, against the French to stave off the progression of that type of government. President Kennedy, in the early 1960s and post-Cuban Missile crisis and the Bay of Pigs debacle, formed what was known as the "SOG" or "Studies and Observation Group," whose members learned unconventional warfare practices. The name belied the member's skills. Their mastery was highly honed and comparable to that of the British SAS and Israeli Mossad. They eventually became known as the Army Special Forces and the Navy Seals.

During the Vietnam war, the SOG teams, consisting of two men from Special Forces and four indigenous soldiers, operated behind enemy lines. The men covertly took photographs, culled intelligence and evidence, captured NVA officers and convoy drivers, and carried out general area monitoring of the Ho Chi Minh trail.

All the collected information was transferred to MACV intelligence analysts, who sent their recommendations to the Air Force's B-52 squadrons and the Navy aircraft carriers in the Gulf of Tonkin, which resulted in attacks that crippled—but didn't completely shut down—North Vietnamese supply routes.

I am sure my mouth dropped open. I was amazed by Bill's grasp of history and politics. He was, without question, extremely well-read. I was about to say something of the kind before he continued, but the overhead speakers crackled, and a deep, booming voice announced, "Attention, all American service personnel. Your flight to Vietnam is now boarding."

We looked at each other, guzzled the rest of our drinks, and walked out into the 100-degree heat. As we made our way to the aircraft, Henry Harris was quiet, deep in thought. For my part, I was still trying to absorb Sergeant Forbes' history lesson.

It felt good that the three of us bonded. There's nothing worse than being alone; there's too much time to think. After take-off and once we reached cruising altitude, we all sat back comfortable in our own space, while readying ourselves for the next leg of our journey to Clark Air Force Base on Luzon Island in the Philippines.

Four hours later the engine noise changed, and the captain announced that we were descending and would be walking out into ninety-five-degree temperatures with 100 percent humidity. As we stepped out of the aircraft's air-conditioned cabin, Henry looked at me, his eyes wide open in surprise at how hot it was. Neither of us had experienced this sort of atmosphere. We could hardly breathe, and when we did, it felt like we were inhaling air from a 400-degree oven. The terminal was just in another soulless airport, but it was cooler than outside, offered a bar and newsstand, and gave us a much-needed opportunity to stretch our legs. So far, the trip had been incredibly long and tedious, and the next stop would see us land in Vietnam.

Back on the aircraft, the three of us grew instantly quiet. Thoughts of Vietnam crowded our minds. As we drew closer to our destination, after twenty-three hours, I realized that the sun had never set. We had been following the sun for the whole journey, but now, as we made our final descent into Biên Hòa Air Base in South Vietnam, it was low in the sky. As we made our final approach, it dropped unceremoniously into the South China Sea as if putting a period to the end of our journey. We landed with a thud, and it was like I had entered a black hole; suddenly, it was real. I grabbed my throat; it felt like something was gripping it and preventing me from breathing.

Darkness enveloped the base; my feelings turned to awe and astonishment. I was in the combat zone about to start a one-year obligation to the army, although it felt more like a prison sentence. The DC-8 taxied and eventually rolled to a stop. The captain told us to remain seated. A minute or two later, an Air Force sergeant got on the plane, "Welcome to Biên Hòa, men, everything is quiet right now, but that could change in an instant. As you get off the aircraft, if you hear 'incoming,' run to the lighted bunkers at the sides of the tarmac leading to the terminal building. You'll be safe there."

I grabbed my overhead bag, swallowed hard, waited my turn to deplane, and then stepped into my destiny.

# CHAPTER 16

# WELCOME TO BIÊN HÒA AIR FORCE BASE

As I stepped out of the aircraft with Sergeant Forbes, the first thing I noticed was the humidity—and the stench. I asked Bill, "What is that foul smell?"

He looked at me and smiled, "That, my friend, is a combination of burning rice paddies and third-world shit."

I wrinkled my nose and thought, *Heck, I have 365 days of this in front of me, and I won't even get time off for good behavior*!

We walked into the air-conditioned comfort of the terminal and over to the baggage claim area. Henry Harris was already there. Bill rummaged in his bag and handed us some small white tablets. They looked like Bayer aspirin. "Guys, here's a couple of sleeping pills each. I suggest you take them this evening; they'll help you get over the jetlag."

As pleasant as it had been to spend time with them, I was eager to get going once I grabbed my duffel bag off the carousel. I shook hands with my two new pals and said, "Good luck, gentlemen, keep safe." As soon as the words came out, I realized that would be tough to accomplish; both would be heading to the front line.

I headed to the line-up for the bus that would take me to the 90th Replacement Battalion at Long Binh. While I waited, I felt a tap on my shoulder. It was Henry Harris, beaming from ear to ear, "Hey, Mr. Miller, do you want to ride with us in the Special Forces Jeep that came to pick up Sergeant Forbes?" I think he thought he was riding with John Wayne. I thanked him but refused. The bus would be just fine for me.

The base was only four miles southeast of the terminal. Once there, I followed the signs for in-processing; I must admit, it felt good to be going through the officer's entrance.

After I finished the paperwork, staff directed me to the barracks to find a spare bunk. I quickly unpacked my immediate necessities, including my shaving kit, shower shoes, and clean underwear. The shower was a slice of heaven: hot, steamy, and long. I let the hot water ease the stress from my shoulders and neck and sluice down my body. It's amazing the places you hold stress. I discovered muscles I never knew existed! Once I'd brushed my teeth, combed my hair, and donned new underwear, I felt like a new man.

The processing clerk told me where to find the mess hall. *Ah!* That was my next stop. I was starving, but a little nervous about the quality of the food. I shouldn't have worried; a large bowl of white bean and ham soup and some hot rolls tasted like the best food you could find on earth. It's amazing what a good, flavorsome meal, a hot shower, and clean clothes can do to lift the spirits; but even after all of that, I was dog tired.

Back at my bunk, I took one of Bill's sleeping pills with a full glass of water and laid my head on the pillow. The next thing I remember is waking up to full sunlight streaming through the windows, fully rested thanks to Sergeant Forbes and his "magic" pills.

I spent the next two days acclimating myself to Vietnam and the base. The sights, smells, the noise, the bustle—it was all foreign to me, but at the same time exciting. Finally, I received my orders to report to the 3rd Squadron, 17th Air Cavalry Regiment—

aka 3/17 Air Cav—stationed at a fire support base called Dĩ An, situated east of the Đồng Nai River, a dozen miles northeast of Saigon.

• • • • •

Early the following day, I was picked up by Jeep and driven directly to a helicopter pad. My driver instructed me to wait for a chopper with a yellow triangle just below the main rotor. I stood in the heat for fifteen minutes, watching the busy base traffic and hoping that there would be no "incoming" while I was standing out in the open. I heard a chopper getting closer, and as it came in to land, the yellow triangle indicated it was my ride. I grabbed my duffel bag and headed over. The pilot handed me a helmet with the cord already connected to the intercom. He smiled and told me to use the rear seat belt to secure my duffel. Over the intercom, he said, "Welcome to A Troop 3/17 Air Cav, I'm Captain Reynolds," and shook my hand. When I noticed the minigun sticking out of my side of the Hughes OH-6 chopper, reality set in with an almighty thud; it was used for attack missions, not only escorting new Warrant Officers. It was then that I began searching for bullet holes.

Captain Reynolds took off and, as we gained a little altitude, I could see the extent of the airport for the first time. I was stunned at the sheer number of people and trucks moving about, and helicopters landing and taking off. My first thought was, *It sure doesn't look like things are winding down here.* Once we left the traffic pattern, we made a sweeping turn and headed south, and I could see below the terrain I would soon be flying over. There were rice paddies in every direction, something I'd only ever seen in a book. It was surprising how flat the land was, with Saigon in one direction and the ocean in another. There was less fertile jungle than expected, even though I knew the army had cleared more than 150,000 acres using Agent Orange, a potent defoliant and, as the world would later find out, was the cause for birth defects, illnesses (including cancer) and even death. Seeing the barren landscape was a powerful reminder of America's impact on this land.

My thoughts were interrupted as the chopper lost altitude quickly, dropping to fly low along a tree-lined river. We were gaining on a distant bridge pretty fast. I looked over at the airspeed indicator; it read 120 knots (130 miles per hour) and closing in on its maximum speed. The bridge got closer, then really close, and I expected, in an attempt to scare me, Captain Reynolds would carry out a quick cyclic climb over the bridge at the last moment. I looked across; he was one hundred percent concentration. When I turned to the front, my heart missed a beat; he was going to fly under the bridge. Far from being scared, it was exciting, unbelievable, impossible—what a rush! As we gained altitude again, I looked across, and Captain Reynolds grinned from ear to ear. I wondered whether I had passed my first test—a test of nerves.

We landed at Dĩ An, and I thanked the captain for a most . . . entertaining . . . ride. After getting into the captain's Jeep, we drove to 3/17 Air Cavalry Squadron headquarters. I'd barely had a chance to catch my breath when the squadron's first sergeant took the captain and me in to meet the squadron commander. Once the sergeant closed the door, we came to attention and saluted. The colonel returned the salute, we shook hands, and he invited us to take a seat. He asked for my personnel file, and after several minutes of intense scrutiny, he said, "Wow! Captain Reynolds, we have a meat cutter in our squadron!"

I was mystified as to why my first career choice had provoked such an outburst.

He put the file down on his desk, and said, "I played football at school with Vince Lombardi, and he used to work in his dad's meat market on Saturdays and during the summer break."

Afterward, I saw the point in having us write our autobiographies as warrant officer candidates. At least I made a tenuous connection with the Lt. Colonel; I wasn't just a number—I was "Meat-Cutter Miller."

"Mr. Miller, you will be filling a vacancy in A Troop. Captain Reynolds will take you over and help get you settled.

At our troop headquarters, Captain Kilcrease, the troop's executive officer, assigned me a "hooch," which I soon discovered was my room, later learning that it also referred to a southeast Asian thatched hut.

He said, "Drop off your duffel bag and then meet me in the Officers' Club for lunch."

I saluted, "Yes, Sir!"

Captain Reynolds showed me the way to my new living quarters and informed me that the only person I needed to salute, when I eventually met him, was the officer in charge of A Troop, Major Dervaes. He showed me the shower block along the way and pointed to my "hooch," which was right next to a volleyball court. You learn not to get attached to where you live in the army because everything is temporary, but it was nice to have an actual room to myself. I threw my bag onto the bed, closed the door, and we headed off to the Red Horse Inn, Officers' Club, otherwise known as the O-Club. XO Kilcrease beat us to it, so we joined him and ordered hamburgers for lunch.

Over lunch, Captain Kilcrease updated me on my immediate schedule. In under an hour, I had an appointment with the flight surgeon for a full physical. Two hours later, I was to do a helicopter check ride in a Bell UH-1 Huey. Finally, at 5:00 p.m., the first sergeant would give me a tour of Dĩ An Fire Support Base, followed by a return to the XO to complete more of what the army loves—paperwork.

The only thing on my agenda of some concern was the check ride in a Huey. It had been seven months since I had flown one, so I feared I might be a little rusty. At precisely 3:00 p.m., I turned up at Squadron Headquarters and met the standardization instructor pilot, who took me to the flight line. I was nervous, and my hands were damp, but I told myself I had this. I was correct; I passed without a problem, and the instructor immediately cleared me for combat duty.

I met the first sergeant for my tour of the base. My first question was, why is it so quiet? He told me that most of A Troop were about two hours south of the base at another fire support base named Sóc Trăng. They'd been there for several weeks. B and C Troops of the 3/17 Air Squadron were also operating in other areas of III Corps.

During the tour, I noticed that the bunkers were in disrepair, some were flooded. The sergeant said there had been no attacks on the base in years, but it was still guarded 24/7 in case a Viet Cong decided to creep in under the concertina wire fence with a satchel charge. I raised an eyebrow when he said this and he laughed, "The VC are sneaky, the satchel charge is an explosive device with handles. If they can get close enough, they'll hurl it into a bunker, an ammo dump, or even a helicopter." As we continued the tour, the sergeant pointed out several manned machine gun pits along the perimeter of the base.

Later, I caught up with the XO for dinner at the O-Club. He shook my hand and congratulated me for passing the helicopter check ride and my physical. I thanked him and sat down.

"So, Mr. Miller, do you feel combat ready?"

I smiled, "I hope so. Time will tell."

During dinner—a cheeseburger this time—I realized that we still had more paperwork to complete, begged off due to exhaustion and asked if we could handle it in the morning? He said "sure," and told me to report to the orderly room at 8:00 a.m.

It had been a long three days with a lot to process. Sitting on my bed, I thought back to leaving Ginger at the Travis Air Base and how heart-wrenching that had been. I'd flown a Huey for the first time in more than half a year—that was stressful. Okay, exciting, but also nerve-wracking. *What if I had failed the check ride?*

The last thing I remember was removing my shoes. I woke fully dressed and reached out for my watch. It was 10:00 a.m.; damn, I was already two hours late for my meeting with Captain Kilcrease. In a panic, I undressed, showered, shaved, re-dressed, and ran to the orderly room. I burst through the door and apologized profusely for being so late.

The XO smiled, "Calm down, Mr. Miller, your ass-chewing days are over. We're all professionals here, just trying to do our job. Just don't make a habit of it." I couldn't believe my ears; this was so unlike basic training. He looked up from his paperwork, "This can wait; let's go and get some chow. Maybe they'll have some eggs and bacon today and not just some oatmeal? A guy can hope, right?"

*3/17th Air Cavalry Squadron Headquarters at Dĩ An*

# CHAPTER 17

# 359 DAYS LEFT, BUT WHO'S COUNTING?

A fter lunch, we completed the outstanding paperwork, and Captain Kilcrease told me I had the rest of the day to get settled into my room. "And, Mr. Miller, introduce yourself to your hooch maid. You'll need to pay her $10 a week; she'll clean your room, make your bed, do your laundry, change your sheets, and polish your boots."

He also offered me his jeep to visit the Post Exchange (PX) at Biên Hòa should I need to purchase any personal items from the store. I accepted his offer, and Captain Reynolds offered to drive. We talked, and I told him I appreciated the XOs thoughtfulness. He said, "Yes, we are lucky to have him here." I'd only been in Vietnam a few days, but Captains Reynolds and Kilcrease had done everything in their power to help me adjust to my new life; it was already beginning to feel less like a prison sentence and more like an almost "normal" job. Looking back, though, I realize how naïve that thought was. I hadn't seen combat yet.

Over dinner, we discussed the hunter/killer missions and our unit's part in them. I already knew the basics. The "hunters" were Scout helicopters that flew low and slow over enemy territory to entice the Viet Cong to open fire and expose themselves. Immediately after the scout received fire, the pilot's observer, aka door gunner, would drop a white phosphorus smoke grenade, aka Willie Pete. This incendiary grenade burned white hot and marked the target for the Cobra gunship overhead. As the scout helicopter pilot shouted, "Receiving fire!" to alert the "killers," he took evasive action evacuating the area as quickly as possible, while his observer fired his machine gun at the enemy. The pilot in the Cobra gunship, 1,500 feet above, came down hard and fast, firing rockets and miniguns to help the scout escape.

What I didn't know was how the Scouts knew where to look. There were thousands of square miles of territory to cover, so I asked, "How do you know where to look for the enemy?"

Captain Reynolds explained, "We are a support unit for American combat units, and sometimes Army of the Republic of Vietnam (ARVN). They get their intelligence from long-range reconnaissance patrols (LRRPs) or from prisoners they've captured. Helicopters drop the LRRPs into known enemy areas to covertly gather information. They actively avoid contact with the enemy. A few days later, a helicopter picks them up and flies them back to base, where analysts review their intel. They look for any information that will help them pinpoint enemy locations. Based on this intelligence, our troop operations dispatch hunter/killer teams to these locations."

I bit into yet another burger—the menu was extremely limited— and thought about what the Captain just told me. So, I asked, "What if you stumble on a heavily armed enemy encampment? How can one gunship hope to wipe them out?"

"In that case, the Cobra pilot will climb to a higher altitude and decide whether to use artillery or request the Air Force FAC (Forward Air Control) send fighter jets to the location to carry out an airstrike."

In response to my furrowed brow, Captain Kilcrease added, "Mr. Miller, you are so lucky, most people only read about history; you will get to see and live history being made here with A Troop."

Captain Reynolds leaned forward, continuing from his previous point, "Sometimes the intel is no good, and we spend the whole day trolling the jungle without making enemy contact."

I pushed my plate away, "Does the enemy ever discover the LLRPs? And, if they do, how do you extract them?"

"Good question, Mr. Miller," Captain Reynolds said, "this does happen, and as soon as we get the call, we go out with a hunter/killer team to provide enough firepower to give them a chance to escape the area and make their way to a nearby landing zone. Our Slick—aka a Huey utility helicopter—will then extract them."

My heart was pumping; this was becoming *very* real; we were dealing with life-and-death situations. We weren't just looking at strategic maps or practicing with fake targets. For heaven's sake, the thought of flying at tree-top level in a tiny helicopter, actively hoping the enemy would fire on you, seemed like the definition of madness. I was glad I wasn't going to be flying the Scouts.

Captain Kilcrease rose and said, "Goodnight, gentlemen. Mr. Miller, you are heading out tomorrow afternoon for Sóc Trăng. You'll go on the ash-and-trash resupply run. When you arrive, report to Captain Womble; he's the lift platoon leader." With that, he waved his arm in farewell and left.

Surprisingly, I got a good night's sleep, had an excellent breakfast, and got myself organized and ready for the next leg of my journey to the combat zone. Shortly after lunch, the company clerk arrived at my room and said, "Sir, the truck to the flight line is ready to depart."

I grabbed my duffel bag and followed him out. The Huey carried helicopter parts and mail. Squeezed into the rear seats were two enlisted men. You could have knocked me over with a feather—one of them was Henry Harris. I laughed and said, "Hi Henry, fancy seeing you here!" We shook hands. I was pleased to see the kid again.

I took the co-pilot's seat and shook Captain MacDonald's hand; he was blond and a couple of years younger than me. "Welcome to A Troop, Mr. Miller." After departing the Dĩ An traffic pattern, visibility became poor.

I asked, "What's with all the smoke?"

Captain MacDonald explained, "This is the time of year where the Vietnamese farmers burn their rice fields. They do it to get rid of the remaining straw after the harvest; it also kills pests and controls disease."

Once we landed at Sóc Trăng, I had a chance to get reacquainted with Henry, or "HH," as I called him. However, we only had a minute or two before his infantry platoon sergeant arrived.

"What was all that about?" Captain MacDonald asked.

"That young private and I sat together on the flight from Travis—he's a nice kid. Now, I see we're in the same unit; what are the odds of that?"

Captain MacDonald nodded, "Sure is a coincidence, there are a ton of units he could have gone to, but he's lucky to be here. He could have ended up in a "straight-leg" combat unit."

I asked him what he meant and that I hadn't heard the term before. He explained, "'Straight-leg' combat units don't have helicopters; they hump around the jungle for weeks on end, looking for the enemy. Nasty work. Your friend will mostly do helicopter rescue missions in this unit and spend every night at our base camp. In his situation, which would you prefer?"

I nodded. For some reason, I felt a sense of guardianship over Henry. It was that big-brother feeling.

We headed to our company area, and he introduced me to Captain Womble, who then took me to meet Chief Warrant Officer Blair, whom I'd be flying with the following day. We shook hands; he was about my height and sported a mustache that made him look distinguished. He reminded me of a typical RAF officer in a British war movie.

Chuck took me to my Quonset hut and showed me where to stow my stuff. Invented by engineers in 1941 at the Quonset Point Naval Air Station in Rhode Island, they were easy to set up and made of galvanized steel. To me they looked like tunnels, but they provided simple and effective shelter.

Sitting on my bunk, he went over unit protocol and explained my role as co-pilot. I learned that Chuck was a veteran; he had extended his one-year tour and had been with the unit for seventeen months. He would soon be heading home.

"Anyway, it's chow time, Miller. Let's go get something to eat."

I followed him to the mess hall, and we walked to the officers' side. Protocol dictated that he introduce me to Major Dervaes. I remembered that I was supposed to salute the major when I met him, so when he stood up to shake my hand, I was disoriented and saluted instead of shaking his hand. Some people in the mess hall chuckled, and I felt like an idiot. The major broke the tension, "Alright, at ease."

He then introduced me to his staff and welcomed me to the unit. "Mr. Miller, as soon as I get a chance, we'll meet and discuss a few things."

I headed off to the chow line, and most of the officers made eye contact and nodded, and several made a point of shaking my hand. One pilot said, "Miller, how long have you got left?"

I grimaced, and replied, "359."

He shook his head, "I don't remember ever having that many days to do. Try counting down the days backward. That might make it seem shorter."

I looked down at my plate. I'd piled up Salisbury steak, mashed potatoes, and corn with lashings of gravy. On the side, hot dinner rolls with real butter. It smelled delicious, and I was starving. I could tell this would be the best army chow I'd gotten so far.

Chuck led me to a table occupied by pilots from the lift platoon. They acknowledged me, and some stood to shake my hand, but most were fully involved with their meals. I wanted to gobble mine up before it got cold! After dinner, we headed back to our quarters. Some played cards or wrote letters; others just hung out, told stories, or cleaned up in preparation for the next day.

Eventually, things quieted down, and everyone turned in. I slept soundly, for a while at least. Then, the sound of explosions woke me, *BOOM, BOOM, BOOM!* They were too close for comfort. I was wide awake in seconds and flat on my face under my bunk. When the blasts stopped, I crawled out and turned on my flashlight. It was eerily quiet—the rest of the men were sound asleep. It only took my befuddled brain a minute to realize that the artillery rounds were outgoing, not incoming. It's amazing how, even when asleep, soldiers' subconscious minds can recognize the difference; sleep is that important, I suppose.

Chuck woke me up at 5:00 a.m. I threw water on my face, shaved, combed my hair, and we headed for the mess hall. During breakfast, Captain Bryant, the operation officer, briefed us on the day's mission. We were to use one of our four hunter/killer teams to support an ARVN unit twenty miles southwest of Sóc Trăng. While they were out on recon looking for the enemy, we, as the lift platoon, would stage on the side of the runway, ready to deploy the minute one of our teams needed rescuing.

Once the briefing was over, I had time to think about the possibility that today could be the first time I flew into enemy territory. The responsibility for potentially saving our team members' lives weighed heavily.

# CHAPTER 18

# FROM THE FRYING PAN, INTO THE (LINE OF) FIRE

A fter breakfast, Chuck sent me down to the flight line to do the pre-flight on our Huey. The responsibility of being a co-pilot on my first mission felt overwhelming; I didn't want to screw up. By the time I arrived, the crew chief had all the inspection panels open, so I took my new pre-flight inspection checklist book, got my flashlight, and began the inspection. I'd barely started and was inspecting the "Jesus" nut that secured the main rotor to the mast when Chuck called up to me.

"Is it safe to fly, Miller?"

"I only just got started."

"Lucky for you, I flew this bird yesterday. Get in."

I climbed down from the mast, dumbfounded that we weren't going to carry out a full pre-flight inspection, but I guessed that he had complete faith in his crew chief. That and, perhaps he didn't want me screwing anything up.

The Scout and Cobra helicopters had already repositioned on the side of the Sóc Trăng runway. There were two other lift Hueys in our team that parked behind us. The major was flying in his command and control Huey, while our three Hueys, with our seven-man aero-rifle team on board, wouldn't be leaving the ground unless one of our Cobras or Scouts got shot down.

Each team was getting ready for takeoff.

After a couple of hours, I asked Chuck, "Is this the routine for the lift platoon? Do we just sit around all day and wait in case a Scout or Cobra gets shot down or has mechanical problems?"

"That's pretty much it, Miller. Most days are long, hot, and boring. But that's a good thing. I hope you brought a good book."

At lunchtime, we unpacked our C-rations. Mine contained crackers and peanut butter both in cans, cans of pre-cooked chicken, noodles and sauce, a pecan cake roll—in a can, and the ubiquitous salt, instant coffee, cream substitute, sugar, a 10-pack of Marlboros, and some Stim-U-Dents, which were basically flat toothpick-type implements for cleaning our teeth. The latter came with instructions, *Clean teeth immediately after eating*; the U.S. Army really cared about our health. At least if I got shot down, I'd have clean teeth!

The food looked awful, but it tasted okay, and there was enough to keep you going throughout the day. Having never been a smoker, I always gave my cigarettes away, which made me popular. I probably could've made a fortune selling them! Dang!

After lunch, the afternoon dragged on; on one hand, I wanted something to relieve the monotony, but on the other, I didn't want to see a helicopter team run into trouble. Suddenly, Chuck's radio burst to life, and I could hear him speaking to the major.

"Okay, Miller, you'll see action on your first day. Beware what you wish for, my friend. We have a Scout down; we're going in."

I jumped into our helicopter, and within minutes, the three Hueys—each with seven aero-riflemen—were heading for the downed Scout. It wasn't long before I could see smoke directly ahead. We were the lead helicopter, and Chuck received instructions again from Major Dervaes. Once the briefing was complete, he said, "It's Paul Chalet again! That mother-f-er is going to get me killed yet! This is the third time he's been shot down and the third time I've had to save his ass. Geez!"

The sheer adrenaline rush of taking off for my first mission, seeing the smoke, the reality of it was like nothing I had ever experienced. I was excited and terrified all at once and forgot what I was supposed to do. I blurted out, "What do I do?! What's my job?"

Chuck glared at me, "What? You've got to be kidding me! I told you last night before dinner and again this morning! You're in charge of the magnetic compass, and that's it! Now, if I get shot, then, and only then, you will take over flying. Got it?"

Embarrassed, I nodded, checked my seatbelt for security, and thought that overseeing the magnetic compass was like being in the rear seat of a tandem bicycle. I was nothing more than a sack of potatoes taking up space. But then it all came flooding back; if Chuck got shot, then flying the Huey was up to me, and I'd be operating the radio too. That was a scary scenario.

I snapped back into the present moment when I heard Chuck shout, "The LZ is hot!"

As we flew closer, green tracers tore across the sky in our direction. Everything happened so fast. Our Cobras were shooting rockets to either side of where we intended to land. Out of my peripheral vision, I could see Chuck crouched low in his seat as we descended toward the landing zone. I quickly did the same, learning on the job. As the distance between us and the ground diminished, our door gunners fired their M60 machine guns, using the source of the incoming tracers as a target. We dropped lower and lower, skimming the ground slowly to allow our seven aero-rifle infantrymen to jump out. Once they were on the ground, we left the area and removed ourselves to a safer altitude to circle with the other lift ship, at 2,000 feet behind the Major's Huey.

My heartbeat slowed a little, and I remembered one of my infantry instructors saying, "You will never forget the feeling the first time you face the working end of an AK-47 assault rifle." Man, he was right!

We hung out far above the action, waiting for the Major's order to go back in and pick up our infantrymen, pilot, and observer. Chuck punched me on the arm and said, "Hey, Miller, how did you like your first combat assault?" I didn't reply. I was still reliving what had just happened when he added, "If you think that was bad, wait until we go back in."

My first thought was, *I wish I had written home last night.*

Then the relative peace was broken when Chuck called, "We're going back in Miller. Brace yourself."

We descended toward the LZ, our Cobras providing cover, peppering the flanks of the landing zone with rockets. Our door gunners fired their M60s relentlessly. With 200 yards to our target, I heard one of the gunners scream over the intercom, "I've been hit!"

Chuck slapped me on the shoulder, "Quick, man that M60!"

As I tried to unbuckle my seatbelt, my fingers weren't obeying instructions as efficiently as I would have liked. After what seemed like minutes—but must have been 30 seconds at most—I took the machine gun from the gunner who had been firing it with his good arm. While helping him out of his seat, I could see he was obviously in a lot of pain as I began firing the belt-fed gun at the incoming tracers.

The second we touched down, our seven infantrymen jumped aboard, one of them helping one of the downed crew into the aircraft. I continued firing as we took off until we were out of range, then looked around to assess the situation. Amazingly, the only person with injuries was the gunner, and one of the team was already wrapping his wound. I returned to my co-pilot's seat and realized that I'd just survived my first combat assault unscathed and hadn't made a mess of my shorts.

On the way back to base, I thought back to my early days in basic training at Fort Ord, when I was skeptical about why we needed such extensive training. Of course, I'd understood that knowing how to fire an M60 could be helpful at some point, but I would never have guessed I'd be using that skill on my very first day of action. I had just witnessed and been a part of a well-coordinated rescue by highly trained professionals. Who would have thought that three Hueys could land under fire in enemy territory, drop off twenty-one infantrymen, take off, and come back later to pick up our troops and the rescued crew? Back at home, I would have called that preposterous. For the first time, I felt grateful for all the army had put me through to ready me for combat.

Once we landed at Sóc Trăng, I watched the medics attend to our gunner and thought, *what are the chances I'll survive a year of this? I may end up going home early—in a box.*

Over the following two weeks, none of our hunter/killer teams got shot down or suffered mechanical malfunctions, so our Hueys were just on the side of the runway from dawn to dusk. I was bored to tears, but at least got to finish Jerry Kramer's book, *Instant Replay.* After our two-week stint, we returned to our home base at Dĩ An.

Once we'd parked the helicopter and completed the necessary administration duties, I headed back to my hooch. There was a large box waiting for me. It was from my dad. I opened it and was surprised to see a reel-to-reel tape recorder and a short message— *talk to it daily.*

There were also two letters, one from Mom and one from Ginger. It was good to read the news and to have survived long enough to read them. For the next few hours, I learned how to use the tape recorder and then answered the letters with a newfound respect for the fact that these could be the last thoughts I'd ever get to share with my loved ones.

*Silver Spur aero-rifle platoon (ARP) standing by in a ready response mode during hunterkiller operations.*

# CHAPTER 19

# READY, AIM, FIRE!

Two days later, I bumped into the infamous Paul Chalet, who seemed to have nine lives. He was a CW2, one rank above me, thick-set, with dark brown hair and a mustache. He looked a little Italian. He was coming out of his hooch next door to mine.

"Damn!" I said. "You look better than your helicopter; all that's left of that is the fuselage. How's your observer?"

He recognized me as a member of the team that rescued him, gave a mischievous smile, and said, "He broke his wrist, but other than that, he's just dandy."

"How soon will you be back on flight status?"

"I have to see the doctor in a couple of days. The usual check-up to see if I'm fit to fly. I feel great—it won't be a problem. Until then, I can hang around here, play volleyball, and chill."

Paul and I became friends and ate together most nights at the officers' club, otherwise known as the Red Horse Inn. It allowed me to learn more about hunter/killer missions and, particularly, his role as a hunter. Paul was tough; he loved the adrenaline rush of being a Scout pilot. He also displayed a dark sense of humor when discussing his exploits.

I asked him to tell me more about the enemy we were fighting. As far as I was concerned, they were ghosts. I'd never seen an enemy combatant, only their tracers and bullets buzzing past my helicopter. He explained that the Viet Cong, with the support of the North Vietnamese Army (the NVA), was a small, agile, and notoriously elusive enemy. He warned me never to underestimate them, as they could blend seamlessly—and instantly—with the jungle surroundings and remain hidden. And noiseless. Like ninjas.

Paul explained that the VC trained its troops not to fire at a Scout helicopter when it was heading toward them because the pilot controlled a forward-facing minigun from a firing button on the cyclic control.

"The only time they'll fire is when we back them into a corner or when they think they have the advantage."

I asked him to tell me more about the pilot's minigun.

"Well, Miller, it isn't so small. Some people refer to it as a Gatling gun, but while it's similar in concept, it doesn't use the same components, and the feed mechanisms are very different. A Gatling gun is hand-operated and fires rapidly, but it's not automatic. Once I press the trigger on the cyclic control, it continues to fire until I release the button. That's good for us and bad for the VC."

Warming to his armament lesson, Paul told me that the minigun could fire 2,000 to 4,000 rounds a minute and was horrendously loud. I wasn't sure I was looking forward to seeing it in action.

I asked why he moved from co-piloting Hueys to acting as bait for the enemy.

"I was beyond bored, so I signed up for Scout training and immediately got addicted to the adrenaline rush. I also liked the fact that I was at the sharp end when it came to finding and killing the enemy."

Several weeks later at the Red Horse Inn, I confided that sitting around on the tarmac for several hours a day, with only brief spurts of activity, was driving me crazy.

"Well, Miller," he said, "I can cure that. I'm sure Captain Kilcrease told you that he likes to see lift platoon members go up in a Scout or a Cobra to get a bird's eye view of the troop's mission. Why don't you fly with me and check it out for yourself?"

I'm usually not the knee-jerk type, but I said, "Sure, set it up."

Walking back to my hooch, I thought, *what the heck have you done? Chalet's been shot down three times, and you just volunteered to fly with him. Are you mad?*

Two nights later, Paul casually dropped this into the conversation.

"Miller, you're riding with me tomorrow. We'll be flying out to Tây Ninh."

Filling in the details, he said that the Tây Ninh firebase was about sixty-five miles northwest of Dĩ An and close to the Vietnam-Cambodia border. We'd be much closer to enemy territory—I swallowed hard. Seeing the look on my face, Paul continued.

"I'll let you fly us to Tây Ninh so you can get a feel for a Scout helicopter. That way, you can get us home if I get shot."

I must have turned a shade of grey because he said, "My observer will be riding in one of the Hueys, so if after the first mission you feel uncomfortable, he can take your place. Being a hunter is not for everyone."

We parted company at about 10:00 p.m., and I headed for bed. I was antsy and couldn't relax, instead tossing and turning for what seemed like hours. I eventually fell into a restless sleep before being startled awake. My heart was pumping out of my chest and sweat dripped from my forehead and the nape of my neck. Flashes of the nightmare jolted me: *my Scout low and slow over the jungle, tracers searing up toward us, bullets tearing into my leg, Paul unresponsive next to me, his eyes still open.*

It was 2:00 a.m. I got up, pulled on my flight pants and boots, and wandered into the fresh air. It was in the seventies and humid—pleasant for Vietnam. I couldn't shake the dream, but I needed rest; tomorrow was going to be intense. Back in my bunk, I fell back to sleep, a disturbed, agitated, fearful sleep. My alarm woke me at 5:00 a.m. After shaving and putting on a clean flight suit, I headed to breakfast feeling like a zombie. God only knows what Paul must have thought of this shell of a man who was going to fly his helicopter. We went to the flight line, where I followed Paul around while he pre-flighted one of the new Bell helicopters, the OH-58A.

I asked, "Paul, how do you like this over the Hughes OH-6?"

Paul shook his head.

"It doesn't maneuver as well as the Hughes, the engine has less power, but on the upside, the cockpit is less cramped. It'll do—it will have to, won't it?"

My experience in Vietnam, to date, had been sitting on runaways waiting for something terrible to happen to one of our aircraft. This morning, however, it felt as if I were part of something far more strategically significant. I looked around; three Hueys, containing twenty-one aero riflemen, the major's command and control Huey, four Cobras, and three other Scout helicopters; my heart was thumping in my chest; this was no dream. I almost felt sorry for the enemy.

We lifted off, and after several minutes, Paul pointed directly ahead.

"See that mountain? That's Núi Bà Đen, otherwise known as Black Virgin Mountain. It's over 3,000 feet high and the tallest in South Vietnam. It's strategically important for the enemy and us. We have a radio relay station on the summit. Therefore, we control the top, but the Viet Cong control the bottom. One night, two years ago, the base was attacked and overrun by the VC. By the following afternoon, gunships and artillery fire drove them off. Twenty-five enemy troops were killed and twenty-four American infantrymen, with another two missing in action. So far, they haven't tried again. However, after I arrived ten months ago, I heard infantry forces from the 1st Cavalry discovered arms caches in tunnels at the base of the mountain. Getting rid of the VC rats scurrying around the mountain is impossible. I have no doubt they will try again. It's just a matter of time."

I quietly absorbed the history lesson; it seemed I had much to learn about the enemy. As we approached Tây Ninh Fire Support Base, I could see a large area around the base that was devoid of all vegetation. Paul quickly filled me in.

"That's the 150-yard kill zone. Rusty barbed wire and razor wire surround the base perimeter. If the enemy breaches the perimeter, there are trip wires that will detonate large oil drums containing a mixture of diesel fuel and napalm."

"That sounds lethal," I said.

Paul grinned, "Yep. If Victor Charlie ever decides to pay a visit, they'll first have to navigate a tricky dance floor. And the oil drums are just the opener."

I noticed that Paul used Viet Cong, VC, and Victor Charlie interchangeably.

"If the enemy troops somehow manage to survive the explosion and the jellied gasoline, there are manned guard huts, protected by sandbags, every 100 feet along the perimeter. Nobody messes with those guys and their M60s and survives. Oh, I almost forgot, on every corner of the perimeter is a deuce-and-a-half with four 50-caliber machine guns mounted on a turret."

As I looked down, I could see the two-and-a-half-ton turreted trucks, machine guns ready.

"Wow, that's impressive! The Viet Cong would have to be mad to attack the base with ground forces."

Tây' Ninh's base was far more extensive than Dĩ An's. For some reason, it reminded me of the Las Vegas strip at 3:00 a.m. It was non-stop busy, a hive of activity. There were helicopters, trucks, jeeps, and GIs everywhere. Once our fleet of twelve aircraft landed, we refueled and repositioned ourselves on a level area beside a runway ready for combat. Our platoon leaders left to attend the morning operation briefing. About thirty minutes later, Captain Estep returned and said, "Chalet, Miller, you're first up."

Remember that old cliché about having your heart in your mouth? Well, I thought I was going to choke. We would be doing visual reconnaissance for an infantry platoon of the 25th Infantry Division. Paul and I walked back to our Scout, and I could see the rest of our team doing the same. I buckled myself in; there was no turning back now. I thought of Ginger and questioned the sanity of risking everything because I was bored. We took off, following Major Dervaes's command and control Huey. I looked at the map coordinates; it was about a thirty-minute flight to our destination. I thought, *Okay, Paul, you can turn this thing around anytime now.*

A few minutes later, Paul told me to get a feel for the M-60. He had me point the machine gun at the 8:00 position out of my door and fire off a few rounds. It felt good to know the weapon worked and that I was not an unarmed, sitting duck. Instantly replacing this reassurance was the sinking feeling that I would soon use the gun against live human beings. Paul's voice over the intercom startled me.

"Miller, here's what's going to happen. Once we reach the map coordinates and get the word from Major Dervaes to begin our visual reconnaissance, we'll drop down to treetop level and start scouting the tree line between the rice paddies and the jungle. Once we locate the guys from the 25th, we'll slow down and start looking for the enemy."

I looked at the sea of jungle ahead and wondered how the heck I was going to spot anything.

"What am I looking for?"

"Anything that looks out of the ordinary: trampled down grass, cleared areas, hell, anything that doesn't fit, even a McDonald's hamburger wrapper," Paul laughed.

A minute or so later, we got a call from the major to begin our visual reconnaissance. Almost as soon as we started our descent, I told Paul I could see some of the 25th infantry guys off to our north, hunkered down in a rice paddy field.

"Okay, I see them! Miller, once we get low and slow, don't be afraid to shoot first if you see the enemy."

Suddenly, we were so low I could give a thumbs up to the infantry guys on the ground. It felt good to support them; the leader and a couple of his men returned the gesture. Paul started flying low and slow, baiting the enemy to draw their fire as we crossed from the rice paddies into the jungle.

A white phosphorus grenade hung on a wire above my helmet, so I could quickly grab it when needed. My job was to drop the grenade the second we drew enemy fire. When it hit the ground, it would explode and dispense the phosphorus, which would ignite the second it came into contact with the air. The resulting smoke would mark the position of the Viet Cong; my job at that point was to return enemy fire using my M60.

All this required ultimate concentration. I can only compare it to driving a car on a cold, icy, and foggy night in heavy traffic. But that doesn't do it justice. We repeatedly continued to patrol the tree line but saw nothing. Paul was in my ears again.

"I can feel that they're down there somewhere, so let's see if the machine gun will bring them to life."

I immediately saw the dark humor in Paul's statement.

I could hear Paul telling the Cobra overheard what we were going to do as he slowed the helicopter even more, concentrating on the tree line. I loosened my seatbelt to allow me to turn a little more to the right; then, I started firing short bursts into the trees. Nothing—if the VC were down there, they were holding fire. Paul's voice came loud on the intercom.

"I'm going to strafe that tree line down there with the minigun."

The sound of the minigun was deafening as it fired thousands of rounds a minute into the jungle. If the enemy was down there, we made them feel extremely uncomfortable. We made a second and a third pass while I continued to fire short bursts from the M60 into the jungle just inside the tree line. What happened next was the scariest thing I had ever experienced.

"Receiving fire!" we screamed in unison.

I grabbed the grenade and dropped it like a hot potato as enemy tracers headed our way from Paul's side of the helicopter. What happened next, happened fast. Almost too fast. Paul made a quick right turn, and, from overhead, our Cobra came in fast, firing its rockets toward the phosphorus smoke. Paul climbed quickly, turned left, and returned to the site of the smoke from the Cobra's rocket attack. Meanwhile, as the Cobra climbed back to altitude, it was tracked by enemy tracers. While the enemy focused on firing at the Cobra, Paul lowered the Scout's nose and zeroed in on the enemy's position. He began firing the minigun at one hundred yards, ten rounds a second out of each of the six barrels. The enemy tracers heading toward the Cobra instantly stopped.

As we took another pass over the enemy position, I dropped another phosphorus grenade to pinpoint their location. Our Cobra returned from above the contact area on its second attack, firing multiple pairs of rockets and its minigun at the new position. As it pulled away and gained altitude, no tracers followed it. Looking at the destruction below me, I was sure there could be no enemy survivors. Paul followed the Cobra to a higher altitude.

"Damn, Paul! That was an adrenaline rush like no other. I am incredibly impressed by the surgical precision of the team."

Our time on station had expired, and we needed to return for fuel and a short break. The second hunter/killer team had already arrived to take our place. We followed our team Cobra back to Tây Ninh. With more fuel and fewer crew members on board, Major Dervaes, in his Huey, remained on station to continue as command and control and to brief the next team on what we'd uncovered. Paul and I rotated with the other teams four times that day, but thankfully the excitement was over, and we exposed no more enemy troops. The infantrymen we went to support were able to continue their mission without running into Viet Cong troops. It was a good day, but did I want to be a Scout pilot permanently? That was the $64,000 question.

*Spur scout pilot Paul Chalet and his observer at*
*Tây Ninh returning from a hunter-killer mission.*
*Mountain in background is Núi Bà Đen.*

*Approaching Tây Ninh for a "first light" mission at sunrise.*
*Núi Bà Đen is on the left side of the photo.*

*Silver Spur aircraft at the Tây Ninh POL "hot" refueling during combat operations.*

*Photo taken from front seat of the Spur Cobra while in the middle of a rocket run in Cambodia in support of 25th Infantry Div.*

# CHAPTER 20

# SCOUT OR COBRA?

L ater that afternoon, on our flight back to Dĩ An, I told Paul that I'd only learned about our use of light observation helicopters as bait to draw enemy fire after arriving in Vietnam.

"Same here. It seems like it's not public knowledge back home and who would believe it anyway."

I was silent for a while, just thinking. It surprised me that Paul didn't know about it either.

"Now that I've seen it firsthand, I realize how perilous it is to be a scout helicopter pilot or crewmember. How the heck do they get volunteers for these risky missions?"

Paul shook his head.

"I suppose in the same way someone volunteers to be point-man in the infantry and lead his men through the jungle searching for the enemy while avoiding booby traps. It's in the DNA. Some feel the need to lead, others like me are addicted to adrenaline."

We fell into a companionable silence for the rest of the journey home, although home was a relative term. I relaxed and watched the flat terrain pass beneath me. I felt different now after having faced the working end of multiple AK-47 assault rifles for the second time. Paul broke me out of my reverie.

"Here, Morgan, why don't ya take over flying this thing for a bit?"

I sensed he was preparing to tell me a story. I was right.

"There's a rumor going around the Red Horse Bar that U.S. Military Assistance Command Vietnam, under the command of General Creighton Abrams, has gathered intelligence from inside North Vietnam, Laos, and Cambodia indicating there is a massive buildup of North Vietnamese armies just waiting to cross the border and attack us now that American forces are departing."

"How does that affect you and me?"

"Well, Morgan, the plan is to send our troops, with air power, into Cambodia, Laos, and North Vietnam to surprise the enemy and hit them hard so we can safely achieve the American force's departure. Our squadron may go into Cambodia sometime in early May to support the 25th Infantry Division."

"Sorry, Paul, I'm confused as to why this invasion will help our forces depart South Vietnam."

"Because, once we succeed, it will set the North Vietnamese armies back a year or more, during which time the U.S. will speed up the training of South Vietnamese forces so we can hand over control of all ground operations to them."

"How can you be so confident it will be a success?"

"Because of our superior air power, namely the B-52 bomber. Morgan, imagine your favorite shopping mall back home being instantly turned into the surface of the moon because two B-52s, wing tip to wing tip, at 40,000 feet dropped 200, 500-pound bombs on it."

I was silent for a few seconds absorbing this information.

"Paul, I keep hearing about *Search and Destroy* missions, but how are they different from *Hunter/Killer* missions?"

"Good question, Miller. As it sounds, the *Search and Destroy* tactical maneuver consists of putting large numbers of GIs on the ground to look for communist units and destroy them. It turns into a war of attrition and, in my opinion, has cost too many American lives. There seems to be a never-ending stream of NVA reinforcements, so we're not winning in terms of attrition. It's more about body count than gaining territory."

"So, you see *Hunter/Killer* missions as more surgical, targeted, and effective?

"Yes, Miller, that's it. I'd like to see General Abrams expand the Air Cavalry *Hunter/Killer* concept. A Cobra and a Scout helicopter with three pilots and an observer could locate the enemy and keep them pinned down until the Air Force F-100s, or our army's heavy artillery wipe them out. I'm convinced this approach would efficiently deal with the enemy threat and cost fewer American lives. Anyway, we'll find out soon enough if the rumor is accurate."

I was impressed with Paul's insights.

"So Paul, you've heard about the disaster that happened at LZ-Xray in November of '65, right?"

"Yep."

"Well, one of my instructors at infantry school was right in the middle of that battle. He told us how instrumental air support was to their survival. He said they would've all been killed without air support. General Westmoreland considered the mission a *Search and Destroy* victory because we lost fewer soldiers than the North Vietnamese."

There was silence for a few minutes until Paul burst out.

"Morgan, why in the heck did you go to infantry school?!"

I grinned, "It's a long story. I'll tell you sometime over a beer."

Lying in bed that night, the one thing I knew for sure was that I did not want to be a Scout pilot. I lay there forever just trying to figure out why I wasn't satisfied with being in the lift platoon. It involved less flying, which meant less risk and a better chance of returning home in one piece. After some soul-searching, I realized that I liked it best when I was in a leadership role—sitting on the sidelines wasn't for me. In the short term, I took Chuck's advice from my first day at Sóc Trăng.

When I had complained about life in the lift platoon being boring, he warned me to be careful of what I wished for. I'd heard that before in my life, but for other people, not me. It seemed like such a cliché; a way for someone to maybe get out of a conversation he didn't want to continue or to get away from someone who bored or irritated him. It was like a "See ya later" throwaway phrase. Now that I was on the receiving end of it, that phrase was anything but a throwaway. Now that it really applied to me, I could finally understand the wisdom behind it.

For the immediate future, I would continue to assimilate myself into the unit as a Huey co-pilot. However, I decided to follow Captain Kilcrease's advice and ask for an orientation flight in a Cobra to help me better understand their role in the Hunter/Killer team. With that final thought, I fell asleep.

Two days later, I saw Captain Moss returning from a mission and approached him. His sunglasses were missing a lens, which made me smile. He looked so odd. I'd heard Captain Moss had a quirky sense of humor but was well-liked and respected, especially for his excellent leadership skills. I introduced myself, and we shook hands.

"Captain Moss, I'd like to see what it's like to fly in a Cobra and experience the Killer role firsthand."

He smiled.

"Sure, Miller! Maybe we can entice you to join the weapons platoon; we always need good pilots. How does tomorrow look?"

I was learning that things happen fast in combat zones. "Tomorrow" came in the blink of an eye!

Early the next morning, we flew out of Dĩ An to Xuân Lộc, a firebase about fifty miles east, with the rest of the Hunter/Killer teams and the lift Hueys. The previous year, the Viet Cong had attacked the base, and a number of its troops breached the perimeter before being driven back by artillerymen, helicopter gunships, air strikes, and a unit of the 11th Armored Cavalry Regiment. The Battle of Xuân Lộc was another reminder of the dangerous combat zones I flew in and out of every day. We arrived at the refueling station first, and Captain Moss directed me to refuel the Cobra.

I jumped out, headed to the petroleum lubricants area, and turned on the pump for the aviation gas. There was a loud hissing noise, and suddenly aviation fuel shot into the air. I immediately turned the pump off, my hands trembling. The distinctive kerosene smell was overpowering; a diesel, oily odor. I ran over to the Cobra and knocked on Captain Moss's window. His head was back, his visor down; he was dozing. My urgent knocking woke him.

"What, Miller?!"

"Sir, we have a major leak over there," I said, pointing to the pump.

He looked down, and said, "I'll be a son of a bitch; when did Leak become a major?"

"No, sir, I'm talking about a fuel leak!"

"I know, Miller," he said, chuckling to himself as if he'd just told the funniest joke. "Let's check it out."

For the rest of the day, I saw the Hunter/Killer mission from the Cobra's perspective. I felt much better being above the action, not acting as bait, and having significantly more firepower. The Bell AH-1 Cobra was fast and heavily armed. It had two wing stubs, one on either side of the helicopter. Each wing contained a nineteen-shot pod mounted inboard and a seven-shot pod mounted outboard. In the nose turret, which could move left, right, up, and down, there was a 7.62mm minigun with a selectable firing rate of 2,000 or 4,000 rounds per minute, and a 40mm grenade launcher with a firing rate of 400 rounds per minute.

The extreme exposure I felt in the Scout was replaced by a feeling of control, of leading the action. By the end of the day, thoughts of serving my time out in the relative safety of the lift platoon morphed into a desire to join Captain Moss's Cobra team.

• • • • •

The rumor Paul mentioned turned out to be true. In the first week of May, our unit's Hunter/Killer operations moved to Quần Lợi

Base Camp, sixty miles north of Saigon. Rocket City, as it was nicknamed, was originally a French rubber plantation. The camp had been turned over to the 1st Cavalry Division years earlier. The division's aviation units consisted of their 1st of the 9th Air Cavalry Squadron, their Blue Max Attack Cobra Platoon, and their 229th Assault Helicopter Company, supported by a company of their infantry.

We flew out of Dĩ An early morning for the flight north to Quần Lợi. As we came in to land, the scene below me was like nothing I'd ever experienced. The Cambodian Incursion had begun on April 29th and was now in full swing. Everywhere I looked, there were men, helicopters, and equipment. Back home, Ginger had written to me about protests against the uptick American involvement in Cambodia and that President Nixon was repeating his intention to leave Vietnam. North Vietnamese and VC troops were building bridgeheads in Cambodia close to the capital Phnom Penh, while South Vietnamese troops backed by U.S. GIs were heading west toward the capital.

We settled into our "accommodation" and went for dinner. Everywhere was buzzing with frenetic energy; you could actually feel it; the sense of purpose, urgency, and intensity was pervasive. I knew I wouldn't be bored sitting beside a runway while at Quần Lợi.

The following day, we learned that our Hunter/Killer teams would support the 25th Infantry Division and work with the 1st of the 9th Air Cavalry Squadron. For the rest of the month, our platoons flew every day from dawn to dusk, except for the four helicopters and aero rifle platoon we left on standby. They were always ready to rescue the crew of a downed Scout or Cobra helicopter.

Our Hunter/Killers flew low and slow, and searched for an enemy skilled at being invisible. My lift platoon did what it did best, move men, supplies, and equipment; that is, when we weren't rescuing our troops. I flew up to twelve hours every other day, resupplying American and ARVN forces at temporary fire support bases in Cambodia.

On one occasion, I flew four days in a row, a task which was beyond exhausting, despite the ongoing adrenaline rush. Flying and co-piloting in such an extreme environment, and for so many hours, had an upside—it turned me into a very confident Huey pilot.

By the end of May, I had clocked in more than 300 hours of combat flight time since arriving in Vietnam. Despite the almost non-stop activity, I remained unfulfilled in the lift platoon. I'd flown a Scout, which was like having a death wish, but after my ride with Captain Moss and talking to some of the Cobra pilots, I realized that flying Cobras was the middle ground I'd been seeking.

The next time I saw Captain Moss, I requested permission to join his platoon.

"I felt you'd circle back to me, Miller; I'll talk to the major and find out the procedure to get you a Cobra transition."

He was as good as his word, because a day later, I met with Major Dervaes. He invited me to sit down and looked at me with serious intent.

"Captain Moss tells me you'd like to transfer to the weapons platoon. I can arrange that, but first, I must evaluate your pilot skills. Tomorrow, you will be my pilot in the command and control Huey. If you pass muster, I'll recommend you for the Cobra Transition School."

I thanked him and was about to stand up to leave. He wasn't done just yet.

"Miller, I never got a chance to meet with you after you joined the lift platoon, and I've been busy ever since. So, now I have you here, let me give you my welcome speech. I expect everyone in A Troop to look sharp every day; your boots should be shined, you should be wearing a clean flight suit, and I expect you to be clean-shaven, although trimmed mustaches are permitted. Most importantly, I expect my officers to act like professionals, especially when drinking at the Officers' club."

I'd heard much of this from my fellow warrant officers and knew that heaven help an officer who got drunk or, worse, became involved in a fight, whether as an instigator or innocent bystander.

"Thank you, Sir. I'll see you in the morning."

As I walked away, I was happy about the possibility of joining the weapons platoon and felt confident about the following day's flight. It added an extra spring to my step.

I slept soundly and woke refreshed for a change. After breakfast, I met the major at the flight line, and we pre-flighted his Huey. After buckling ourselves in, the major started the bird, hovered over the runway, and made the takeoff. I was in the right front seat with the major to my left. Once we reached 3,000 feet, Major Dervaes turned the controls over to me, told me we were going to an area in Cambodia, and gave me a compass heading to maintain. *Okay,* I thought, p*iece of cake! This is going to be like an aircraft proficiency check ride.*

During the thirty-minute flight, he told me that he wanted me to fly at 3,000 feet in a left-hand orbit over the Cobra once we reached the map coordinates.

The *piece of cake* turned into an arduous, ten-hour day. Although the major took back control, every hour for about ten minutes, I did the rest of the flying. As the sun began to set, we returned to Quần Lợi. I shut down the helicopter and got out; the major was already standing next to my cockpit door, his hand outstretched to shake mine.

"Great job, Miller. You are now a member of the weapons platoon. I'll get you a Cobra transition as soon as this Cambodian Incursion is over."

That put a smile on my face. Nothing would thrill me more until I eventually returned home to Ginger and my friends and family. Or, so I thought.

*North end of Quần Lợi where the serviceable remains of French rubber plantation owner structures still remained.*

*South end of Quần Lợi airstrip where control tower, tactical operations center and Spur Cobra maintenance tent was located.*

*Enroute to Xuân Lộc for a mission while flying over weather.*

*Me as a new gun platoon Cobra pilot*

# CHAPTER 21

# WITNESSING THE PERILS OF WAR

On June 3, 1970, Captain Moss made a point of welcoming me to the gun platoon. He told me that I would be flying into Cambodia the next day with Bob Dibbern, a senior Cobra pilot. I met Bob when I first arrived, but we hadn't had an opportunity to talk since then. Bob was around six feet tall with sandy blond hair and blue eyes. He could have been one of the Beach Boys! My first impression was that he was mature, although I suspected he was younger than he appeared. Later, in the Officers' Club, he told me that he had been in Vietnam for 11 months and was looking forward to going home.

The next morning, we did all our pre-flight work, followed three other Cobras hovering out to the runway at Quần Lợi, then took off for Tây Ninh for my first day with the weapon's platoon. On one hand, I knew what to expect. By that time in my relatively short stint, I'd already seen enough operations from the co-pilot seat of a Huey but sitting in a Cobra gave me a whole new perspective. I felt like the new boy at school. I needed to prove myself worthy of Captain Moss's faith in me.

After the thirty-minute flight, we refueled, parked, and waited for the platoon leaders to return from their briefing. I stood with Bob, Scout pilot Bill Wallace, and his observer when Captain

Moss and Captain Estep—who was in charge of all Scout pilots—
returned. I looked across at Pilot Wallace. He had short, brown
hair and a solid build and looked every inch a "hunter," on edge
and anticipating action. There was no "down time" with him and
others of hunter status. I didn't catch his observer's name, but he
was a heavy-set man with dark brown hair. I thought they made a
good looking team, intense, ready at all times, and all about getting down to business.

Captain Estep spoke, and with map in hand, showed us the
area over which we would be doing visual reconnaissance. It was
a Cambodian village seven miles west of the border. Intelligence
had identified this hamlet as a possible sanctuary for enemy soldiers, suggesting that the villagers were supporting NVA soldiers
arriving there. The location boasted a healthy supply of fresh water and vast rice fields.

Everyone was dead silent as they walked to their helicopters.
Each of us was facing our own demons; fear of failure, fear of being maimed or killed, fear of the enemy; even fear of success. In
my case, it was my first time flying a Cobra into a combat zone.
For Bob, it was crossing the border and going back into enemy territory during the final days of his stint in Vietnam. Wallace was
a relatively new Scout pilot and would be relying heavily on his
more experienced observer, Specialist Gillett. Although I had experience flying into Cambodia several times already as a member
of the lift platoon, this felt very different. Someone could outline
your role all they liked, but it was always just theory until the action began. I felt extremely anxious.

Bob and I buckled up and took off. Bill followed Major Dervaes in his Huey, and we followed the Scout to the designated map
coordinates. It wasn't long before we arrived over a vast area of
farmland. The major instructed Bill to begin visual surveillance
and fly low and slow along the jungle perimeter within the prescribed operational area. We descended, following the Scout, and

adopted a left-hand orbit. Within minutes of Bill flying at treetop level, his voice came over the radio.

"I've spotted a communication line—there's a cable down there on a freshly traveled trail."

He turned and went in for another look to confirm what he and his observer saw. We watched as the Scout got closer to the suspected enemy haven. Bob's voice came over the intercom again.

"I have a bad feeling about this."

I immediately tightened my grip on the minigun sight handles. No sooner were the words out of Bob's mouth than we heard static, then Bill screamed that they were receiving fire.

The Scout instantly flipped over and crashed to the ground; the explosion destroyed the helicopter. I had no doubt that Bill and Gillett were dead. Before I got the exclamation point on "Damn!" Bob made a quick left turn and rolled in, firing his rockets to the west of the crash site on the incline above it. I fired the minigun at our rockets' point of impact. Bob got off six pairs of rockets before he ended his run at the treetops and then began to climb to a higher altitude. Tracers zinged past our cockpit. In a surprising move, Bob stopped his climb and went into a smooth, steep, descending left turn to head back to the tracers' origin.

"Fire that damn minigun Miller!"

At treetop level, the rockets erupted from their tubes and flew straight for about twenty meters, exploding just as we flew over them. The shockwaves rocked the helicopter. Later, I found shrapnel from our own rockets embedded in the outboard rocket pods and bullet holes in our tail. Once we reached a safe altitude, I had a chance to think about what just happened. Bob's quick thinking and exit strategy adjustment allowed us to escape almost unscathed. Had he continued to climb, we would have been sitting ducks.

Once we were at altitude, I could hear Bob talking to the major; I tuned out for a few seconds to regain my composure. The Air Force Forward Air Controller (the FAC) had been monitoring our company's radio frequency from high overhead. Over the radio, I hear Toy-16 call out to the major, "Spur 6, would you like a set of fighters?"

❧ The major responded in steady, rapid-fire speech, "Roger! Have them contact Spur 31 on this frequency."

Spur 31 was Bob's call sign. While waiting for the fighters to arrive, we continued making rocket runs to keep the enemy pinned down. We heard the major call our Tactical Operation Center, the TOC, requesting another Hunter/Killer team to relieve us. A few minutes later, a radio call came in from the inbound jets.

"Spur 31, this is Hawk One-One. We are at 5,000 feet and have a Tally Ho on the smoke from the jungle. What's the situation?"

"Hawk One-One, our Scout helicopter was shot down by heavy automatic weapons fire. The target is fifty meters west of the burning crash site. Do you have us and the target in sight?"

"Roger, Spur 31. Sorry about your loss. We will make our runs south to north with a right break."

My nerves buzzed with anticipation. I was about to witness my first tactical air strike. In the distance, I saw an Air Force bomber moving toward our location.

"Bob, what kind of bomber is that?"

Bob laughed.

"That's not a bomber, Miller; it's two F-100s in tight formation. Watch them separate when the lead jet starts its bomb run."

"Spur 31, this is Hawk One-One; we are commencing our bomb run."

"Roger, Hawk One-One. I have you in sight. We'll stay clear."

The first jet rolled in, dropping two napalm bombs on the target. The leader's wingman followed with two 500lb MK-82 general purpose bombs. Hawk One-One made another radio call.

"Spur 31, we also received automatic weapons fire and would like to make two more passes with our 20-millimeter and minigun."

"Roger that, we will stand by."

After the jets' third pass, we heard, "Sorry, Spur 31, that's it. We are out of ammo."

"Hawk One-One, nice job! Thanks!"

We could hear the major briefing our replacement Hunter/Killer team, Spur 39, which was on its way from Tây Ninh.

"You need to make that crash area safe. We must get our aero rifle platoon on the ground to recover our downed crew. There is a FAC overhead, call sign Toy-16, who can send another set of fighters if you need them. I have to refuel but will return as quickly as I can. Stay alert and be very careful!"

"Roger, Spur 6."

After refueling, the major returned with our third Hunter/Killer team, and the lift Hueys with their aero rifle teams, to the crash site. By the time our recovery mission was completed, it was midday, and marked several hours since the enemy shot down our Scout. Luckily, it went off without any interference from the enemy. Our Huey took the downed pilot and his observer to the hospital landing pad at Tây Ninh. Our unit continued visual reconnaissance around the village for the rest of the day, although we saw no enemy activity.

The following morning, I flew down to Dĩ An for the memorial services for WO William T. Wallace and his observer, Specialist-4 Jerry C. Gillett. I was with Captain Estep, Lieutenant Kelly, who was in charge of the aero rifle platoon, and his platoon sergeant. The service would be held at the squadron chapel at the base.

As I walked into the chapel, I saw Captain Kilcrease seated near the podium next to the squadron chaplain. I took my seat next to Lieutenant Kelly and the other members of our unit. There were no flag-draped coffins, just a table next to the pulpit. On it, two pairs of black leather boots supporting two black Stetson cavalry hats featured the names of our two fallen crew members and our unit's crossed sabers insignia.

The chapel was silent, the mood somber. We'd lost two good men; it could be one of us next time. Grief lingered heavily in the air, stilling our voices and even our thoughts. I was sad, but somewhat detached. We'd lost two brave warriors, but I barely knew them. I'd only met Bill Wallace early the previous day, and as for Jerry Gillett, I had never spoken to him. They were my brothers, and they were strangers.

The chaplain's words interrupted my thoughts.

"Gentlemen, may we remember that these two fine young men made the supreme sacrifice here in Vietnam while fighting for our country. They had their whole lives ahead of them. Unfortunately, their loved ones and we will never know what they could have achieved, but I feel they were the embodiment of everything we all can hope to be. God bless Warrant Officer Wallace and Specialist Gillett, and may God welcome them home."

It was indeed a solemn service, but it had also been noticeably short. I left the chapel feeling the men deserved more accolades and recognition for giving their lives for someone else's cause. So, instead of receiving the solace I was hoping for, I left with a feeling of emptiness. I asked myself, *what were we fighting for?* My fear was that I might never know.

*Myself, David Toms, Charlie Neal, J.C. Moss and Ed Marzola
taking a break between flights out in the area of operation (AO).*

*Spur hunter-killer operations area in Cambodia.*

*Joe Jackson*

*Robby Hodge*

# CHAPTER 22

# MAYDAY! MAYDAY!

The mood back at Quần Lợi after the funerals was subdued. The deaths of our Scout crew cast a long, dark shadow. On my days off, I'd get up, shower, shave, dress, go for breakfast and then relax. The routine was almost comforting in a way; it offered a level of stability and safety. It made me feel anchored; as if there was some sense to all the craziness around us. All too soon, I'd be putting myself in harm's way again. I always kept a notepad with me to record anything that came to mind. Back at base, I'd dictate my thoughts into my dad's tape recorder. It helped me feel that my family was close, that if I didn't return, they could listen to my voice going on about mundane things such as my living conditions—which were better than I had expected—as was the food. Hopefully, upon my return home, I'd listen to the tapes again and laugh at how unexciting things appeared to be.

Ordinary things counted when you lived in a camp; they took on greater importance. My toiletries had been running low since I'd been in Quần Lợi because there was no PX store; nor was there an opportunity to make a trip to Ben Hoa to visit the PX there. So, I wrote to Ginger asking her to send me shaving cream, toothpaste, and hand lotion because my hands were cracked and raw. I also told her when I expected to be back in Dĩ An so we could talk by phone. We had a somewhat complicated communication system. When I wanted to speak to Ginger, I used the landline at Dĩ An.

My call went to a MARS radio station in Vietnam, and they transferred it to a ham operator stateside who patched it through to a local operator, who then transferred the call to Ginger's landline. Due to this convoluted routing, we had to plan well in advance especially because I'd usually call her at noon my time, which was 2:00 a.m. for her.

With a few days left in President Nixon's incursion into Cambodia, I was flying with Spur 38 pilot Dave Tela. Our unit was heading to Tây Ninh for a regular hunter/killer mission. However, within minutes of leaving Quần Lợi, we heard Cobra pilot Jim Elkin yell, "Mayday! Mayday! Mayday! Stiff control! Landing immediately!"

Looking over my right shoulder, I could see the Cobra losing altitude quickly; it sounded like the pilot had little or no control of the aircraft. Seconds later, Elkin's helicopter slammed into the ground. Because Jim continuously keyed his mic all the way as he fell to the ground, there was no way for my pilot Dave Tela to tell him to switch his hydraulic control to system two. Had Dave been able to contact him, Jim could have possibly regained control of his Cobra.

Major Dervaes quickly took control of the situation. He turned his Huey around and told the rest of us to maintain a left-hand orbit at 3,000 feet. The major's voice boomed in my ear,

"Spur 19, recon the area for enemy activity. Over."

Scout Pilot Larry Sherrer slowly descended to tree top level and scoured the area. Receiving no fire and seeing nothing suspicious, he declared the area "cold." I could hear the major instructing Captain Womble, the lift platoon leader, where to land his three Hueys and to deploy his twenty-one infantrymen to secure the area. Major Dervaes said he was going to land close to the downed aircraft. The infantrymen secured the area, retrieved the pilot and co-pilot, and loaded them into the major's helicopter. Men guarded the perimeter of the crash site, while others stripped the downed Cobra of its minigun, radio, and any-thing else that could be useful to the enemy.

The operation took twenty minutes. As Major Dervaes and Captain Womble prepared to head back to Quần Lợi, the major's voice came over the radio, "Spur 35, Spur 39, destroy Jim's Cobra." The helicopter received extensive damage, but we never left anything for the enemy.

Back at Quần Lợi, the major called us all together and told us that both pilots had died on impact. You could have heard a pin drop. We were stunned—no one said a word. I'd witnessed four deaths in two weeks and had difficulty processing it. This time was worse because I knew both pilots well. I paced around, trying to work out what could have gone so drastically wrong to cause such a devastating crash. I needed to talk it through with someone, but everyone seemed to be in shock. No one was in the mood to talk. I felt a hand on my shoulder; it was Dave Tela.

"Jim Elkin and I went through flight school and Cobra school together. I knew his wife. He was a good friend."

It felt strange that Dave was so calm, almost cavalier, about losing his friend and fellow Cobra pilot. I expected he would be more broken up, not coming to me to provide solace. But then he put it into perspective.

"Morgan, we've lost several pilots and crew during the nine months I have been here. Today, you witnessed your second fatal event; this time, it involved pilots you knew. That makes it per-sonal. But I guarantee you; there will be more fatalities—that's the reality of war."

I nodded but couldn't think of anything to say. Dave continued.

"Did you know that Jim's co-pilot was going to take over the gun platoon when Captain Moss goes home, which is not too far away now? This has been a sad morning for the troop."

Before the crash, we were on our way to Tây Ninh. However, since Major Dervaes had been talking to the 1st of the 9th Air

Cavalry control center about the loss of our two pilots, they sent their hunter/killer teams to take our place at Tây Ninh.

Things gradually returned to normal, or as normal as things could be under the circumstances. An hour later, one of our hunter/killer teams took off for Cambodia, and Dave and I were back in the rotation, waiting our turn to join the day's hunter/killer operation again. With time to kill, Dave made a surprising statement; he felt Cobra pilots in Vietnam were unknowingly being used as test pilots. I asked him to explain.

"Since the Cobra arrived in the fall of 1967, it has acquired a bad reputation. There have been rumors about stability control and tail rotor problems occurring while hovering with a left rear quartering tailwind."

"What does this have to do with this morning's crash?" I asked.

"I talked with the Huey pilot who recovered the two Cobra pilots. He told me that the aircraft had hit the ground with terrific force, suggesting the pilot had experienced a hydraulic control problem—in this case, a collective pitch problem."

"So, he couldn't control his altitude nor how fast they were dropping?"

"Yes, Morgan, that's it. Sometime ago, I talked to another flight school buddy, Ed Soliday who is our Cobra maintenance officer. He told me that, unlike the Huey, the Cobra has two separate hydraulic lines serving one servo. Because of the Cobra's Stability Control Augmentation System (SCAS), the pistons in the flight control servos are constantly moving, like the shock absorber on a car traveling at high speed on a washboard dirt road. Ed's opinion was that this constant movement could cause heat to build up in the servo cylinders, causing wear of the seals over time and resulting in possible bleed-through between the two systems. If true, this condition could cause hydraulic fluid to leak out, followed by a loss in hydraulic pressure, causing the servo to seize up and make the helicopter uncontrollable."

I nodded, and Dave continued.

"Picture a garden hose going to a sprinkler head with four arms—now replace the sprinkler head with a helicopter's four servos; pitch, roll, collective and tail rotor. Over time, the sprinkler water stops coming out of one of the sprinkler arms. But, when you turn water off and back on again— think switching from Cobra system 1 one to Cobra system 2, the Cobra's hydraulic pressure returns to normal and all four arms of the sprinkler work. That is, until the hydraulic pressure drops again causing one of the sprinkler arms to stop again."

"So, let me get this straight, Dave. The Cobra has one hydraulic reservoir, which supplies two separate lines to the same control servo. If one line fails, a pilot can switch to the other."

"That's correct, Morgan, but we were never taught that one of the four control servos can fail by itself, while the other three work normally. That's where it gets dangerous, and I am positive this is what happened in today's crash."

What Dave had told me made sense, but it indicated that the crash should have been preventable. We didn't see any action for the rest of the day; it was routine reconnaissance with no sign of the enemy. The next day, several pilots rode the ash-and-trash Huey down to Dĩ An for the memorial services. I was not one of them. While waiting for our turn to fly, I mulled over everything Dave had told me.

*Myself and Dave Tela sitting on Spur Cobra #171 ammo bay door while on standby out in the area of operation (AO).*

# CHAPTER 23

# WHERE'S HENRY HARRIS?

**B**ack at Quần Lợi on a rest day, I heard that one of our
Scout helicopters had been shot down in Cambodia, just
north of Lộc Ninh. News traveled quickly around the
camp, especially when it involved a downed aircraft. Everyone
was eager to hear who the crew was and whether they were okay.

I later learned from fellow Cobra Pilot Dave Toms how it all
went down and that someone I knew well was involved. This
was the story as I heard it. Captain Cook, who was our operations officer filling in for Major Dervaes, had been flying our
Command-and-Control helicopter when enemy fire shot down
one of our scout helicopters. He called the TOC and requested
the deployment of our aero rifle platoon to recover the downed
pilot and observer. The rescue was quick and easy, with no interference from the enemy, and neither crew member had life-threatening
injuries. It seemed to be a successful mission; that is, until, back at
base, the infantry platoon sergeant did a head count of the infantrymen on the rescue mission. He was one man short.

The sergeant looked at his twenty-one aero riflemen and asked,
"Where's Henry Harris?"

Everybody started talking at once, asking each other when
they last saw Henry. Emotions ran high; leaving a man behind in

enemy territory was about the worst thing a team could do. Captain Cook witnessed the headcount and immediately ran to report the situation to Major Dervaes. With only about two hours left of daylight, the Major ordered our hunter/killer team to follow his Huey to the landing zone to search for Henry. Once on the ground, they spent ninety minutes looking for Henry, but as they lost the light, the major had to order the team back to Quần Lợi.

Back at the base, the major and Lieutenant Kelly decided to call in a K-9 team from the 25th Infantry Division. They hoped that, at daybreak, the dogs might get a scent of Henry. Major Dervaes also requested help from the Special Forces A Team that oversaw base security at Quần Lợi.

The following day, a platoon of our infantry, the K-9 team, Major Dervaes, Lieutenant Kelly, and a six-man Special Forces team thoroughly searched the area. It wasn't long before one of the dog handlers found dog tags at the side of a trail. Major Dervaes confirmed they belonged to Henry Harris.

Lieutenant Kelly and our aero rifle platoon widened their search in the area surrounding the spot where the dog tags had been found but came up with nothing. Later that morning, the Special Forces team leader met with the Major and Lieutenant Kelly. They decided that half his men would head west along a known trail in the direction of Phnom Penh, and the remaining men would head south from the Cambodian border to Lộc Ninh and ultimately An Lộc.

They hoped they would find clues to Henry's whereabouts and possibly capture a prisoner. Meantime, the Special Forces team leader suggested Major Dervaes extract his team and return to Quần Lợi, where he would receive daily updates.

Back at base, the major announced he would update everyone that afternoon. The whole camp was on edge, and solid information was in short supply. We gathered in the troop area by late afternoon and the major filled us in on what happened since Henry Harris went missing. There was a sense of disappointment and despair that he was still missing and almost certainly in enemy hands suffering heavens knows what indignities and even torture.

A week later, the Special Forces team leader informed the Major that, aside from the dog tags found on the first day, the team that headed south had seen no other clues on their hike to An Lộc. He suggested that Henry may have been taken north to a POW camp about sixty miles further into Cambodia and added that his other team was still searching to the north and that he'd get back to the major as soon as he heard anything.

The Cambodian incursion was drawing to a close. In a few days, the U.S. would pull out of Cambodia. Our unit would begin moving back to Dĩ An. Henry Harris' whereabouts were the main topic of conversation at the base. He was a young man, a rookie soldier, and ill-prepared for the horrors of war. I thought about him often and prayed that one of the Special Forces team would find him soon.

Back in Dĩ An, Major Dervaes got permission from our 3/17th squadron commander for a one-day unit stand-down to celebrate Independence Day and the end of the Cambodian incursion. On July 4th, the scout platoon challenged the weapons platoon to a softball game. I played first base. There was a lot of beer consumed that day, and the game was boisterous, to say the least. We all needed to let off some steam. Our weapons platoon won, which was the icing on the cake. After the match, our squadron cooks barbecued steaks and manned the chow line, serving both enlisted men and officers.

Later, after dinner, Major Dervaes gave a short speech about the part we had played in the Cambodian incursion and thanked everyone for a job well done.

Later, he played his guitar and sang a few country western songs. Most of his unit gathered around to listen, and many joined in on the songs they knew. There was a feeling of peace, a moment to relax, but it was tainted by thoughts of a young man, far from home, imprisoned in a foreign land. That is, if he was not already dead. At 8:00 p.m., a group of us went to the troop area to watch the movie; *She Wore a Yellow Ribbon*, starring John Wayne.

All too soon, it was morning, and we went back to looking for the enemy. However, the area was quiet. The American and ARVN forces had destroyed the enemy's Cambodian sanctuaries and disrupted their supply lines.

Major Dervaes left for home the following week, and his replacement took over A Troop. At his first officer's meeting, "The New Major" told us there would be no changes to Major Dervaes' policies. He underlined this by saying, "We are all professionals here, and I will expect all officers to act accordingly." Then he surprised us further, "One thing will change, however, and that is the way A Troop flies to the area of operation every day." We all looked at each other, not understanding why he would make this change.

"From now on," he said, "the Scout pilots will fly low, looking for the enemy *en route* to the AO. Any questions?"

You could have heard a pin drop. His remark took every ounce of oxygen out of the room. I glanced around and all I saw was the sort of look you get when there is an awful smell in the room, and everyone is looking for the culprit.

After this meeting, a group of us headed to the Red Horse bar, where the new guy in charge was the hot topic. One Scout pilot said, "What planet did this guy come from? You can't see much detail flying at 100 knots, 100 feet from the ground! And even if you did manage to spot something at that speed, it would be almost impossible to return to that exact spot to investigate further. Doesn't he know that?"

More pilots came in, and we moved from the bar to some hastily pushed-together tables. The mood was one of astonishment and anger. The new policy change was stupid and downright dangerous. One after another, Cobra and Scout pilots listed the safety issues that arose from this new procedure. The discussion got heated. Major Dervaes' replacement was not off to a good start.

He was not well liked or respected, and we all just referred to him as "The New Guy" for the rest of his command. We all missed Major Dervaes, that's for sure.

I found my attention drifting away from the conversation. I thought about Henry Harris. I was sure he was still alive. Yes, he was young and a little naive, but he was no patsy—he was stronger than he looked.

*JC Moss – a swing and a miss on July 4, 1970*

*Craig Johnson re-arming 20mm cannon at Tay Ninh*

*044's "Have a Nice Day" turret with minigun and grenade launcher*

# CHAPTER 24

# COBRA SCHOOL

July 1970 saw the Military Assistance Command Vietnam (MACV) continue to send some units home and move others around Vietnam. This was in preparation for the eventual withdrawal of all American forces from Vietnam.

On August 1, I was having breakfast with Captain Moss when he handed me my orders to attend Cobra Transition School in Vũng Tàu. I was to report the next day and take enough personal items to last two weeks.

I had twenty-four hours to prepare, so after breakfast, I returned to my hooch and made a tape recording to send home. I spent the next hour telling my family that I was going to Cobra school, updating them on what was happening at the camp and other seemingly mundane bits of information that I knew would help them to visualize me here in Vietnam. I told them that Henry Harris was missing and how worried I was about his welfare. I packaged the tape, addressed it, and took it to the orderly room for mailing. While there, the clerk told me Lieutenant Devane would take me to Vũng Tàu in the ash-and-trash Huey. I returned to my hooch and began leafing through the Cobra Operation Manual. Flying a Cobra was very different from flying a Huey. The Huey was more of a transport helicopter, whereas the Cobra was a gunship. They both had the same engine and transmission, but everything else was different. The Cobra only had two seats and was much narrower. It accelerated faster and had a higher top speed than the Huey—it was aggressive rather than lumbering workhorse. I enjoyed flying it and looked forward to learning more about the operating systems.

I woke early and headed for breakfast. As I left my hooch, I blinked and shaded my eyes; there wasn't a cloud in the sky, and the sun was already relentless. I met Lieutenant Devane at the flight line a little later, and we climbed into the helicopter. The lieutenant was a signal officer. He had a cushy job managing a team of five men repairing helicopter radios, which is why he volunteered to pilot the ash-and-trash on most days; Lieutenant Devane was a good guy and felt he should contribute more.

Once we were seated in the helicopter, he handed me a map and said, "Okay, Miller, you're the navigator."

I looked at him and said, "You haven't planned the flight?"

Smiling, he said, "Nope, I thought you'd handle that."

I looked over the map and located Vũng Tàu, about fifty-six miles southeast of Dĩ An on the coast. While climbing out of Di An FSB, I told Lieutenant Devane, *aka Sparky 6*, to head south and climb to 5,000 feet. He leveled off at 5,000 feet, just as we crossed over Nha Be Naval Base and I told him, "Turn left to 130 degrees. Vũng Tàu is forty-eight miles straight ahead."

"You know, Morgan, Vũng Tàu used to be an in-country R&R destination, so the quarters should be pretty nice." I felt a small surge of anticipation—a private room, a comfortable bed, non-army sheets, good food, maybe even pictures on the walls. I was beginning to think I was going to a hotel. *Steady on, Morgan.*

Once I could see the Vũng Tàu runway, which was ten miles away, I called their control tower and got clearance for a straight-in landing. After landing safely, we quickly made our way to the admin office, and I checked in for the course. An efficient, young clerk with a wide toothy smile told me there was a pilot meeting at noon in the mess hall and gave me directions. Sparky 6 handed me my travel bag and said, "Good luck, Miller. See you in a couple of weeks."

Another clerk took me to my room. I looked at my watch; it was only 9:30 a.m. Lieutenant Devane was correct; the billets were one-hundred percent better than my hooch in Dĩ An. It was a large single room with a table, chair, closet, and a view of the beach. It may not have been heaven, but it was heaven to me.

I unpacked and wandered outside. I first wanted to look at the helicopters I'd be flying, so I walked over to the flight line where five Cobras were waiting for their new pilots. I was impressed; they were much newer than the ones we had back at the base. I made my way to the maintenance shed and waved hello to the mechanics working on three Cobras. One of them, a short guy a little younger than me, came over; he had short brown hair smudged with grease. We had a brief conversation about the Cobras before I made my way back to find the location of the mess hall. It was still forty-five minutes before the meeting, so I returned to my room to relax and think about what the next fourteen days would bring.

I was early and the first person to arrive, so I chose a seat. There were AH1G Cobra flight manuals at each seat, along with the course syllabus. I flipped through the pages and remembered how technical and descriptive it was. The room gradually filled up, and everyone nodded in acknowledgment as they entered it.

On the stroke of noon, a major entered, and everyone stood.

"Take your seats, gentlemen. I am Major Bowers."

He was tall, a fraction taller than me. He looked like an athlete, fit, not an ounce of fat—and alert, someone I felt would be easy to respect. He wore an Army Rangers patch on his left shoulder and aviator wings on his left chest. This man was well qualified and had the necessary experience and credibility to run this training school. I inwardly smiled; *so far, so good.*

He introduced the course, outlined the syllabus and added, "Because you are all experienced pilots, this is a condensed version of the four-week course taught at Fort Hunter/Stewart, Savannah,

Georgia. Monday through Friday starting at 7:00 a.m., breakfast will be available in the mess hall. At 8:00 a.m., half of you will attend class on the Cobra's operating systems and the other half will receive flight training from our highly qualified instructors. At noon, lunch will be served. At 1 p.m., you'll change places. I hope that's all clear?" The major introduced us to our Bell helicopter technical instructor and our army Cobra flight instructors. My flight instructor was CW2 Rick Normand. He was 5'10" and heavy-set—a second-tour Cobra pilot.

The next morning, breakfast was at 7:00 a.m. At 8:00 a.m. I walked to the flight line with half of my fellow transition pilots. We rotated two-hour flight training sessions which included pre-flight and post-flight critiques. After our lunch break, we had four hours of ground school taught by a Bell Helicopter technical representative from Rhode Island. He had a New England accent which changed words with Rs from "car" to "cah." I found his accent fascinating and amusing. He taught us the finer details of how the helicopter's operating systems worked, what they did, and why they were there.

By the middle of the second week, we learned that the Cobra had two hydraulic pumps, which supplied the hydraulic pressure to systems one and two, but that the fluid came from only one reservoir. This got me thinking about what had happened to Jim Elkin. His cries, "Mayday! Mayday! Mayday! Stiff control! Landing immediately!" rang in my head.

At the end of the class, I asked why there wasn't a warning sensor in the single hydraulic reservoir, which would let the pilot know if the fluid was low. The instructor said, "Well, Mr. Miller that's a good question, I'll do some research and get back to everyone with my findings."

The transition course was intense, fast-paced, and unrelenting. There was a feeling of urgency that I had not experienced during training back home. Long days followed each other without a break. I could see the stress building in the eyes of some of my fellow participants. Vietnam was different; this training could mean the difference between life and death: my life and death, so I focused and soaked up the information like a sponge.

After three days of flight training with Rick Normand, I began to see that he was going to be the best flight instructor I'd ever been trained by, civilian or military. I noticed he'd do things that only experience can teach you—war zone experience—little things that could keep the helicopter in the air and save your life. Like when making a rocket attack, you need make damn sure the Cobra's trim ball is centered, otherwise the rockets will not go as intended. If you have your scout helicopter or friendlies close by, they could be killed.

Fourteen days later, only two pilots out of the twenty enrolled in the course failed the final flight check ride. Luckily, I was not one of them.

After an informal graduation ceremony, I hitched a ride back to Dĩ An on a 1st Cav helicopter. Back at base, I sought out Captain Moss and presented him with my certificate. I was officially now a Cobra pilot. He glanced at it, shook my hand, and congratulated me. I asked him how things had been at camp; he raised an eyebrow and rearranged his face into a grimace.

I said, "It's the 'The New Guy,' right?"

He didn't say anything, but I could have covered a five-lane highway if I'd read between the lines. One thing was clear; I'd hit a nerve; it was "The New Guy," alright. I wondered what new strange policy changes he was trying to push through this time. Or was it something else?

Over the next few days, I tried to discover the reason for the Captain's grimace, but whatever the platoon leaders knew, they kept it close to their chests.

No one was speaking; it was as if they were hiding military secrets.

*Claude Devane having returned with assorted helicopter blades*
*and parts for the maintenance team.*

# CHAPTER 25

# THE TOP-SECRET MEETING

During August, the 1st of the 9th Air Calvary Troop moved south from Quần Lợi to Lai Khê, and our A Troop Squadron moved from Dĩ An to Quần Lợi to replace them. These troop movements were a continuation of what we experienced the month before; some American ground forces were returning home, and the Army of the Republic of Vietnam (ARVN) infantry ground units were taking their place. However, the U.S. Army hunter/killer teams still had a job to do.

At Quần Lợi, my Cobra pilot buddy, Mike Billow, saved me a bunk.

"Hey Morgan, we have ARVNs guarding the base perimeter. How about that shit? We're the only American unit here."

"That's called Vietnamization of the war, Mike, and it doesn't give me a warm and fuzzy feeling. How about you?"

"No, it's a scary thought. I'll be sleeping with one eye open, that's for sure."

ARVN officers received U.S. army special forces training, and knew what they were doing, but the average enlisted Vietnamese soldier was not as trained or as motivated. They came from hunter-gatherer traditions and showed little respect for American soldiers trying to help them live in a free, democratic society. At

Quần Lợi, the fact that ARVN soldiers were responsible for base security was disturbing. It was like moving to a small town and witnessing the professional, full-time fire department replaced by less-experienced, conscripts.

I was already missing Dĩ An, where Biên Hòa PX and downtown Saigon were only a jeep ride away. Calling home from Dĩ An may have been convoluted, but at least it was possible, and the local Vietnamese barbers were a lot better than having a roommate hack away at your hair.

Quần Lợi was remote, with fewer comforts of home. On a positive note, due to being higher above sea level and nestled among rubber trees, it was cooler and less humid than Dĩ An. Shortly after unpacking, Captain Moss arrived at my hooch and told me that the commanding officer wanted to talk to me ASAP.

"Really, Captain? What's up?"

He raised his eyebrows in what was beginning to become shorthand for, *It's "The New Guy" again,* and said, "Just go to the orderly room. I have to go and get Bill Yount as well."

I arrived at the orderly room ahead of Captain Moss and Bill. When they arrived, the major called us into his office. We came to attention and saluted. Bill was a new Cobra pilot; he was the same age as me, heavy set, about my height, with light brown hair. The best way to describe him was to say he was reserved, but that was putting it mildly. He didn't say much and rarely offered an opinion on anything.

"Gentlemen, thanks for coming. Take a seat."

It only took me a few seconds to recognize that standing beside the major was my old high school buddy, Skip Newman. The last time I'd seen him was stateside at the University Lanes bowling alley with his girlfriend. I had to control my amazement and prevent my jaw from dropping open because I knew that Special Forces operate with a high level of secrecy, and I didn't want to cause him any trouble. However, we made brief eye contact, which was enough acknowledgment.

The major cleared his throat and said, "Gentlemen, early this morning, the Special Forces team leader here at Quần Lợi updated me on the status of our Henry Harris. Sergeant Newman, would you take over?"

"Yes, Sir. Gentlemen, we have known about a POW camp in Cambodia about ten miles east of Phnom Penh for a while, from our Special Forces guys on the ground. We strongly believe that Henry Harris is a prisoner there, and we need to get him out as a matter of great urgency because we feel the camp is preparing to close down. They will kill Harris or move him further north if that's the case. We don't have time to get official approval for a rescue attempt through our line of command, so we are hoping A Troop will assist with the rescue."

I looked over at Captain Moss and Bill. The captain had an eager, interested look on his face. Bill kept his cards close to the vest. Sergeant Newman walked over to the far wall of the office and pulled a curtain back to reveal a map of Cambodia. He pointed to a circled "X."

"The camp is near the Mekong River, about eighty miles west of Quần Lợi and ten miles east of Phnom Penh."

After answering a few questions, he ended his briefing. The major thanked Skip, shook his hand, and said he would contact him tomorrow with a decision. The major then turned to look at us.

"The reason I have invited you, Mr. Miller and Mr. Yount, is because you are mature men and our most experienced co-pilots. To be clear, I am asking—not ordering you—to consider undertaking an unofficial, top-secret mission that could very well get you killed. We are talking about flying into Cambodia and rescuing Henry Harris with the help of a Special Forces team on the ground in the area. Mr. Miller, you would be promoted to Pilot in Command for the mission and your team would consist of Mr. Yount, Sergeant Newman, a door gunner, and the crew chief. I intended to join you on this mission; however, Captain Moss convinced me that if the squadron commander called—or worse— "turned up unexpectedly and found me absent, it would be . . . problematic."

I raised my hand and was about to speak when the major stopped me.

"Mr. Miller, I don't want an answer from you now. But let me be clear, this is not an order. I want you and Mr. Yount to think this over tonight and let me know in the morning. Remember, what you just heard is top secret; it does not leave this room. You are all excused. I suggest we meet tomorrow morning for breakfast at 6:30 a.m."

We stood as one, came to attention and left the room. Once outside, Bill and I wished Captain Moss a good night and headed back to our hooch. Laying on our bunks, neither of us said a word; there was much to consider. I thought about what Ginger would say if she knew I was voluntarily risking my life to save a virtual stranger; I hoped she'd understand. And how could I live with myself if I turned my back on Henry?

Finally, feeling like I had a load of bubble gum in my brain, I sat up, looked at Bill, and said, "I need a drink; what about you?"

"Sounds like a good idea to me."

We walked over to the Officers' Club. At Quần Lợi, it was known as the Bunker for no better reason than it had been the command bunker when the 1st Cavalry occupied the base. We ordered our drinks and joined a group of our Cobra colleagues, Mike Billow, Joe Jackson, Dave Toms, and the new pilot, Robby Hodge, at a large table. No sooner had we sat down than Captain Moss marched through the door like a man on a mission. On his way to the bar, he walked past our table and invited me and Bill to join him. It sounded more like an order than an invitation, though.

The other guys smiled as we got up. In such a tight-knit community, it didn't take rocket scientists to know when something was up. By the time we got to the bar, the captain had three shots of tequila lined up—I got the feeling they were all his. He asked what we were drinking, and I ordered a rum and Coke; Bill had a

Budweiser. We sipped in silence for a while until the tension became unbearable. Suddenly, Captain Moss blurted out.

"Well? What have you decided?"

Bill focused on his beer. I took a long sip of my rum and said, keeping my voice low, "To clarify the situation, rescuing Henry is not only unauthorized; we'll likely be shot down and killed. Of course, we could survive, be captured, and spend the rest of our days at the Hanoi Hilton. On a slightly more positive note, we could succeed and end up in Fort Leavenworth charged with heaven's know what—dereliction of duty, stealing a Huey and invading Cambodia single-handedly." I smiled, trying to lighten the mood. In more ways than one, it was a suicide mission.

Captain Moss grinned, "Worst case scenario, gentleman, if you survive, that is, you might need the services of an attorney. But at the end of the day, you will be following orders, even if those orders were framed as a request."

"Does that mean you're on board with this mission, Captain?"

"I am not saying that I'm NOT on board. Perhaps you need to sleep on it."

"You mean, lie awake all-night thinking about it?"

Bill was as silent as Charlie Chaplin on the topic. He just sat stoically drinking his beer.

"The reality is this: the major and I needed two pilots who we believed had the skills and experience to get in and out safely. You two were chosen because you are older and more mature than the other pilots and offer the best odds of getting a positive result."

My drink was almost empty, and I contemplated another.

"This might be Henry's only chance. I'm not sure if I told you, but I sat next to Henry on the long flight to Vietnam. I got to know the kid. I heard about his family, his home, and his dreams—we bonded. I think of him like he's my brother. I have no option; I need to do everything I can to save him."

The emotion in my words was such that Captain Moss put his hand on my shoulder. Then, he looked at Bill, who was now on his third beer. Bill pursed his lips, lifted his chin, and nodded. He was in. With a rueful grin, the captain toasted us both with his last shot of tequila.

I broke the tension, "Captain, I need to get my head around the logistics of this mission, is there somewhere private where we can start planning?"

"Relax, Mr. Miller. Finish your drink, maybe order another, and then we'll head to the Tactical Operation Center. That's where A Troop commands and directs its hunter/killer operations, so they've got maps we can use."

Bill and I knew the location of the TOC, but we'd never been inside. We ducked under the door and into the bunker. Captain Moss went over to a large, grey metal cabinet and dug out aeronautical charts. It didn't take us long to find a map showing Saigon north to Quần Lợi and a second one showing Quần Lợi west to Phnom Penh. Bill and I taped the two maps together and cut off what we didn't need. Bill used a ruler to draw a straight line from where Highway 13 north of Quần Lợi crossed from South Vietnam into Cambodia and then west to the POW camp near Phnom Penh.

Next, Bill took the plotter, figured out the mileage and heading, and then computed the flight time based on ninety knots of airspeed. We all took our time scrutinizing the terrain, which appeared flat, mostly jungle with intermittent open spaces. After we plotted the route, I said, "Sir, this would be a piece of cake if, that is, it wasn't over enemy territory and at night. I'd feel much better if an Air Force radar plane was overhead just in case we have mechanical problems."

Captain Moss smiled grimly and shook his head.

"Gentlemen, there are currently only five people on the planet who know about this mission, and three of them will be on board the Huey."

After Captain Moss put the maps back in the TOC cabinet, we climbed out of the bunker and into the night air. It was hot and humid, sweat dripped into my eyes, and I felt a lump in my stomach.

"Thanks for the briefing, Captain; it's good to have an idea of what we are getting into and the logistics we need to consider."

When we got back to our quarters, Bill spent a few minutes watching four of our roommates play poker. There were a lot of chips in play, but in the big scheme of things, the risks the card sharks were taking paled in significance when stacked up against what we had just agreed to undertake.

Lying on my bunk, I thought about how little Bill had said about the rescue mission; he took the strong silent type to a new level. But I already knew we'd both be telling the major at break-fast that we would rescue Henry Harris—or die trying.

*Officers mess hall at Quần Lợi*

*Quần Lợi outdoor motion picture theatre in troop hooch area*

*Tactical Operations Center entrance at Quần Lợi*

# CHAPTER 26

# PREPARING MENTALLY FOR THE BIG NIGHT

I t was 2:00 a.m., and everything was quiet except for the endless drone of someone snoring loudly in a distant bunk. I was lying in bed thinking about the flight and going over the details repeatedly. Sleep came only in waves, and I soon dozed off again, only to be awakened by the other hooch pilots getting ready to start work. It was 5:00 a.m. I turned and looked over at Bill; he was awake but just staring into space, so I didn't disturb him. There was no need to be up yet, but I went with some friends for breakfast—scrambled eggs, coffee, and the usual fixings.

Heading back to my hooch, I bumped into Bill leaving for the mess hall to have breakfast and meet the major, so I decided to walk with him—I thought another coffee might help clear the cobwebs. Mike Billow, returning from a pre-flight, joined us. After going through the chow line, we wandered to the officer's section and sat down. No one spoke; I drank my coffee, and the other two concentrated on their food. Fifteen minutes later, Mike dropped a bombshell.

"So, which one of you is going to be the major's pilot tonight?"

I was stunned; *what the devil; how did he know?*

I said, "How the heck did you find out about that?"

"I got the word from the Cobra crew chief while I was pre-flighting."

Looking across at Bill, I said, "We don't have any details yet, and we can't talk about it even if we did. It's on a need-to-know basis only."

Bill added, "Mike, it's the major's plan, but he is not going. Just me and Morgan."

Mike said, "Okay! Mum's the word."

Mike was only twenty and a little wet behind the ears, so I decided to change the subject before somebody overheard our conversation. I liked Mike; he was almost six feet and slim, with dirty blond hair. He was unsuccessfully trying to grow a mustache, probably in an attempt to look older. The major's comments about needing mature co-pilots were on point. I knew Mike signed up for the army's rotor wing flight course when he was only eighteen, and I'd always meant to ask him why; this seemed like an opportune moment. He smiled, eager to tell his story.

"After high school, I went to Stanford University as a biology major, but during my first semester, I learned from a friend that the army had a helicopter course that didn't require a college degree. I'd always wanted to fly, but it was expensive—definitely out of my reach."

I interrupted, "I can relate to that; I paid for my own civilian flight training for four years before getting drafted."

"Yeah," he said, "the week after I learned about the helicopter course, I went to Redwood City, California, and talked to an army recruiter about the program. He assured me there was no obligation and suggested I take a test to see whether I was a potential candidate. A week later, he called and told me I'd done well on the test and wanted to sign me up for the army warrant officer flight training program. I asked what commitment I would have to make, and he said five years from graduation."

Mike took a sip of his coffee, which must have been cold by now, and continued, "I said I'd think about it. Two weeks later, I decided to leave Stanford and join the army."

Talkative Bill said, "Wow!"

"I held off telling my parents until the week before I was due to leave for Fort Polk, in Louisiana. Not surprisingly, they were mortified. Their first thought was that I was giving up Stanford for the inevitability of going to Vietnam. In the end, they supported my decision, albeit reluctantly."

I put my arm on his shoulder, "You, young man, are very mature for your age. I wouldn't have had the maturity to make a decision like that at your age." As soon as the words left my mouth, I thought, *heck, I'm only a half-dozen years older than this guy.* War sure does age you quickly.

Breakfast over, I left the guys, walked over to the maintenance area, and introduced myself to Ed Soliday, the Cobra maintenance officer. I needed something to get my mind off the rescue mission, so I quizzed him on the recent Cobra crash. The mechanics of the hydraulic system were still puzzling me. We talked for a couple of hours, and I understood the system better. The problem was the more I knew, the more questions it raised.

Back at my hooch, I found Bill lying on his bunk, staring at the ceiling—again. His "man of few words" routine was becoming trying.

"Bill, are you ready to discuss our flight?"

He sat up, swung his legs to the floor, and looked at me, "Now that I know the particulars, I'm fine with the mission, Morgan. What about you?"

"I'm okay, I think. I'm going for a long walk after lunch. I need to mull it over to ensure I've considered it from every angle." It was the unknowns, those unexpected situations that tended to get you killed; I wanted to spend some time thinking about the "what ifs."

Bill laid back, put his arms behind his head, and said, "Okay, well, I'm going to rest up for a while before lunch. We've got a busy night ahead of us." I admired his stoicism, but that just led me to wonder what he was truly thinking.

For the next hour, I made a tape to send to Ginger, speaking into the microphone as if I were talking to her; although a one-way conversation, it made me feel closer to her. I was careful to sound normal as if I wasn't just about to go on what could be a suicide mission. Sure, it was dangerous, but I knew we'd make it back—hopefully with Henry.

Bill and I went to get some lunch at the mess hall. Obviously, by the set of his jaw, he'd been thinking, "I think we should take two M16 rifles and a couple hundred rounds of ammo, along with eight or so boxes of C-rations and five, one-gallon jugs of water."

"You mean in case we get shot down and miraculously survive?" I said, laughing.

Straight-faced, Bill said, "On my first tour, back in '67, I was with the 189th Assault Helicopter Company, and that's what we always took when flying over dangerous territory. At the time, we were based at the Pleiku air base in the central highland's region, and almost daily, we resupplied the Special Forces base, near the Cambodian border. We also flew Special Forces teams into Cambodia and dropped them off in the middle of nowhere. We'd return a week later and pick the Special Forces guys up with a McGuire rig—that was scary stuff."

I'd forgotten the depth of experience Bill had and was eager to hear more. He was doing an excellent job of keeping my mind off our impending mission. I asked him to explain a McGuire rig; I'd never heard of it. This was the most I'd heard him talk—ever.

"It's a long nylon rope with a heavy sandbag attached to the end, designed to penetrate the jungle canopy when dropped out of the helicopter. We'd drop the rig, and somehow, I never knew exactly how, the Special Forces team members attached themselves to the rope. Once my crew chief got the all-clear from their leader, the pilot and I would slowly lift them clear of the jungle. Once our crew chief gave us the all-clear, we'd fly slowly to a nearby clearing and gently set them down. We'd hover while they disconnected themselves from the rope, then land and pick them up and take them back to Dak Pek special forces camp on the Laos border, all the while hoping that we wouldn't come under enemy fire."

"Wow, Bill, I've never heard of that strategy and technique. Was it exciting, scary, rewarding?"

Bill shook his head, "All of those things, Morgan. I tell you, those Special Forces guys are nuts. They spend their lives in enemy territory and do stuff you wouldn't believe. It's like they have no fear. It was good to be supporting them, though."

With Bill's great story bouncing off my brain cells, I decided to take the walk I'd promised myself. I needed to calm my nerves. I would soon be working closely with the guys Bill had just described as "nuts." Their lives would be in my hands, and so would Henry's.

Quần Lợi was located on a colonial-era French rubber plantation, and many of the original buildings were intact. I walked to the end of the runway, around the mansion, and discovered the old swimming pool, which until only a few years ago, had still been maintained and was used by the 1st Cav. It was empty. I stood for a few minutes, imagining our soldiers diving from the high boards in what would have been a beautiful setting. Today it looked sad, forgotten, and it was out of bounds.

The large, two-story plantation house looked as if someone could still be living there, but I could see no window coverings; the rumors I had heard about occupants were obviously incorrect. Snooping around, I discovered some outbuildings, including an implement shed containing broken equipment, an empty storage building, and what appeared to be a bunkhouse for plantation workers.

I looked at my watch; it was time to head back now that I had worked through my thoughts about the mission and putting my life on the line for a young man I hardly knew.

CHAPTER 27

# FINAL PREPARATIONS

As I walked back to my hooch after visiting the plantation house, still dreaming of what it would have been like to swim in the pool back in the day, I passed the first revetment. Huey 369 was parked there, and I considered giving it a pre-flight, but there were too many people around, and I didn't want to tip anyone off that I would be using the bird later.

I decided to sit in the cargo bay for a while, the night's mission playing on my mind. The crew chief interrupted my thoughts.

"Are you flying with the major tonight?"

A little too quickly, I said, "No! Where's he going?"

I didn't know exactly how much the crew chief knew; the rumors were rife in the camp. If he knew about the mission, one of the four of us in the know must have blabbed. On the other hand, he might be bluffing to encourage me to spill the beans. That wasn't going to happen.

He looked at me intently for a few seconds and then said, "I don't know, but I was told the bird was going out tonight after dark. So, can I help you with something?"

"*Nah*, thanks. I'm just here to think about my wife and family, and this is the furthest helicopter from my bunk." Of course, I knew that he would be unceremoniously awakened by the major's clerk shortly before midnight and told to get his ass to the flight line.

I stood up, smiled, and headed back up the flight line. I'm sure the young crew chief knew something was up. I glanced at my watch and calculated the time left before take-off; six hours. The day seemed to be never-ending. It felt like I was treading water—I just wanted or perhaps needed—to get on with the mission. Then it dawned on me, *shit, I was supposed to be meeting the major at 6:30 p.m., as in now*!

I ran to the orderly room, and once there took thirty seconds to catch my breath. The first sergeant pointed to the major's open door, and I went in, glancing at my watch. Captain Moss was speaking to the major about the mission plans. Bill was sitting quietly, taking it all in.

"Sir, I'm sorry I am late."

"No problem, Mr. Miller. Mr. Yount told us you were on board with this mission. Take a seat."

Captain Moss continued telling the major that we had all gone to the TOC the previous night and planned the flight. The major asked to see the flight plan, and Captain Moss rolled the maps out onto his desk. After they were flattened out, the major moved his finger over the line of flight.

"How are you going to find where Highway 13 crosses the Cambodian border? It'll be pitch black."

"Sir, we will fly the runway heading until we intersect the due north, 00-degree radial from the electronic navigational system in Saigon. At that point, we'll turn right and track outbound on that 00-degree radial, which goes right over Loc Ninh. Then, for a positive time and distance starting point, I will call Saigon approach control, call sign Paris Control for our exact position on that radial. According to my calculations, that checkpoint is seventy-five miles from the Saigon VOR."

"Nice job, Mr. Miller! Staff Sergeant Newman, do you have any questions?"

"Not currently, sir."

"Okay, gentlemen . . ."

I quickly interrupted the major's attempt to close the meeting.

"Sir, Bill and I estimated the approximate weight and balance for the mission, and we think we should leave the door gunner behind to save weight. We don't know what the terrain will be like when we land, and it will be crucial to be as light as possible when we try to take off with seven of our guys on board. We have Sergeant Newman with us; he can take the door gunner's place."

"Good point, Mr. Miller; I agree. Anything else?"

"I think that's it, Sir."

"Okay! The mission is a go! I'll meet you at the flight line at 1:45 a.m., that's seven hours—go get some rest."

Captain Moss turned to us outside the major's office and said, "I'll bring you two M16s with 200-round ammo belts. I'm on duty at the TOC this evening, so I'll come and wake you at 1:00 a.m. I'll bring the flight map."

As the captain was about to leave, Bill said, "Excuse me, Captain, what about the water and C-rations?"

"Yes, sorry, I'll get those right now. See you at 1:00 a.m."

As Captain Moss walked away, I said to Bill, "That's it? I feel we've forgotten something."

"It's in God's hands now, Morgan, but my gut tells me we'll be fine."

I looked at my watch as we walked back to our hooch. Six and a half hours to what could be a turning point in my life, or perhaps the end of it. I noticed the mail clerk had dropped off some mail. It was lying on my bunk, and for a moment, I felt a sense of guilt—what would my family think of me risking my life on such a dangerous mission of dubious legality?

There was a tape from Ginger and a letter from my grandmother. I was about to open the letter when a group of my roommates returned from the bunker. I took my Craig recorder and Ginger's tape outside to get some privacy and avoid answering any difficult questions.

It was incredible to hear Ginger's voice, so clear, vibrant, and loving—I missed her so much. Listening to her brought her closer, in spirit at least. She caught me up with life stateside; all was good with our friends and her family. She said she had dinner with my parents every Wednesday night, which she very much enjoyed. The only time I became a little emotional was when she excitedly told me that she wished our R&R would come sooner because she missed me so much. The next several hours were going to be as far removed from R&R as I could imagine. I was so pleased that I'd sent her a tape before this mission. In case . . .

When I got back to my Quonset hut, I found it unusually quiet, almost eerie; my roommates avoided eye contact. The unsubstantiated, although factually correct, rumor had obviously spread like wildfire. Nobody felt they could, or should, say anything about the not-so-secret-secret mission.

I was dreaming of being poked in the chest by an NVA guard. I could smell his sweat, the meal he had recently finished. I looked up to see Captain Moss poking me hard.

"Mr. Miller, it's 1:00 a.m. we're live."

Bill was already dressing. I washed my face and brushed my teeth—I wanted to face my destiny clean and tidy, at least.

The three of us headed to the mess hall and raided the refrigerator. I prepared a pilot's mission meal: I cut a biscuit in half, spread it with mustard, and added a slice of Spam. My beverage of choice—Coke. Bill looked disgusted at my "meal" and dug deeper, grabbing a couple of cooked hot dogs from the back of the fridge. It wasn't fine dining, but it would do.

Captain Moss came up behind us and patted me on the back.

"Are you guys ready?"

"Yes, sir, it's odd, but I'm not worried about this mission for some reason. Should I be?"

He grinned.

"That's why you two were selected for this mission. Over the last few months, you've both proven that you are cool under fire. You'll be fine."

Walking down the flight line, I chewed on my "disgusting" breakfast and saw a flashlight inspecting the helicopter. It was the crew chief.

I said, "Good morning, young man. Is it ready?"

"Sir, I'm confident this bird is airworthy, but I assume you will do your own inspection?"

"Roger that," I replied.

As I walked around the revetment to the helicopter's left side, I saw the major talking to Staff Sergeant Newman.

"Good morning, Sir," I said, and saluted.

"Good morning Mr. Miller, Mr. Yount."

I turned to Sergeant Newman.

"Are we still departing at 1:45 a.m. prompt?"

"Yes, sir."

"Sergeant, I have 1:25 a.m. on my watch, and it's the 15th of August."

"I have the same, Morgan."

I said, "Bill, would you pre-flight the right side of the bird while I do the left?"

When Bill and I met at the tail rotor, I asked, "When was the last time you piloted a Huey?" It was a rather belated question, but I needed to hear the answer on the flight line.

"*Uh* . . . It's been a while." The hesitation was a surprise, but to use an old cliché, it's like riding a bike; you never forget how. Combat experience was sometimes more important. As the captain had implied, clear heads and cool in combat, that was what counted, and Bill had that in spades.

I asked the crew chief to double-check that all inspection panels were closed and to get back to me. I saw Bill shining his flashlight on the water jugs, the M16s, the ammo belts, and the six boxes of C-rations stored behind my seat. I shook Sergeant

Newman's hand as he maneuvered himself into the rear door gunner's seat. I put on my helmet and bullet stopper, fondly known as a chicken plate, and buckled up. Captain Moss handed me the map through the window. Over the intercom, the crew chief, now seated on the other side of Skip, said, "Sir, all panels are locked, and everything is secure."

"Roger that," I said. I shook Captain Moss's hand, swallowed hard, and said I would see him soon. I opened the map and, using the red lens of my flashlight to protect my night vision, checked the flight plan for the trip. After talking briefly to Captain Moss, Bill got in, buckled up, and said, "Okay, Miller, fire this thing up! Let's go get Henry."

# CHAPTER 28

# THE RESCUE MISSION

The increasingly high-pitched whistle of the Huey's turbine engine winding up always raised my heart rate a little, and today was no different. It meant the start of a mission—all systems "go." I switched on all radios and dialed the due north, 00-degree radial from the Saigon VOR into our VOR radio and set the altimeter—also known as barometer pressure indicator—to the field elevation of 530 feet.

Tonight, I had no doubt I would need all the help I could get navigating in total darkness and blackout conditions. I made a radio check with my team and received confirmation from Bill, Sergeant Newman, and the crew chief. All set, I began hovering out of the revetment and moving onto the runway. The torque meter indicated forty pounds, and all instruments were green, so I lowered the nose. This allowed the Huey to sink a little as it went through transitional lift and continued to move forward. I increased the climb-out airspeed to sixty knots and reminded Bill on the intercom that I was going to maintain runway heading while climbing until I intercepted the 00-degree radial from the Saigon VOR. As I approached 3,000 feet, the VOR began to center, and I carried out a standard rate turn of three degrees per second to a heading of due north.

"Paris Control, this is Army 369, squawking 1200. I am approximately seventy miles north on the 00-degree radial, over."

"Roger, 369, we have radar contact sixty-eight miles north on a heading of 00. Say request, over."

"Paris, I just wanted to ensure you could pick me up. Thanks. Over and out."

I turned off the transponder to conceal our flight direction as we continued our climb on a north heading. We were alone.

I was now totally focused, my powers of concentration honed to a knife edge. Lives were at stake, including mine. I planned to cross the border over Highway 13, at the town of Loc Ninh, at 5,000 feet. From there, I'd make a course correction to 280 degrees west.

I announced over the intercom, "We should arrive at the contact point in about forty-five minutes."

Approaching Loc Ninh, I asked Bill to take over flying so I could check our position on the map. I needed him to be comfortable flying the Huey if I became incapacitated. *It was better than thinking wounded or killed.* I looked up; it was a clear night with no moon, just the millions of stars above to guide us.

Twenty minutes west–northwest of Loc Ninh, I told Bill that we had another twenty-five minutes of flying time to the pickup point.

"Roger that, Morgan."

Minutes later, Sergeant Newman came over the intercom and told us that he had been attempting to make radio contact with his team on the ground, but with no luck so far. Making contact was imperative. I wondered whether enemy forces on the ground were searching the skies at the sound of our rotor blades. They knew the *thwap, thwap, thwap* of a Huey well. I felt my anxiety kick up a notch, and the knot in my stomach was growing from the size of a baseball to a football.

Ten minutes later, Newman reported that he successfully made radio contact. The ground commander asked us to turn our landing light on for a count of five, so he could make a positive ID. I thought, *we'll be sitting ducks for a few seconds.*

I did as instructed and could see a faint white light in the distance. Bill changed direction a little to home in on the light. I remember saying to Mike Billow that our mission was on a need-to-know basis; now I was in the same position, and I needed to know from Sergeant Newman the geographical and topographical details of our landing spot. Without accurate information, we could screw up our approach, and we might only get one chance.

Sergeant Newman's voice boomed in my ear.

"Make a steep circling approach over the light."

*Great, it's pitch black, and all we have is a pinprick of light— nothing wrong with that. Shit!*

Bill's tinny, echoey voice came over the intercom.

"Morgan, should I make a power descent down to 2,000 over the target?"

"Hell no, that will increase the rotor blade." *Whop, whop.*

"OK, I'll reduce power and maintain 90 knots."

As the light loomed closer, Bill brought the Huey's nose up and reduced power a little, which slowed our airspeed to 80 knots as we continued to drop from the sky. At 2,000 feet, Bill leveled off, increased power, and began circling the light.

"Morgan, I could do with your help with the controls."

"Roger, I'm on it."

This was tricky. Sergeant Newman leaned forward, looking out the front window next to me, and searched the ground. Then I heard him on the intercom.

"Land to the right of the light, heading west. Over."

Bill's voice was strained.

"Tighten your seat belts! We're going to land this bird."

He reduced his turning radius, leveled out on a heading of 360, and slowed his airspeed to sixty knots. At an altitude of 900 feet, he continued his turn and descent, stopping his turn at 270 degrees. As the light from the ground grew larger, we could see the Special Forces guy guiding us into land. Bill slowed the chopper for landing and touched down. My heart rate exploded. I couldn't see his face, but I felt sure Bill was as calm as a cucumber.

Sergeant Newman was out of the helicopter a few seconds before we touched down and immediately took a fighting position next to his teammate, who had guided us in.

"Bill," I said, "where is everyone?"

"I was thinking the same thing, Morgan."

Then we heard explosions, and they were close. I looked at my watch; we'd been on the ground for just a minute—it seemed longer. Sergeant Newman's voice erupted in my ear.

"Only two of my guys are here; the rest are on their way. They'll be here shortly."

*"Shortly," what the hell did that mean?* I squirmed in my seat, the feeling of exposure rising every second we were on the ground, deep in enemy territory. *Okay, Morgan, breathe deeply, keep it together, remember you're here to get Henry.* The word "shortly" kept playing over and over like a broken record. I wanted "shortly" to be now!

I busied myself scanning the instrument panel, and everything looked good. The seconds ticked by—there was nothing we could do but wait. It was nerve-wracking, and I could feel sweat running into my eyes. I licked my lips; *how could they be so dry when my forehead is sweating?*

I must have zoned out for a second because I was brought back to reality by a voice. "Sir, all eight are on board. Let's get the hell out of here!"

Impulsively, I shouted, "Eight?! That's one more than we planned for."

More explosions, this time closer. We needed to get the heck out of Dodge, and now.

Sergeant Newman assured me.

"Relax, sir, it's under control. We have a prisoner. He's handcuffed and seated right in front of me. Just let me know if the extra weight is becoming a problem during takeoff, and I'll kick his sorry ass out the door."

I was shaking, and so was the ground around us. We were receiving fire, and if we stayed on the ground any longer . . . I hollered at Sergeant Newman.

"How steep do I need to make our departure? Like now, please!" There was dead air for just a second or two, then Skip's voice came back calmy.

"On this heading of 270, you have more than two football fields of level ground." *BOOM*! A shell landed, and something zipped through my side window, leaving a dime-sized hole. *Shit*!

Needing no further encouragement, Bill pulled the bird off the ground, and we began to move forward. As we did so, the torque indicator read that we were just over our maximum of fifty pounds. *BOOM*! As we went through transitional lift, another round exploded immediately behind us; they were zeroing in on us.

We had no landing light, and there were trees surrounding the clearing. Two football fields didn't feel enough. *Dammit, I can't see*! Bill was a study in ultimate focus. The helicopter began picking up speed. I scanned the instruments, glowing green; we were at a little over 500 feet. *Was it enough*? Bill switched on the landing light for two seconds; we had to see how close we were to the trees. We were clear. Our altitude was increasing; at 700 feet, I knew trees were no longer a problem. My breathing steadied, and Sergeant Newman's calm voice came over the intercom.

"Okay, Mr. Miller, three of our rescue team are wounded, but none are critical. We have Henry safe and sound, but a little worse for wear and our prisoner is right in front of me."

At 1,000 feet, Bill began a standard rate left turn to 100 degrees. I turned the VOR indicator to 180 as we climbed to 5,000 feet. Once there, I unbuckled my seat belt, turned around, and over the intercom, said, "I'd like to congratulate everyone on a successful mission. Good job!"

Bill, ever the professional, said, "Hold on there, Morgan, we still have to get back to Quần Lợi."

I agreed, then ignored him and high-fived the team one by one. I was in an adrenaline rush, and relief flooded over me. Damn, it felt good! As soon as I had the chance, I went back to check on Henry Harris. Although it was wonderful to see him, I could see he wasn't quite sure what was happening. He showed no signs of recognizing me.

Back in my seat, I buckled up, checked the VOR to ensure it was still on the Saigon frequency, and double-checked the 180-degree radial. We were still too far away to pick up a signal. Finally, our VOR indicator came alive; we were going to make it. Forty-five minutes later, we reached Lộc Ninh, and Bill began his descent from 5,000 feet with a shallow turn to the southeast. I called our TOC.

"Spur control, we are about twenty minutes from touchdown. Over."

"Roger that. This is Spur 36. Welcome back. How did it go? Over."

"We picked up everyone, and we have a prisoner on board. Spur 36, could you get a jeep out to the end of the runway with its headlights on to guide us in? We'll be landing to the north. Over."

"Roger that. Over."

Ten minutes later, we saw the Jeep's headlights shining out of the darkness like a benevolent monster leading us home. Bill requested I take control of the helicopter; I'd more experience with night landings at Quần Lợi. I remembered my early flight training instructors; they drummed into us to trust our instruments, not our fatigued brains, after a high-stress mission. It was pitch-black save for the Jeep's lights. I settled myself into my seat; my approach needed to be spot on.

I couldn't see them, but lurking on either side of Quần Lợi's narrow runway were 100-foot-high rubber trees. It crossed my mind that they would not feel like rubber if I hit them. Disorientation—caused by stress and tiredness—was the leading cause of failed landings at night, so I focused primarily on my instrumentation, using the lights from the Jeep as a secondary guide. Flying directly toward the Jeep's headlights on a heading of 210 degrees, I flew over the Jeep, made a left turn to a heading of 180 degrees, and maintained that heading for one minute. I then began a left standard-rate turn and rolled out on a heading of 310 degrees at 1,500 feet above sea level, 1,000 feet above the runway. My teardrop turn lined me up perfectly with the runway about one mile out and directly behind the Jeep. I began my descent, turned on my landing light, and checked all my instruments were glowing green. The Jeep passed beneath me, and I came to a hover about 100 feet down the runway next to the major's revetment. I then hovered over and parked the bird in the major's spot. I shut the helicopter down, and for a second or two, the only sound was the *thwap, thwap, thwap* of the rotor blades slowing to a *swish, swish, swish*. Everyone was glad to be home safely—well, everyone except for the prisoner.

I opened my window to let some air in, and immediately Captain Moss was there, thrusting his hand toward me and shaking it vigorously.

"Well done, Morgan; I knew you could do it!"

I had no chance to reply before he left to go and congratulate Bill.

A Special Forces medical tech and our troop medical tech were already doing triage on our wounded. They left for our unit infirmary within minutes while the rest of the Special Forces team headed in the opposite direction with the prisoner.

I looked at my watch; 4:00 a.m. It felt later.

A lot later.

# CHAPTER 29

# THE DEBRIEFING

I stepped down from the helicopter, took a few paces along the flight line, and immediately felt faint. My knees buckled, my mouth was parched, and I had to hold onto Captain Moss's shoulder for support. He grabbed me and held out a canteen of water. I drank like I'd been stranded in the desert for days. My head cleared, and I could once again stand without support. I heard the captain asking Bill about the rescue.

"It went fine, sir, but it was very stressful,"

Bill said this in his measured way of speaking that failed to match the words he was saying.

"Are you feeling okay now, Mr. Miller?"

"Yes, sir, I'm fine now. I think it was just the rush of adrenaline catching up with me; it went to my head."

"Okay, guys, head to the orderly room; Staff Sergeant Newman will handle the debriefing."

I was feeling better. Bill put his arm around my shoulder and said, "We did good today, Morgan, real good."

The major's clerk laid out seats in the orderly room. As we waited for the others to arrive, it was good to unwind and reflect on the incredible rescue we just successfully undertook. The major walked through the door with our medical tech and Henry. I quickly got up and shook Henry's hand. He looked like he had

been through the wringer and then some, but I thought he was
holding up surprisingly well.

"Mr. Miller, you were part of the rescue? Thank you! Thank
you!" As he said this, tears welled up, and he rubbed them away
with the back of his hand. I was so glad I had played a part in getting him home safely. He sat next to me, and I introduced him to
Bill, who also received Henry's profuse thanks.

Captain Moss arrived with a carton of ice-cold beers and Cokes
just as the major prepared to address us.

"What you are about to hear does not leave this room.
Understood?"

As one, everyone in the room said, "Yes, sir."

"Over to you, Staff Sergeant Newman."

Captain Moss guarded the door, although the likelihood of anyone being up at this hour was small.

"Gentlemen, let me give you a little background to this mission.
After 1968, it became too dangerous to insert Special Forces teams
into enemy territory by helicopter; the risk of being shot down
increased alarmingly. This brings us to this morning's mission.
Planning started two weeks ago at 2:00 a.m. when a six-man Special Forces team parachuted from a C130 transporter at 25,000 feet.
Once on the ground and regrouped, the men hiked through the
night and set up camp on a small hill overlooking the POW compound the following day. From this vantage point, they watched
the camp's activity for several days, gathering enough intel to
form a rescue plan. Early in the surveillance, it became obvious
that the NVA was planning to move the camp. At that point, we
knew we had to take action immediately. At 2:30 this morning,
three team members moved to rescue Henry here, code-named
Henry-6. Once the team had their target—that's you, Henry—they
headed for the pickup point, about two miles from the compound.
Any questions?"

We were all so fascinated by being given an inside look at a
Special Forces mission no one said a word.

"Okay, then. As we were about to land, one of the team warned me that tracking dogs were barking at his six o'clock and that three of his team were boobytrapping the trail with Claymore mines. He radioed me that he could see the chopper and would arrive at the landing zone any moment, followed shortly by the rest of the team. Once we landed, I jumped out and took a defensive position. Within a minute or so, I could see two team members coming out of the jungle; one was wounded, and the other was helping Henry. The rest of the team arrived shortly after, and we were able to take off before things got too nasty; although I understand Mr. Miller here had a close encounter with some shrapnel. With that, I'll turn things over to the medical personnel."

The medic looked over at Henry with a smile.

"Well, Henry, you've lost a lot of weight; you are extremely dehydrated and malnourished. Nothing too surprising there. You're a young, fit guy, so we'll take you to the army hospital in Saigon and return you to the healthy young buck you were before your unfortunate adventure."

Henry, as always the polite and humble guy he was, smiled and thanked the medic, who continued his briefing.

"Two of the Special Forces team members have some nasty cuts and bruises, and the third man has a bullet in his thigh, but they will be fine too."

After the debriefing, we sat there for a bit, talking amongst ourselves and enjoying our well-deserved beers. Outside, the camp was starting to come to life, so the major thanked us and wished us a good night, but not before giving everyone the day off to decompress. As everyone was leaving, I crossed the room and sat next to my old high-school buddy, Skip. He was an impressive soldier and a remarkable man.

"Remember when we ran into each other at the bowling alley before I went to Fort Ord?"

"I sure do," he said, taking a final slug of his beer.

"Well, if you'd told me then that we'd be flying into Cambodia on a top-secret, cross-border rescue mission together, I would've called you crazy!"

"Yeah, right, Morgan. It's funny how life turns out. I'm always amazed by coincidences. By the way, I appreciate that you didn't say you knew me at that first meeting. I tend to fly under the radar as much as I can."

"No problem. This mission never happened. In fact, I have never seen you before in my life!"

He stood, shook my hand, clapped me on the shoulder, and said, "You did good today, Morgan; you're a great pilot."

With that, he walked out, and I never saw him again.

# CHAPTER 30

# BECOMING A TEST PILOT

I'd been flying missions with all the Cobra aircraft commanders for a couple of months. However, I'd spent every other day flying with Dave Tela for a week or more when he mentioned he wanted to discuss something with me when I had a moment. I knew he was heading home in early September, so I thought he might want to revisit our conversation about the mechanical issues with the Cobra's hydraulic system. After a quiet day flying close to the Cambodian border, he suggested we go to the officer's mess hall and grab a bite to eat. Once we sat down, he asked, "Morgan, would you be interested in taking over from Ed Soliday when he goes home in a few weeks?"

I was stunned.

"Wow! Dave, am I hearing you correctly? You want me to put myself forward for Cobra maintenance officer? That's a stretch, isn't it? I'm a pilot, not an AMOC-trained maintenance officer. Besides, I'm looking forward to being a Cobra aircraft commander; it's what I've been training to do for the past three months."

"Morgan, management has asked me to see how you feel about this position. One thing you should know is that Ed had no experience either when he started. As maintenance officer, you don't get your hands dirty; it's a supervisory position, and of course, you have to flight test the Cobras after repairs and after each 100-hour inspection."

I had a sinking feeling in the pit of my stomach. I was a Cobra pilot, not a test pilot. Dave, also a Cobra test pilot, broke into my thoughts.

"The 3/17 squadron and the 1st Aviation Brigade were tasked to find someone that had taken the Army Maintenance Officer Course for the job, but they've struck out. If they can't find someone with all the relevant qualifications, the next best thing is a respected Cobra pilot with common sense who's reliable. That's where you come in."

"I'm flattered, Dave, but compliments don't make me any happier. Has all this come about because you and I were chatting about the Cobra's hydraulics?"

Dave smiled, "Well, you didn't help your cause by grilling Ed about Cobra hydraulics the morning before Henry's rescue. By the time the search for a candidate went from Captain Carothers to squadron headquarters and then to the 1st Aviation Brigade—who failed to find anyone—it ended back on the captain's desk. At that point, Captain Carothers called a meeting with the major and Captain Moss—who is also close to heading home, by the way—to identify a Cobra pilot that would best fill Soliday's boots. Moss asked me who would be the best person for the job, and I recommended you without reservation."

"Quite the story, Dave. I suppose I'm honored that anyone would think I could do the job, which sure comes with a hell of a lot of responsibility."

"Morg, there's a strong upside here for you. You'll be on the inside and can drill down into the Cobra's inherent hydraulic problem."

"I've simply been tasked with seeing if you are interested. Would you do me a favor and at least talk it over with Ed before making any decision?"

I nodded. I had a lot to think about. The next day I flew the ash-and-trash Huey to Dĩ An and, while I was there, took the opportunity to talk to Ed. The massive maintenance hangar was busy; mechanics worked on three Cobras, two Hueys, and three scout helicopters. There was something sad and unsettling about seeing the three formidable gunships stripped down and exposed. It struck me how the lives of Cobra pilots were in the hands of these mechanics and, of course, the oversight of the maintenance officer. It was a little like going backstage at a theatre—the actors get all the glory, but the people behind the scenes make the play come to life.

After giving me a tour, Ed and I sat on some empty rocket boxes in the shade just outside the hangar and talked for a while. I learned that he had been a flight engineer with United Airlines, and he'd signed up for the warrant officer candidate flight program rather than be drafted. Ed talked a little about his family and said he was looking forward to going home. Then he went over the day-to-day responsibilities of the job and assured me that if I took it on, I would be inheriting a first-rate team of mechanics. He looked at his watch and said, "Morgan, Captain Carothers wants to meet you."

There was a well-orchestrated, maybe well-intended, plan to sweep me along in a sea of goodwill, flattery, and call to duty. The captain gave me a broad smile as I walked into his office. I wasn't sure whether he was my new best friend or Dr. Death.

"Mr. Miller, you've been recommended by Captain Moss and Chief Warrant Officer Tela for the Cobra maintenance officer and test pilot position. Based on what I have heard about you and their favorable recommendations, I think you would make an excellent leader for our Cobra maintenance team. If you accept the position, you will attend the two-week AMOC—sorry, that's Army Maintenance Officer Course, in Phu Loi base camp, just north of Saigon."

The captain paused and stared at me; I don't think he blinked once. I felt cornered. I was apprehensive and conflicted, but I knew I was expected to say something, "Sir, perhaps you could tell me a little more about the job and your expectations?"

"Well, Morgan, once a helicopter has flown 100 hours, it has to undergo an inspection according to the manufacturer's guidelines and then be test flown by an authorized test pilot—which will be you—before it goes back into service."

I'd noticed that he had said, *which will be you.* The noose was tightening. I felt my forehead beading with sweat—*was it really all that hot in his office?*

"After the test flight, if you deem it airworthy, you sign the logbook, and the Cobra goes back into service. Your primary concern is meeting the Cobra mission requirement of having four flyable Cobras available daily. That's the bottom line."

There it was again, the presumption. It sounded like Captain Carothers wanted me to start right away. The degree of urgency was almost palpable. *But I had time to think about it, didn't I?*

Later that afternoon, I flew back to Quần Lợi with Lt. Devane. I was quiet; all I could think of was that before this all came up, I was satisfied with my army career path—it felt right. But now?

I hadn't been back to base for more than half an hour when I was summoned to the major's office. "Well, Mr. Miller, will you take the job?"

I stuttered and heard myself say, "Well, Sir, er, um, um, I'll go wherever you need me most." It wasn't that I didn't want the job, but I was conflicted and felt I'd lost control of my future. I suppose that's what the army does to you.

A week later, Captain MacDonald handed me my orders to attend the 1st Cavalry Division's army maintenance officers' course and flew me to Phu Loi base camp, where I met my four classmates.

As I had come to expect, I was to take a crash course (pun intended); the program, when delivered stateside, spanned thirteen weeks; here, the instructors had condensed it into what they cozily called a two-week familiarization course.

On day one, the lead instructor informed us that he would focus on the documentation and procedural skills required to maintain helicopter logbooks. A second instructor would teach us how to perform a detailed component inspection, such as the tail rotor pitch change link tolerances. I leaned over to the guy sitting next to me and said, "Try saying that three times fast." He smirked but said nothing; he didn't look like he'd been out of school long and was still afraid of getting detention.

The lead instructor explained that we were responsible for ensuring that the serial numbers for driveline parts if changed during an overhaul, were updated in both logbooks. One logbook was kept in the Cobra, and the other in the maintenance office. We also had to record the work's completion date and the total aircraft flying time. I was again anxious about the level of responsibility and the complexity involved in managing a maintenance department. The instructor paused and looked at the four of us.

"Okay, I know this sounds complex and convoluted, but safety is our No. 1 concern. In any case, you'll have a clerk to help you with all this. But, and I must emphasize this—it's your job to make sure it all gets done and done properly."

Toward the end of the first week, we had sessions with a Bell Helicopter factory representative and Lycoming Engine technical representative. Interestingly, they talked about the faults and flaws of the Cobra and its engine. I squirreled this information away for future reference.

The second week was a lot more interesting, but no less challenging. Two instructors taught us how to perform the maintenance test flight, including autorotation, and what to look for during the flight. I paid particular attention to this part of the course. I felt a heavy burden of responsibility for the young pilots who'd be trusting me to ensure their birds were flightworthy—that they weren't going to get them killed! I thought of Jim Elkin. I could still hear him, "Mayday! Mayday! Mayday! Stiff control! Landing immediately!" That memory is as strong today as it was over fifty years ago.

On our last day, we learned that our two primary instructors would still be available to answer questions once we were back at our bases. Even though it was a short course, the instructors packed a lot into it, and I left feeling more confident about my ability to take over Ed Soliday's job. With my Cobra test pilot orders in hand, I returned to Dĩ An in a Jeep and waited for transportation back to Quần Lợi.

Maybe I was a step closer to solving the mystery of the Cobra's lethal hydraulic issues. Only time would tell.

*Spur Cobra 097 wreck after engine –*
*transmission short shaft failure.*

CHAPTER 31

# HENRY HARRIS' STORY

On my return to Dĩ An, I reported to the A Troop orderly room. The clerk told me that Captain Kilcrease and the first sergeant were in a meeting at squadron headquarters next door and added that Quần Lợi had been under heavy mortar and rocket attack while I was away.

I asked whether there were any casualties. He shook his head.

"None reported so far, but one of the fuel storage tanks was destroyed. I'm not sure how long the XO will be, I can come and get you when he returns."

"Thanks, I'll be in my hooch."

An hour later, the clerk showed up and said that Captain Kilcrease had requested my company in the O-Club at 5:00 p.m. It was only 4:00 p.m., so I put on my rubber shower shoes and wandered to the showers. Hygiene was so important in this climate; the last thing I wanted was to get jungle rot in my privates or on my feet. In any case, I wanted to make myself presentable and be ready for whatever else my superiors threw at me.

I arrived at the club fifteen minutes early; the XO was already there. He immediately reiterated what the clerk had told me about the attack at Quần Lợi and added that A Troop had been without fuel for several days because Highway 13 was closed.

"Due to this, our squadron commander asked for help from the 1st Aviation Brigade, and three days later, after meeting with the air force, fuel and supplies were delivered using C-130s, and we were back in business—albeit rationed."

"Jeez, a lot has happened in the two weeks I've been away. But why is Highway 13 closed?"

Captain Kilcrease shook his head slowly.

"At the same time the NVA attacked Quần Lợi, an ARVN supply convoy from Phu Loi heading to Quần Lợi was attacked on Highway 13, halfway between Lai Khê and An Lộc."

I was stunned; we hadn't seen this level of enemy activity for some time.

"What happened?"

"The lead tank ran over a mine and was disabled. It blocked the road. The ARVN infantry riding in the trucks came under vicious attack, and most were killed. The officer in charge in the second tank put out a mayday call. The 1/9 Air Calvary at Lai Khê responded with a hunter/killer team supported by a command-and-control Huey."

Captain Kilcrease paused and took a swig of his coffee, grimacing because it had gone cold. He continued.

"The scout pilot quickly located the enemy and dropped a WP grenade. This allowed the Cobra to do what it does well, it fired every rocket it had at the enemy position with pinpoint accuracy. However, it was just a drop in the ocean, it took the 1/9 guys two days of heavy fighting to wipe out the VC forces that attacked the convoy. Retribution may have taken a few days, but it was total. Of course, all the food, ammo, rockets, and supplies were lost."

"If the highway is still closed, how are we getting fuel and supplies?"

"Air Force C-130s have been delivering all the supplies. I don't know about you, but I need a drink and some food. Are you hungry?"

"Yeah, I could go for a cheeseburger," which was pretty much my stock answer.

Over dinner, Captain Kilcrease filled me in on the rest of the comings and goings at the base and the move to Quần Lợi. Walking back to my hooch later, I thought about the logistical nightmare the XO had faced since I'd been gone. He had to keep Dĩ An operating with shortages of food, JP-4 fuel, rockets, ammo, and helicopter parts.

When I arrived at the orderly room the next afternoon to pick up my mail, it came as a huge surprise to see Henry Harris there. Boy, it was sure good to see him! He'd filled out a lot and no longer looked like you could knock him over with a feather. We shook hands.

"Henry! What are you doing back here?"

"This will sound crazy, sir. I know I could have, probably should have, gone home but as I told Captain Kilcrease, I want to get back to my friends in A Troop. I want to finish my tour."

His answer surprised me, especially for someone so young.

"Why the heck would you want to do that?"

"Three reasons, it feels good to be part of the aero-rifle platoon and rescue downed pilots and crew. It's very rewarding. Second, I want to even the score a little by getting an NVA soldier in my rifle sights. Third, I want to pass on what I've learned to the new guys."

I was surprised by Henry's words; he was a different person than the young man I spent all that time talking to on the flight over to Vietnam. All traces of naivety had disappeared; recent events had hardened him to the core. I was impressed that he wanted to do the honorable thing and complete his tour with his buddies.

"Henry, meet me in the mess hall for dinner tonight at 6:00 p.m."

The grin was still that of the young man I'd met on the plane.

"Sure thing, sir!"

I went back to my hooch and thought about Henry and all he'd survived. According to my sources, he hadn't spoken a lot about his ordeal. I didn't think that was healthy, so I planned to broach the subject over dinner.

After a few hours thinking about my new job, I made my way to the mess hall. Henry was standing at the door waiting for me. We both lined up and got the chicken fried steak and mixed veggies. I noticed Henry's plate was piled high. It had been three weeks since we got him home safely, and I could see that the novelty of having a good meal had not worn off. That big brother feeling swept over me again. *What was it about Henry that made me feel so protective?*

We ate in companionable silence, although satisfied grunts and sighs regularly came from the other side of the table. At last, I broke the ice.

"Henry, do you feel ready to tell me your story? Maybe start with what happened at the landing zone? I think it will do you good to talk about it."

I immediately regretted asking him the question and possibly pushing too much, too soon. In this job, you never knew what would set someone off and how long the effects would last. I'd seen soldiers maintain a stiff upper lip in the midst of horrifying terror and others crumble in more simple boot camp exercises. The demons were always there.

Henry barely looked up, pushing the last few morsels of food around his plate with his fork. His candor both relieved me and shocked me at the same time.

"To tell you the truth, sir, I don't have the first damned clue what happened after getting off the helicopter and taking up a fighting position. I was knocked out—I have no idea how. I remember waking up, and it was quiet, too quiet. The LZ was empty; I couldn't even hear the Huey's rotor blades. My head hurt, and I felt nauseous."

I nodded but said nothing. This was his story.

"I must have passed out or dozed off because the next thing I knew, there was a bunch of VCs pointing their AK-47s at me. They didn't look happy. I grabbed for my weapon and tried to stand up, but a rifle butt to my head ended that attempt. I fell back to the ground, and they kicked me in the ribs. As I curled up like a baby and tried to protect my head, they kicked me in the back. I was scared, Mr. Miller, real scared."

"That's okay, Henry; I would have been scared too."

"An officer showed up, and I could tell he was an officer because he barked at the men, and they stopped beating me. The soldiers stepped back in deference, and the officer helped me to my feet. He pointed at me and gave them what sounded like several orders before leaving. One of them pulled my arms to my sides and then back so the other one could put a straight bamboo pole through my elbow joints. The first soldier then tied my hands together in front of me with communication wire. I thought, *shit, this is going to be very uncomfortable*, and then things got worse. Two more guys approached me and ran a piece of wire around the pole, between my arms, and around my neck."

"One of the soldiers got right in my face; I could smell his breath. A sour smell; it almost made me retch. He shortened the wire between the pole and my neck. Then, one of the jerks pushed me hard. I fell onto my right shoulder; it took all the wind out of me. I looked up and saw the officer stride over; he looked angry. I panicked when he pulled his gun, but he put it in the soldier's face and spat out something in Vietnamese—I could see the saliva droplets on the jerk's face. He pointed to my canteen of water, which was on the ground close to me, and one of the men picked it up and attached it to my web belt."

"I'm so sorry, Henry. What happened next?"

"The men formed up ready to march; there were ten of them. They put me in the middle, and we started walking along a fairly wide jungle trail. The bugs were awful, they were biting, and getting into my ears, my nostrils, my eyes, and I couldn't brush them away. I remember thinking that *horses in the field back home on the farm must feel like this*. We hadn't gone more than fifty paces when the wire began cutting into my neck. I stopped, shouted, and tried to point with my fingers to my neck. The soldier next to me pulled out his knife, which scared the shit out of me. He looked at me with dead eyes. I saw no sympathy, but neither did I see hatred. He yanked on my shirt, pulled it out, and cut a piece of the tail, wrapping it around the wire. Seeing my dog tags, he ripped them off my neck and threw them to the ground."

I didn't say anything, just shook my head. There were tears in Henry's eyes. I reached across, laid my hand on his forearm, and when he looked up, I smiled and nodded my head.

"A few seconds later, we were on the move again. I had to walk hunched over because of the bamboo pole, but if I bent too far, the wire was unforgiving. It would easily have slit my throat. We walked all day. As the sun started to go down, they set up camp. One of the men sat me down with my back to a tree; right next to me was a rotting log crawling with red ants. I prayed they'd keep themselves on the log. My guard loosened my hands enough that I could point to my mouth. Then he called over to one of the others, and he gave me a bowl of rice and took my canteen off my web belt."

"Just rice, Henry? No meat?"

"Yes, sir, just the rice, but it sure tasted good. I was hungry by that time. I won't bore you with the details, Mr. Miller, but this routine went on for maybe two weeks. Eventually, we got to their base camp; it was situated on a wide river. They untied me, removed the pole, then shoved me into a raised bamboo hut—that sure felt good. I massaged my hands and wrist for a long time and then laid down and slept for God knows how long. When I woke up, the sun was low in the sky, it was late afternoon, and someone arrived with water to fill my canteen and gave me a bowl of rice. I was surprised to find scraps of meat in it, although it crossed my mind that it might be dog. I told myself it was pork and wolfed down the whole bowl using my fingers. I wasn't going to share so much as a grain of rice with my rat companions who were constantly scurrying around."

Henry's story was taking an emotional toll on me; my heart went out to this poor boy. I wasn't sure I could have survived the ordeal he went through. I excused myself and went to the latrine, more to splash water on my face than to use the facilities. Back in the mess hall, I picked up two fresh coffees and took them back to the table. Henry looked up and thanked me profusely as if I was doing him a great service. It brought home the humility of this young man.

"The soldiers hadn't emptied all my pockets, so I reached for the photo I carried of my mom, dad, and my girlfriend. I looked at that picture for a while, and I'm not ashamed to say that I cried for a while. I got out my handkerchief and hidden packs of iodine tablets I had in my thigh pockets, broke it in thirds and I carefully put one into my canteen. The officer who had made sure I was not too brutally treated visited me with another officer and a guard. They said nothing, just looked at me. The guard retied my hands in front of me, and they left."

Henry took a sip of his coffee and seemed to drift off, lost in his nightmare memories. I wondered whether he'd had access to any sanitary facilities while in the camp, but I didn't want to ask. He was a private guy. However, I assumed he just used the corner of the hut. I doubted he would want to talk about it to me. Maybe there were other dark things that he would never talk about—to me or anyone. I hoped that would never be the case. Looking back, so many men died from PTSD from the war we never should have been in. I drank my coffee in silence until he was ready to carry on with his story.

"Mr. Miller, this went on for weeks, I lost track of time. I got rice and water once a day, usually in the afternoon. Always with the same unidentifiable meat. I could see glimpses of the camp through the cracks in the bamboo enclosing the hut, and I got the impression that I was the only prisoner. The camp looked virtually deserted; I counted twelve NVA soldiers at most. Oh, and it had the loudest rooster I have ever heard!"

222 • MORGAN MILLER

Henry's mood lightened; it was good to see him laugh at the memory of the rooster.

"Sir, that damn rooster never waited until sunrise before sounding off. His conditions were better than mine, that's for sure; maybe even better than the guards because he had five or six hens to keep him company."

Henry smiled and shook his head at the thought of the rooster and his harem. Then, as quickly as it had brightened, his mood darkened again.

"After a couple of weeks, I realized I was alone, and the chances of being rescued were about as good as getting eggs from that damn rooster. I thought about trying to escape, but I didn't know where I was or where I would go, even if I was successful. I have to admit, Mr. Miller, I was ready to give up. Then, I thought about God and that he was with me and had a plan, even if I didn't know what it was. It was little things that kept me going, like singing my favorite songs and thinking about my family, especially my girlfriend, Molly. I needed to survive for them; I couldn't let them down. Many nights, when I was in the depths of despair, I recited the 23rd Psalm."

Henry closed his eyes and spoke softly.

"The Lord is my shepherd; I shall not want. He maketh me to lie down in green pastures: he leadeth me beside the still waters."

He went silent, then he opened his eyes, looked intently at me, and said, "I knew that if I died, I wouldn't be alone, but the isolation began to play with my head. The night before the rescue, I sobbed uncontrollably out of pure fear. My body shook convulsively; even the rats left for a while."

I interrupted, "We knew they were going to move camp, Henry; that's why we had to get you out of there. We'd never written you off; we were always going to come for you. It just took some time to find you."

"I know, Mr. Miller, but I surely felt lost and abandoned at the time. The Special Forces guys scared the life out of me. I didn't hear them break into the hut. The first thing I knew was a hand across my mouth and someone speaking English telling me to follow them. The relief was overwhelming, and I felt like breaking down in tears all over again, but I knew I had to hold it together. They half-dragged me to the cover of the jungle, about a hundred yards or so away, and then stopped to ask me whether I could manage a two-mile hike."

Henry's eyes were bright now. I laughed.

"What did you say?"

"I said, bring it on. Are you kidding? I feel I could run the two miles, just show me the way, man! Of course, it was a tough two miles, and I stumbled and fell a lot, but I always got up with the help of those guys. They live up to their title of 'special,' that's for sure. There was no way I was going back to that damned camp. Once I was in the helicopter, the sense of relief was overwhelming, and I thought of my family and girlfriend and wondered whether they even knew what had happened to me. Perhaps they thought I was dead. I don't remember much about the flight back to base; I must have dozed off. I sure was tired."

I told him that we had all been worried about him but that on the flight back, he'd been breathing normally and didn't seem in any medical distress.

"Once we landed, I was lifted down and put on a stretcher. I looked up and asked one of the guys where we were; when he said Quần Lợi, I cried with relief. I was safe. They took me to the infirmary; it felt so clean, it smelled so good. It was the first time in my life that I actually thought the hospital smell was pleasant! The hut that had been my home for months stank. It stank of me, of rotting vegetation, of rats, of my own urine and feces. It sure felt good to be somewhere sanitary. The medics checked my vitals and asked me whether I had any pain. I told them I was fine except I was really hungry and was told that it would be a while before I could eat normally again. Next the Major popped in. 'I need to take Henry to the debriefing.' Medical tech said, 'Yes sir. While you're gone, I will go to the mess hall and warm you a bowl of the chicken soup we had for diner.' That's when I came to the orderly room and saw my rescue team, including you, Mr. Miller. I don't think I've ever been as thankful in my entire life.

"The next day, I was flown to the big army hospital in Saigon. Shortly after I got into my bed, a doctor came in to check my vitals and my range of motion. He put pressure on all my organs, asking if I had any pain, and I told him I didn't. A nurse drew my blood and got a urine sample. A little later, the doctor came by and told me that I'd be OK and that he'd check in with me the following day. The next few days were like living in luxury. I got three meals a day, even if they *were* small; I took long, hot showers and slept in a soft, clean bed."

He went quiet again, and I wondered if he was reliving those few days of normalcy, which seemed like the ultimate luxury. Henry came out of his momentary daydream and continued.

"I had a visit from Army Intelligence, and I pretty much told them what I am telling you now. I slept a lot the first three days. Nurses checked my IV drip regularly and I heard one say my blood count was low and that they were adding vitamins or something to the cocktail."

"Did any of the top brass visit?" I asked.

"Yes, on the fifth day, I was amazed to get a visit from the 1st Aviation Brigade Commander. I thought he might want to quiz me about my ordeal, the prison camp, and the rest of it. I was surprised when he dragged up a chair and talked about his family and asked me what my life was like back home. He was interested in the farm and my parents and said he bet my girlfriend was missing me and that he was missing his wife. He stayed an hour, and I enjoyed his company it was tremendously comforting. Later, Captain Kilcrease and Lieutenant Kelly popped by to tell me they were making the necessary arrangements for my trip home. That's when I told them that I had no intention of going home until I'd finished my tour. In fact, I said, I couldn't wait to get one of those mother-effer's VCs in my rifle sights."

I was a little shocked that "my" young Henry was talking about wanting revenge, understandable as it was. I told him that I didn't think staying on was a wise decision.

"You aren't the only one that thinks it's crazy. The following day, I got a visit from the hospital psychologist. Man, he was boring. Question after question, and then he tried to talk me into going home. He said, in his opinion, I'd been through enough. I talked it over with him and told him point blank that I was not going home, and that it was important to me to pass on what I knew to new guys to improve their chances of returning home safely. And that, Mr. Miller, is my story."

I felt exhausted. I remembered the psychology course at Grossmont college and the professor telling the class that if you ever run into someone who has suffered extreme mental hardship, let them tell their story. It eases their burden by fifty percent by offloading half their burden onto a sympathetic listener. But this was more than offloading. It wasn't as if a friend was sharing a story about delayed flights on vacation. Because we were in a war together, every experience was shared physically, mentally, and emotionally. You didn't have to be in that bamboo cell with Henry eating rice and mystery meat every day to feel his anguish, fear, and hopelessness in your own body and mind. It was almost as if I shared in his PTSD too. I don't think Henry ever really knew he had PTSD, but his next statement pretty much convinced me of it.

"I'm tired; I think I'll head to bed."

"Hold up, Henry, don't go yet. Let's decompress together over a couple of beers. Wait there; I'll be right back."

When I got back to the table, he was resting his head in his hands. He looked up, and something had changed in his demeanor, he looked different, more relaxed, and he'd got a lot of emotion out with the telling of his story. I gave him his beer, and he said, "Thanks for listening, Mr. Miller; I really appreciate it."

We clinked bottles, and I said, "Everyone in this unit greatly respects you, young man. You have improved everyone's morale by insisting on returning to finish your tour. Your actions have shown everyone that this war is personal and that what you went through should have value. Your desire to help new guys learn your combat skills so that they will have a better chance of also going home is admirable."

He looked embarrassed.

"Henry, telling me your story in such detail is a cathartic process; I urge you to be open and share your story with others. The more you share it, the less power it will hold over you."

I could see him processing this, and after a few seconds, he said, "I think you are right, sir; getting it off my chest has helped."

"Could you do one more thing for me, Henry?" He nodded and drained his beer. "Go and write a letter to your girlfriend and your parents and tell them what you've been through and how you feel now that you've come out the other end of the ordeal. They deserve the truth, don't you agree?"

He pursed his lips, grinned a little, and said, "You're a good friend, Mr. Miller; I'll go and write that letter."

*Leroy Johnson and Ed Soliday preparing for test flight*

# CHAPTER 32

# WAY TO HANDLE THE CREW!

I t was mid-September when I reported to the maintenance hangar at Dĩ An. Although the weather was beginning to change, it was still hot, but the rain we'd had for the past two weeks eased off and the day was almost pleasant. Ed was returning from a test flight, so I waited for him to park and walked over to help him with the post-flight inspection.

"Thanks, Morgan; let's head to my office, and I'll give you an overview of your new Cobra maintenance team."

In his office, he handed me a notepad. On it was a list of all the crew members I would soon inherit with notes about each one. I asked him why the top six men's names were circled in red.

"Those guys are experienced, competent, and dedicated. You won't have to worry about the quality of their work; you can rely on them to do a good job."

"What about the rest, Ed?"

"Some are new and need to learn the job, some of the others—well, you'd probably be best without them altogether. None of those nine should be left to work alone; always pair them up with one of the top six mechanics."

I flipped the page, where Ed had listed the names of the Lycoming and Bell Helicopter Tech representatives I could call if I ran into any problems.

"Thanks, Ed, this is useful," I said as I turned to the next page and saw the name Sergeant Babcock boldly circled in black. I knew that Babcock was the top NCO in charge of all the mechanics and crew chiefs for the 575th.

"Why is the maintenance sergeant's name here?"

"Morgan, Babcock is full of himself and constantly causes roadblocks. He's a by-the-book pain in the ass who makes dumb decisions and causes us production delays."

"So, you're not his biggest fan," I said, smiling, "what does he say when you call him on the delays?"

"His stock answer is that he is just following army regulations. We've had heated arguments where I've told him to forget the damned regulations and that we have to respond to combat conditions here in Vietnam. He ignores me and carries on as normal. The men can't stand him. Anyway, he's your problem now, Morgan. Good luck."

I would have to wait and see how best to handle him. The last thing I needed was a spanner in the works. I smiled at my groaning metaphor. And, thinking of spanners, I asked Ed what the most common recurring maintenance problems were on Cobras.

"Good question; the tail rotor pitch change links for one, and the intervalometers cables that carry the electrical current that fires the rockets because our 605th tech supply is usually out of stock of both. Another big headache are the radios because of the frigging constant moisture—it never damned well stops raining."

We both turned towards the door as we saw Captain Carothers and his replacement Captain MacDonald heading our way. They invited us to lunch at the Red Horse bar. Ed agreed and told them we'd meet up there.

The cool breeze had ramped up to a steady wind, which made hearing each other during the Jeep ride up to the bar difficult. It did, however, give me a few minutes to reflect on the huge responsibility I was about to inherit and, of course, the risk involved in being a test pilot. On balance, though, I found myself relaxing. *I could do this.*

We got to the bar first and found seats at the back of the room. Ed had only just started describing his first meal when he got home when Captain Carothers and Captain MacDonald arrived. Captain Moss had joined them. We ordered our food and fell into comfortable conversation. Once the food arrived, I realized that the three captains had invited us to lunch as an impromptu going-away party for Ed. They each spent time thanking him for all his hard work in ensuring enough mission-ready Cobras were available. Captain Carothers said, "Especially with all three radios working!" while slapping Ed on the shoulder. The unexpected impact made him spill his drink. It was a jovial lunch, and although I felt a little like a third wheel, it was good to see firsthand the respect the job garnered from those on the front line.

As we rose to leave, they all wished Ed luck on his next assignment back in the States . . . whatever that might be. As we stepped out of the Red Horse Inn, the heat hit us, the wind died, and even the cool breeze disappeared. Rain was imminent. On the ride back to the maintenance hangar, Ed asked me if I had any more questions.

"No, not at this time. But I am sure that after you're gone, dozens will pop up."

And with that, I felt nervous again.

When I arrived at the 575th hangar the next morning, I learned that Ed and I were immediately getting down to business; I was to ride with Ed on my first Cobra test flight. I settled into the back seat, from where I would be doing my test flights in the future, and Ed gave me a running commentary from the front seat over the intercom. Ed hovered to the end of the runway and began the test flight with a hovering autorotation to ensure the transmission disengaged from the engine. Having one's helicopter's ability to remain airborne relying solely on aerodynamic forces rather than the engine is a scary proposition. I'd done it before in training, but it never got easy; it was super unnatural. Once we got that out of the way, he began climbing out of the Dĩ An traffic pattern to a higher altitude. His voice was tinny over the intercom.

"Morgan, the army designed these test flight maneuvers to test each helicopter's performance at the limits of its operating ranges. So that's what we are going to do now."

My palms were sweaty as we leveled off at 3,000 feet and Ed made banked 180-degree turns, first left and then right. "Okay, the bird feels good. Now we're going to do the VNE test." This tested the maximum airspeed of the aircraft. Ed lowered its nose, and increased power. We began a thirty-degree dive, and the dial in front of me rapidly rose to 190 knots. He slowly raised the nose forty degrees and left the power setting on high as we commenced a high-performance climb. I watched the control panel; the vertical speed indicator maxed out and stayed that way until we were back to 3,000 feet very quickly. Once there, Ed reduced the power and leveled off.

"Shit, Ed, I've never gone that fast in a Cobra, let alone climbed that high so fast. It was a wild ride, that's for sure!"

All I heard was Ed laughing. His last maneuver was an autorotation from 500 feet over the runway. This was a step up from the earlier autorotation, where we switched the power back on after ensuring the engine disengaged. This final test would see us recover from a simulated engine loss and skid to a stop on the ground with only the lift produced by the rotating rotor blades. All pilots perform these autorotations as part of their semi-annual proficiency check rides, but always with an instructor on board. Once Ed left, I would be required to do this maneuver as part of each test flight before returning the aircraft to flight status. Of course, if the freewheeling unit in the transmission didn't disengage, I could, hopefully, turn the power back on and land.

After the test flight, I had a new respect for Ed and a wagon-load of more fears to contain and control. *This was serious stuff.* Knowing that I'd need time to get up to speed, seven of our nine Cobras were mission-ready on the day he left. This gave me a little breathing room. The day after Ed left, I asked Mike Worthen, the mechanics' team leader, to call a team meeting. I assured my new team that none of Ed's procedures would be changed for the time being and that if, at a later date, I felt changes needed to be made, I would talk them over with the platoon sergeant before implementing them.

During my first month in charge, I worked closely with Mike and Ed's list of six reliable mechanics. I familiarized myself with the maintenance routine and the procedures for meeting the unit's goal of four flyable Cobras daily and gradually became more comfortable and confident with my job and team.

I knew that each aircraft commander had an attachment to his favorite aircraft. It was like when you hear about certain baseball players who carry good luck charms or practice certain habits before a game. There was never any proof that their superstitions worked, but in their heads, well, if they thought something was lucky, who could argue with them? So, one of my early goals was to get each pilot's aircraft back to him ASAP. To ensure this happened, when a Cobra came in for maintenance, I allowed my team to cannibalize parts from other Cobras, which were down for maintenance to speed up the process. All was going well, and my first month went smoothly, although I still had to deal with the deliberately combative Sergeant Babcock.

A week later, Captain MacDonald called a meeting in the hangar with every member of the 575th Maintenance Detachment in attendance.

"Men, in three days, we are moving the entire detachment to Quần Lợi. Later today, several 8' x 8' x 8' Conex containers will arrive outside our hangar. You must gather your equipment and begin packing everything into these containers."

The groans were audible, and as I looked around, there wasn't a pair of shoulders that wasn't slumped with the weight of the world on them. The job was manageable here, but moving to another base camp and setting up there was going to be tough.

"Men, I know this is a difficult decision to comprehend, but the squadron commander says that with A Troop moving permanently to Quần Lợi, the maintenance detachment should also be there. This is the army, and we follow orders."

Apparently, a rumor had been circulating for a few days, but it hadn't reached my ears. Talk about being thrown in the deep end; I'd been in charge for only a month and now had to move the whole shebang sixty miles north!

After the meeting, I walked with my team to the Cobra side of the hangar. I hadn't gone more than half a dozen steps when team leader Mike Worthen fell into step next to me. He looked agitated.

"Sir, you realize this maintenance move will slow the Cobra turnaround time. The logistics are shit. Currently, our parts supply is a twenty-minute truck ride away. When we are at Quần Lợi, we'll need to get them from the Phu Loi base camp—that's a thirty-minute chopper ride. Then once you land, you have to add in the time it takes to find a Jeep to pick up the parts and bring them back to the helicopter."

He was on a hot roll, so I didn't say anything. I just let him finish his rant.

"That's not the half of it; if any parts don't fit in the Jeep—like rotor blades, for example, we'll have to use the Tec Supplies truck to haul the blades out to the helicopter, then use the 605th forklift to load them into the helicopter, then return the truck and the forklift. All that takes a lot of time, sir. Plus, instead of having a big, enclosed hangar fifty yards from the runway like we have here, we will have to use the helicopter tent right alongside Quần Lợi's dust-plagued runway. Sir, this dusty, dirty environment is the last straw; we will never be able to maintain four mission-ready Cobras."

"Take a breath, Mike; I can assure you we will not fail at Quần Lợi—I won't let that happen."

"I appreciate your confidence, sir, but I am not looking forward to the move and the negative shit that will spew forth from our worthless maintenance sergeant. But I will work through it and give it my best."

Mike was twenty-two, and already a great leader and well-respected by his team. He was honest and straightforward, and I appreciated those traits. His outspoken rant may have bordered on insubordination, but everything he said was true—except the part about us failing. The one thing that concerned me was his hostile criticism of Sergeant Babcock. I would have to deal with that situation sooner, not later.

Mike split his team so he had one group packing and the other ensuring we finished repairing the three unflyable Cobras that remained in the Dĩ An hangar. As promised, flat-bed trucks began arriving at dawn the following day. They were loaded with containers almost as quickly as they arrived. When it came time for the convoy to depart, there were two M60 tanks; one led the way, and the other took a rearguard position. Overhead, one of our hunter/killer teams provided additional protection. It was an impressive operation, and I thought for a moment it would have been nice to be on the lead tank.

Once the convoy left the compound, I went to the maintenance hangar to see how the remaining two mechanics were doing with the Cobra and when the first one might be ready for its test flight.

Specialist Lamon said, "Later this afternoon, sir."

"Okay. Let me know when it's ready."

I was a little antsy; this would be my first solo test flight. To take my mind off it, I walked into the office and helped the clerk finish packing logbooks and technical manuals—a tedious job at best. But it worked. Time passed. When Specialist Lamon came into the office to let me know I could do the test flight, I was ready for any distractions. Lamon must have sensed my nervousness because he offered to help me with the pre-flight. At the flight line, I asked if he'd like to join me.

"Are you serious, Sir? Yes, I'd love to come along for the ride. I'll go grab a helmet."

When he returned, I was already in the rear seat. He climbed aboard and buckled up, and I started the bird and did a comm test.

"Can you hear me, Specialist Lamon?"

He raised his hand in acknowledgment, and I said, "I'm going to reposition the Cobra to the end of the runway to allow the fluids to warm up. Then, I'll do a hovering autorotation, land, and we'll do another maintenance check."

The first part of the test flight went without a hitch, and the recheck showed no issues, so we took off and performed the rest of the required maneuvers right over the runway.

Everything was good, except Specialist Lamon hadn't said a word since we took off after the recheck. At first, I thought it might be because it was his first ride in a Cobra or that he was merely allowing me to concentrate on my tasks. Once we landed and parked the helicopter, I asked him why he hadn't answered my radio calls.

"Sir, my intercom stopped working once we reboarded after the hovering rotation."

"Well, that explains the silence. Put your helmet back on, and we'll do a comms test."

The intercom wasn't working, something I would not have discovered if I had done the test flight solo. If I had returned the Cobra to flight status, the discovery would not have been made until the aircraft took off for a mission. My stomach lurched—that would have been embarrassing and, more to the point, potentially dangerous, if not deadly.

Lieutenant Devane's avionics tech quickly fixed the fault, and I returned the helicopter to active flight status with my first signature as a test pilot in the aircraft's logbook. At dinner later, I sat with Captain MacDonald. He asked about my first test flight and whether I foresaw any immediate challenges. I brought up what Ed had told me about the army's rules around having to return an unserviceable drive line part before being able to get a replacement. I told him this was unworkable in a combat situation. He could think of no immediate solution but promised to look into it.

As we left the mess hall, I said, "Sir, I have returned Cobra 171 to flight status and would like to fly it to Quần Lợi in the morning and check on how my team is doing and whether they are fully back up and running."

Early the following day, I flew to Quần Lợi. After landing and parking, I walked toward the helicopter maintenance tents, and Mike met me halfway.

"How's it going, Mike?"

"Surprisingly well, sir. We are almost ready to work on Cobra 097, which is down for its 100-hour inspection."

"That's great; I brought 171 to replace it."

In the Cobra area, I was pleased to see that Mike covered our three metal Conex containers with canvas tarps and arranged for another Conex to be placed between the repair tent and the runway to block some of the ever-present dust. I checked the containers; everything had been neatly organized and stored. By the end of the following week, everything was in place at Quần Lợi. A few weeks later, I asked Mike if he had any complaints.

"Do you mean other than the rocket attacks from the enemy?"

"Come now, you don't enjoy the occasional sprint to the bunker? Anyway, they have terrible aim, they rarely hit anything close by," I said laughing.

"Mr. Miller, to be honest, I'd like to lose four or five of our weaker team members. I don't need fifteen guys to work on two or three Cobras. They are getting in the way."

Ed had mentioned that Mike had been a construction foreman before enlisting in the army. He could recognize slackers instantly and knew they were a drag on the better workers and slowed down production. My experience working in organized labor before the army had been that it was impossible to maintain quality control with too many guys working on one project. I witnessed this problem firsthand while working with the mechanics back at Dĩ An.

I asked Mike to give me a list of the redundant mechanics and met with Sergeant Babcock the following day to request that six mechanics be reassigned. He asked me what the problem was, and I told him that they made too many mistakes and negatively affected the attitude of our good mechanics and overall production. His eyes popped wide open, "Well, Mr. Miller, it worked fine under Mr. Soliday!"

"That's not what I heard, Sergeant. And, in any case, I'm in charge now. We're a long way from our parts supplier and can't afford to have a new part cross-threaded just because a mechanic wasn't paying attention."

I looked the sergeant up and down. He was about 35 but old beyond his years; he was slack and lacked any discernible personality. I thought he could get lost in a room with two guys. I'd been watching him, and never once had I seen him supervising any of his men back in Dĩ An, but you could always find him in his office with his feet up, drinking coffee. In a combat zone, lazy people were dangerous. Mike told me Babcock had been in the army for fifteen years and was on his second tour in Vietnam.

We talked about the issue for a bit longer, and all I got from him was arrogance. He was defensive and stuck out his chin and chest like a strutting peacock. Ed was correct about the sergeant. It was time for him to get his wings clipped.

Later, after discussing the situation with Captain MacDonald over dinner, he suggested the sergeant might feel excluded. He told me to place all team instructions through him to see if that improved his attitude. He pointed out that this was standard army operating procedure, and it appeared the sergeant was a stickler for protocol.

The captain sat back, and I could tell he was contemplating what he had just said, "Having said that, I'll talk to Sergeant

Babcock tomorrow; it might be a good idea to find out firsthand what his problem is."

I thanked him; I could push that particular concern to the back of my mind, at least until tomorrow. I bumped into Captain MacDonald the following day and was surprised to learn that the sergeant's attitude toward the captain was so poor he relieved him of his position on the spot. He didn't tell me anything more, but I wished I'd been a fly on the sergeant's wall when it went down! My respect for the captain was already high, but it rose a few notches after his swift HR action.

"Morgan, I'm calling a meeting of the 575th Maintenance Detachment tomorrow at 10:00 a.m. at the troop common area, where I'll address the entire team. You notify Mike Worthen; I'll notify the Huey and Scout team leaders."

At the meeting, Captain MacDonald addressed test pilots, crew chiefs, and mechanics alike.

"Our mission here at Quần Lợi is vital; efficiency and accuracy are paramount—the lives of our colleagues are on the line every day. It has come to my attention that your platoon sergeant has not always been supportive, and in some cases, his attitude has been detrimental to the efficient running of this detachment. I have relieved him of his position, effective as of yesterday. He will be transferred immediately."

There was silence, and I could see people looking at each other in shock. This was Captain MacDonald showing that he would stand no insubordination from anyone, no matter who they were. He continued.

"From now on, I want every one of you to pay attention to what you are doing. Don't be afraid to ask questions. You are all on notice; do the job right the first time, or you will be transferred to the aero rifle platoon or the mess hall. Any questions?"

Silence.

"Okay then! Let's get back to work."

238 · MORGAN MILLER

Outwardly, my face was stern as I looked out at my team. Inside, however, I was pleased as punch. It was just what the team needed; stellar leadership and decisive action. As the meeting broke up, I could see positivity on the men's faces and in how they talked about what they just witnessed. I was feeling good, and it brought home the importance of solid leadership.

Back in my office, I reflected on my decision to take Specialist Lamon on my first test flight. I'd allowed him to look behind the scenes, and he now saw the importance of getting maintenance done correctly—he had skin in the game. I announced that I would take other Cobra mechanics with me on test flights, which caused quite a stir. Commitment levels went up noticeably, morale was better, and the men had newfound pride in their work because they were immersed in the process from beginning to end. They understood it as a real-life process, not just a practice run or diagrams on paper.

One afternoon as the sun went down, I saw three unflyable Cobras, one in our tent and the other two outside. This was par for the course. I looked at the paperwork: bullet holes, hydraulic leaks, inoperable radios, armaments that didn't work—the usual. One of the Cobra gunships only needed its 100-hour inspection, which meant it would be a quick turnaround back to flight status. Out of nine Cobras, we were constantly repairing damaged aircraft as quickly as possible to maintain our mission-ready commitment. Enemy interactions were becoming more frequent, so my team had to work long hours to keep up. Hopefully, this might be easier now that the platoon sergeant had been relieved of his duties. Cobra crew chiefs began taking their 100-hour maintenance orders directly to Mike Worthen instead of the sergeant. They could discuss the aircraft's problems—especially the recurring ones—and make targeted plans of actions to correct them.

This allowed Mike to supervise the work directly with the mechanics. It was a change to the command structure, approved by Captain MacDonald. It transformed the mechanics' and crew chiefs' attitudes—responsibility for maintaining all our helicopters was now firmly on the backs of the men doing the work.

Not everything was improving though; we struggled to keep four Cobras flyable daily due to difficulties in getting parts. I talked the situation over with Captain MacDonald, who suggested we fly the ash-and-trash helicopter the following day down to our direct support maintenance company, the 605th, and talk to Commander Captain Fight about the parts problem.

On the flight to Phú Lợi, I brought up Henry Harris. I told Captain MacDonald that I didn't think Henry should be returning to the aero rifle platoon and wondered if he might have a position for the young soldier. He told me that Captain Cook had already taken care of the issue, and that Henry would work for him in the Tactical Operation Center.

Over the intercom, I said, "Wow, that's a great idea! It looks to me like everyone from General Putnam on down doesn't want Harris back in the area of operation. How did Captain Cook get that past the Major?"

I couldn't see Captain MacDonald's eyebrows move, but I'm sure they did because the silence was deafening. After landing at Phú Lợi, we went to the 605th Maintenance Depot to meet with Captain Fight as arranged. He explained that turning in a defective part in exchange for a new part was the army's way of keeping track of inventory. However, since his depot was the last stop before unrepairable helicopters were sent back to Corpus Christi, Texas, for a complete overhaul, he might have a way around the problem. He smiled; if we'd been in a movie, I am sure he would have looked over each shoulder to see if anyone could overhear our conversation.

"I'm not telling you this, but if you were to bring a couple of your guys here after dark to remove parts from helicopters in the boneyard, I think you might find that my guys might have accidentally forgotten to lock the gate."

Captain MacDonald's eyebrows rose up.

"Really?"

We followed Captain Fight outside and took a tour of the boneyard; many of the aircraft were beyond repair, and a few had parts missing. It was a sad sight. Captain MacDonald said, "I think we should sleep on it before making a decision."

Captain Fight nodded and added, "At the moment, there are slim pickings, but we sometimes get a helicopter that has only suffered a hard landing. If, in conversation, I was to let you know when that situation occurred, well then ..."

I looked at Captain MacDonald.

"This would save two or more days of maintenance delays. It could save lives."

Without moving an eyebrow, he almost imperceptibly nodded, and a conspiratorial smile began forming at the corners of his mouth.

*Assorted Spur aircraft in the Army's 1st Aviation Brigade "boneyard" for III Corps based helicopters.*

CHAPTER 33

# TRANSITIONAL MONTH FOR A TROOP

September 17th started out as a pretty ordinary day at Quần Lợi Airfield. The humidity was high, but the temperature was reasonably pleasant. Dave Toms was standing at the nose of his Cobra; he and his team were getting ready for their mission. Earlier in the day, one of our hunter/killer teams left on a mission to support an ARVN unit northeast of An Lộc. Cobra pilot Ed Marzola flew in the front seat that day. He was training and evaluating Chief Warrant Officer Bonello for his pending Aircraft Commander check ride.

The peace was suddenly broken when someone came running out of the communications bunker, yelling, "Marzola has been shot down!"

Dave had been smiling and joking, but now his face hardened as he climbed into the back seat of his Cobra, yelling to Tom Barnett to mount up. Once airborne, Dave and Tom headed northeast toward the Cambodian border. Although Barnett, who had come to us from the UH-1 platoon, was a pilot, he hadn't been through Cobra transition school, a fact that would prove to have an effect on the outcome of the day.

Joe Jackson followed suit in his Cobra, forming on Dave's wing. Both Cobras were airborne in under two minutes. The two gunships flew hard and fast, gaining altitude slowly to accelerate their arrival on station.

We learned from the major, who was in his command and control Huey, that Ed had been able to get airborne and exit the area; he and Dave Bonello were safe. Unfortunately, Dave Tom's Cobra had been shot down, and they were severely injured.

A couple of days later, I flew to Long Binh in a Huey with Mike Billow, Ed Marzola, and Al Fleenor to visit Dave in the hospital. When we walked into his room, my heart sank, he was in traction, covered with bandages, and IVs were sticking out of both arms—he looked darn miserable. As soon as he saw us, though, he perked up.

"Hey guys, thanks for coming; I was beginning to think you'd forgotten me!"

"Never," I said. "We brought the Huey so we could roll you right out of here when nobody's looking. We're short-staffed, and you can oversee the tactical operation center while Mike Cook's on R&R."

"Right, Morgan, I'm going nowhere fast. The doc told me I have multiple compound fractures in my spine and a shit load of other problems."

The ever-present disinfectant hospital smell, the constant beeping of the machines monitoring his vitals, and the nurses pushing past us to tend to their patient underlined Dave's statement. We grabbed chairs and gathered around Dave's bed.

"Well," I began, "I've got the key players in this mission in one place; I'd like to hear how it played out."

Dave raised his hand; his face was drawn and ashen.

"I don't think I'll be able to talk for too long, but I'll start."

Al said, "Take your time, Dave; I can fill in some details when you've had enough."

He took a deep breath, his eyes squeezed tight for a few seconds, and then he began.

"As we approached the contact point, we saw Ed's Cobra on the ground; it was in a clearing, and the rotors were still turning. He was coming to a hover, and I thought he was attempting to get out of there. I could see the enemy's location and initiated a rocket run to give him cover. After blasting the enemy, I pulled out of the run. I looked for Joe, anticipating he would follow me with his rocket run, and I was preparing to give him cover. However, I saw that his Cobra was leaving the target area. At that point, I wasn't sure whether Ed had cleared the area. I radioed Joe and told him I was heading inbound for another rocket run to assist Ed."

"Sorry to interrupt Dave, but I still don't understand what happened to you, Ed," I asked. "Were you shot down or not?"

"Well, sort of," Ed said, "after feeling the dull thud below my seat and seeing smoke coming through the floor. I knew it was a life-threatening situation. I quickly took the controls back from Bonello and notified our Scout helicopter that we were making an emergency landing to investigate the damage."

"What did you find?"

"Well, as I said, smoke was coming from the ammo bay. After landing and getting out, I opened the ammo bay door and saw smoke coming from the grenade canister. The last thing I needed was for those 250 rounds to explode, so I quickly stood on the ammo bay door and yelled to Bonello to hand me the fire extinguisher from behind his seat. I emptied the extinguisher onto the grenade launcher and used my survival knife to pry out the ruptured grenade and then lobbed it into the trees. Bonello was still in the back seat, and I signaled him to change seats so I could resume control in the backseat as AC. Once we were airborne, I reported our situation to the major, and he ordered us to return to Quần Lợi."

I shook my head.

"That must have been scary. So, Dave, you had no idea Ed had exited the area and was out of danger? Or that Joe had been ordered to head back to base?"

"No, I didn't. I engaged the target on the second rocket run and began taking fire from the side. I could feel the impacts thudding my aircraft, causing my stability control augmentation system to pitch our nose down. I was looking forward and straight at the ground. Not good. My first thought was, *I'm going to die*; my second was *keep this chopper flying*. My training kicked in, and I pulled back on the cyclic, which leveled the aircraft so I could figure out somewhere to put the aircraft down safely."

Ed asked, "So, at that point, did you have any idea what damage the incoming rounds had done?"

"I was convinced that the initial rounds had destroyed the SCAS electronic control unit and were hitting the fuel cell area, so I headed to the landing site I'd selected. Incoming rounds slammed into us relentlessly, and I could see smoke coming from the air vents. It was an acrid smell, bitter, and I could already feel a burning sensation in my throat."

Mike said, "Amazing! How the heck did you get the chopper down?"

"With great difficulty. Smoke was filling the cockpit. Visibility was dropping; I knew making a safe landing would be tough, not to mention by that time, we were having difficulty breathing. In front of me, I was shocked to see Tom trying to open his canopy door instead of jettisoning it—a rookie mistake. To make things worse, he hadn't secured his turret gun sight, so it was floating around the cockpit. The poor guy was so scared and confused, he became frozen."

Somebody said, "Shit!"

Dave rested for a minute. His face was taut, and he was breathing heavier. We waited for him to continue.

"I screamed at him more than once to leave the canopy alone and stow the sight; we were going in for a hard landing. Keeping the aircraft level was impossible; I had no clear reference points. I prayed that we wouldn't hit the ground on our side or, worse inverted. I moved the cyclic counterclockwise to its maximum extent in the hope that it would stabilize us all the way to the ground. I learned later that although we hit the ground hard, we were in a level position. The last thing I remember was being enveloped in total grayness before everything went black."

Dave's head dropped back, and he closed his eyes. I watched his right-hand curl into a fist.

Ed looked over at Al and asked, "What were you and the Major doing in the command and control Huey all this time, Fleenor?"

"We could clearly see that Dave was taking fire. Tracer rounds from the 51-cal were hitting the side of his aircraft. The Cobra's large side-silhouette offered itself up to the enemy; it was a sitting duck. It was gut-wrenching to watch those tracer rounds pound into the Cobra. The major was losing it; he was pounding the dash with his fist and yelling at Dave, even though he knew he couldn't hear him, 'Toms, maintain control! Keep that machine flying!' It was almost as if Dave could hear the major because it looked for a second as if he was regaining some control and heading for the clearing. We could see smoke, so we knew Dave would struggle to get a visual. We watched helplessly as the Cobra hit the ground and started burning. Then, we watched Chodara's scout helicopter land next to Dave's burning aircraft and watched Sergeant Purcell pulling Tom and Dave out of the wreckage."

Dave opened his eyes but didn't focus on us—he was back there. The three of us paused, looking at each other, then Mike said softly, "What happened next, Dave?"

"I have no idea; as Al said, Louis Chodara managed to land his aircraft near us, and he and Sergeant Purcell pulled Tom and me out of the burning wreckage."

Ed turned to Mike.

"Hey, Mike, you've been sitting there pretty quietly. How were you able to help?"

"Things happened a little differently for us. Patterson was my front seat that day. As soon as we got our assignment, we cranked up the Cobra and took off with our scout. I immediately began hearing reports about Toms and Barnett, and how they were in enemy contact involving a 51-caliber machine gun. Shortly after, I heard over the radio that a heavy-fire team of two Cobras from the 1st of the 9th Air Cav had been dispatched to the area in response to Toms and Barnett being shot down. I radioed Operations that I was heading to help and sent my scout back to Quần Lợi. As I approached the area from the West, I could see the two Air Cav Cobras circling at altitude. There was a lot of yelling from their radios concerning what to do about the enemy's 51-cal. There was some discussion about whether the gun was being remotely controlled. It was suspicious that the area around it had received a ton of rockets, but the gun was still firing. Knowing my bird was equipped with the 20-millimeter Gatling gun, and that from my location at a distance, I was in a better position to assess the situation, I took over the mission and calmed everyone down. I told them to follow me in a daisy chain attack order, which made us a fire team of three and allowed us to unload 20-mil bullets and heavy rocket fire on the enemy gun position. This maneuver cleared the way for our slicks to land quickly, set up a perimeter, and pick up Toms and Barnett."

Dave stirred, and as one, we turned toward him.

"My memory is a little hazy, but I remember a couple of infantrymen grabbing me by the arms and dragging me towards a waiting helicopter. It's funny what you remember. Although I kept drifting in and out of consciousness, I recall being dragged and upset that my pistol had caught on a bush. I must have passed out; the next thing I remember was lying on a helicopter's hard, cold floor. My back hurt a lot, and I drifted in and out of consciousness. I remember the pain, the joy of hearing the *whop, whop, whop* of the rotor blades, the comfort of someone laying their hands on me and telling me I was going to be okay, and then darkness. Then I arrived here, broken and ready to be fixed."

Al said, "This is a good hospital, Dave, from what I've heard. You're in good hands."

"Yes, they've looked after me well, but I'll be leaving for the States next week; the doctors here have done all they can, but apparently, I need more specialized care."

To lighten the mood, Ed changed the subject, "Have you had any other visitors?"

"Yeah! One of our rescuers, Sergeant Purcell, popped in yesterday. He was here having some of his bandages changed. You should have seen the big scabs from burn blisters on his face. He got them from a couple of our rockets, which fired inadvertently because of the intense heat, while pulling me out of the back seat. I think he will be left with some pretty good scars. He's also mentioned some hearing loss. I thanked him for what he and Louis Chodara did for Tom and me and told him how courageous I thought they were, and how deeply I am indebted to them. They are heroes in my eyes."

"Tell us about Tom, Dave," Mike said.

Dave looked down at his hands and said, "He wasn't as lucky as me."

He took a deep breath and continued.

"Tom was also brought here after the crash, but he died a day later from renal failure. His spinal cord was severed in the crash, paralyzing him from the neck down."

I said, "I'm sorry, Dave. I know that's been eating on you. But you must think of yourself now and work hard on your recovery. What is your prognosis?"

"Well, besides the compression fractures in my spine, I have first, second, and third-degree burns on all the exposed areas of my body, a fractured sternum, and a fractured wrist. I will need some major surgery followed by extensive physical therapy. However, by the grace of God, I'm alive and on the road to recovery, even if it's going to be a bloody long road."

We all fell silent, and then Dave cleared his throat and quietly summed things up.

"You know, I don't think there will ever come a day when this incident doesn't come to mind. I will forever be grateful for the heroism of Purcell and Chodara. Similar stories have played out across Vietnam; my heart goes out to all the brave men we have lost during this insane war. I will be eternally grateful to God for watching over us all that day."

"Amen," Ed Marzola said.

Within seconds, Dave was asleep. We left quietly. There, but for the grace of God . . .

*Lou Chodara, John Kelly, and Mike Billow*

# CHAPTER 34

# PICK-A-PART RAID
# IN THE BONEYARD

Losing our third Cobra pilot, Tom Barnett, weighed heavily on my mind for the next few weeks. The pointless loss of a promising young man was something I had to process and, almost guiltily, push aside so I could focus on my work. Keeping Cobras in tip-top shape would help save more lives, and I took my responsibility seriously.

It was the beginning of October, and there'd been a Cobra parked next to the control tower ever since I took over from Ed. I hadn't given it much thought; I was too busy. But on this bright, sunny day, I asked Mike about it. "We call that POS636." I looked inquiringly, and he said, "Piece of Shit."

"Ah, yes, sorry, I'm slow today. I remember this bird from when I was in the weapons platoon; it wasn't one of my favorite aircraft back then. But why aren't we repairing it and getting it back into service?"

Mike shook his head, "It's more than we can tackle at the moment; its engine is so weak no one wants to fly it, and the fuel gauge is as unreliable as a clock with no minute hand. We don't have the parts, and it's too big a job to do here."

I walked around the POS and said, "Mike, I want to resurrect this old gal when we have some spare time. It's a waste just sitting here when we need as many Cobras as possible."

Mike smiled and said, "No time like the present; we never really have spare time, do we? Let's take a look at it right now."

The first thing we discovered was the battery was dead, so I asked Mike to go and get an auxiliary power unit while I inspected 636. After a few minutes, I could see the fluids were all okay, and after checking its logbook, I saw it was manufactured in 1967 and had 3,800 hours of flight time. In terms of Vietnam and our A Troop, it was the oldest Cobra we had. I first thought the engine was kaput, worn out, and not worth repairing—it would need a whole new engine. Mike came back with the power unit, and we started her up. At flight idle, all the instruments were in the green, so I took her to full power for ten minutes, then shut the old girl down.

I turned to Mike, "I think we should take her up tomorrow and see how she flies."

"Okay, Morgan, I'll give her another complete pre-flight to ensure she's fit to fly. Sir, why don't you get a hold of Joe Jackson the AC? He is abandoning the aircraft because of the gas gauge and the weak engine."

Later that evening at the Officer's Club, I sat down with Joe and asked him what the problems were with Cobra 636. "I assume you know about the faulty fuel gauge, but the big problem was it lacked power. The engine would only pull about 89 percent on the N-1 gauge, with a full load of rockets, miniguns, and 40mm grenade ammo, making it unsafe to operate in the area of operation."

This was helpful information; the Cobra should be pulling 92–94 percent. I told Joe we would see if we could fix the problems and get her back in service. He laughed and said, "Good luck with that." It's difficult for pilots to renew their faith in an aircraft that has attained the status of a POS.

The next day, engine techs Decker and Henry reported that the turbine engine had built up a lot of gunk and needed flushing out. They would use a concoction of Tide detergent and walnut shells mixed with water and powdered milk. They were wrong if they thought they would surprise me with this cocktail of strange ingredients. The Lycoming tech rep had told us about this fascinating method at test-pilot school.

Once my team did all they could with the Cobra, I took it for a test flight. As I lowered the nose for takeoff, the gas gauge showed half-full. Even though I knew we'd filled the gas tank, my immediate thought was, *we did check the gas, didn't we?* I shook this unnerving feeling off but empathized with previous pilots who would have been forced to continually check their watches to ensure they were aware of the two-hour flying window before needing to refuel.

After one pass around the traffic pattern, I did a maximum performance climb to check the torque and N-1 gauges. Joe was correct, it was a struggle to get the torque to forty-five pounds, and the N-1 would only reach eighty-nine percent. I concluded that the engine in 636 was too weak to be used in combat. Back on the ground, I went to see Captain MacDonald and told him that, in my opinion and that of the engine techs, the engine needed replacing, along with the fuel gauge.

"Well, Morgan, we can't do that here, so I suggest you fly 636 to our direct support maintenance company and get them to do the work." The following day, for safety, I followed Lieutenant Devane in the ash-and-trash Huey to Phú Lợi. I arrived safely, but the flight confirmed that 636 was indeed a piece of garbage. LT. Devane carried on to Dĩ An and agreed to pick me up on the return leg.

I briefed Captain Fight, filled out a work order, and he said the work would take two weeks and he'd keep me posted on their progress. I had time to kill while waiting for Lieutenant Devane to return from Dĩ An, so I joined Captain Fight for lunch.

A week later, he called and told me they had some problems with 636 and asked if I could hitch a ride on the ash-and-trash helicopter and meet with him? Back in Phú Lợi, the next day he showed me the new Lycoming TH-53-B engine and fuel cell, which was ready to be installed. We discussed the mechanical issues his team had discovered. He explained that as the helicopter had to be put in an airframe jig for support to replace the fuel cell, did I want to replace the center of the cockpit Plexiglass?

"One other thing, Morgan, if you can leave it here for another two weeks, we can repaint the bird and give old 636 a whole new look!"

I was excited, "Wow! Yes, it's going to be like a whole new aircraft. Let's do it!"

I had four hours to kill before my ride arrived, so I asked the captain if I could borrow his Jeep to visit the PX and pick up some personal items.

Two weeks later, I returned to Phú Lợi to pick up a nearly-new 636. It was parked outside the hangar sporting its beautiful new paint job. I went into Captain Fight's office, signed the work order, and thanked him. "Morgan, the Lycoming tech is here. Would you like to speak to him?"

The tech was a tall, friendly guy. We shook hands, and he said, "So you're the first guy that gets to fly the freshly painted Cobra with the new engine? Lucky you."

I asked him whether the rumor that the new Lycoming engine had more power was true, and he confirmed the gossip. "It has more torque because of the new titanium combustion chamber." We talked for a few minutes about technical stuff before I walked outside.

Captain Fight asked me to walk with him to the boneyard. There stood a crashed, but complete, Cobra. He said, "We may forget to lock the gate tonight, Morgan." What a great opportunity, I knew I had to return after dark with a few guys and strip the valuable driveline parts before someone else got wind of this bounty.

I was happy about flying 636 back to Quần Lợi and seeing how well it performed, but even more excited about getting my hands on all those precious driveline parts. On the flight home,

I studied the torque meter, N-1, and airspeed indicator. Cruising at 140 knots, I had forty-five pounds of torque and eighty-eight percent on the N-1. Even though the Cobra wasn't carrying ammo, I could quickly tell the new 636 had lots of power in reserve. Halfway to Quần Lợi, my mind returned to the opportunity of getting back to the 605th after dark to strip the crashed Cobra before it got shipped back to Texas. Back at Quần Lợi, I made a high-speed pass right down the middle of the runway, letting my team know that 636 was back. After parking in her revetment, I saw Mike Worthen coming down to help me secure her.

Mike reported that his team was all caught up, and Cobra 439, our newest aircraft, was ready for me to test fly. I told him that he could release the rest of his team but that I wanted him to go on the test flight with me. We did the maintenance operations control on the Cobra and took off. The sun was setting, so I did the autorotation before putting her through the rest of the test flight procedures. On the way back to Quần Lợi, I told Mike the only thing required was to adjust the trim tabs on the main rotor blades because they were a little off track. After landing, we adjusted the trim tab, and I signed the aircraft off—another Cobra ready for flight.

Without explanation, I told Mike that after dinner, I needed him to gather his four best men with their tools, and lighting equipment and meet me at Huey 368 at 9:00 p.m. He looked curious but said nothing. Later, we all met at the Huey and headed for Phú Lợi. A little over an hour later, we were at the boneyard gate, which was, as promised, unlocked. Under cover of night, I instructed the guys to remove all the Cobra driveline parts: engine, transmission, main rotor hub, blades, tail rotor drive shaft, and tail rotor assembly. While they were busy wrenching, I went to the bar to get them some beers. Captain Fight was tending the bar. I quietly thanked him for his help and ordered the beers to go.

When I was last at Phú Lợi, the captain had offered me a Conex to put the parts in, so we didn't have to try to fit them in the

Huey. I returned to Mike Worthen with the beers and pointed out the Conex container where we could store the parts. He said the team would be done in about three hours and would need a way to move everything to the Conex container. I returned to Captain Fight, got the key to the hangar, and went back to the boneyard with a forklift. As parts were removed, I hauled them to the container. By one in the morning, we were heading back to Quần Lợi.

I headed straight for bed; in the morning, I had big plans for my team, getting 636 mission-ready. Over breakfast, I told Mike that I'd changed my mind. I wanted 636 to have a heavy-hog configuration—four 19-shot rocket pods instead of the standard two 19-shot inboard and two seven-shot outboard. I asked him to tell Ed—aka Tank—Carson to check the sighting of the rocket pods before rearming.

In my opinion, the best configuration for a Cobra on Hunter/ Killer work was the 52-rocket pod set up with the minigun and 40-millimeter grenade launcher. However, with its new-found power, 636 was ideal as a heavy hog and gave us three different armament configurations to effectively respond to the enemy. We also had three Cobras with the XM-35 system, a 20-millimeter Gatling gun that fired 750 rounds per minute and would put a hole in a half-inch-thick piece of steel.

If one of our hunter/killer teams found the enemy, we could send out Cobras 155, 202, or 097 with their 20-millimeters, or 636 with its seventeen-pound rocket pods, any of which should eliminate the enemy. If the enemy threw more at us than any of these configurations could handle, we always had the Air Force for backup.

I kept Cobra 636 in reserve because even though it was like a new aircraft, no one trusted her, even though she was my new secret weapon. No one knew what the future held for that gunship!

Over the next few weeks, we made regular trips back to the "secret" container in Phú Lợi, exchanging old parts for the ones we'd liberated from the crashed Cobra. This on-hand supply of driveline parts significantly reduced the time it took to get Cobras back to mission-ready status.

*David Bonello*

*Me, Claude Devane, and Harry MacDonald*

*Decker A. Decker*

CHAPTER 35

# THAT DARN STICKY WICKET!

I was doing a maintenance operational check (MOC) on a helicopter when the siren broke the peace of a November afternoon. Someone was down. Seconds later, Specialist-4 Busto, one of my mechanics, came running toward me shouting, "Mr. Miller, Captain MacDonald needs you to join him in OH-58 down the flight line."

Grabbing my helmet, I got out of the Cobra and headed for OH-58; I could see the rotor blades beginning to turn. Once in the air, he told me that AC Craig Johnson had made an emergency landing, west of Lộc Ninh, in Cobra 097, due to a stiff cyclic control. A sense of *déjà vu* swept over me, and my mind went straight to Jim Elkin, "Is he okay? Did he get the bird down without crashing?"

"Yes, Henry, he's fine, and the Cobra sustained no damage, but we need to extract him and figure out what's wrong with the Cobra. Any thoughts?"

I noted that the captain had used my given name rather than my middle name, which is what I was always known by. I wondered whether the informality was a show of camaraderie, reflecting that this would be my first decision in the field, away from the security of Quần Lợi.

257

"Hard to tell, Sir," I answered, "without checking the servo compartment."

As we got closer, I could see Captain Cook's command and control Huey, followed by the three lift Hueys, which had already dropped off our aero rifle platoon circling the area.

As we were about to land, I could see Craig and his co-pilot standing with Lieutenant Kelly, our infantry platoon leader next to the Cobra. The rest of the platoon were spread around the clearing providing protection, although, thankfully, there was no sign of the enemy.

We landed and I jumped out and walked over to the Cobra. "So, what happened, Craig?"

"The cyclic control suddenly began to stiffen up, it was crazy; I knew I had to land while I still had some control."

"Smart move, Craig. This is what I suspect happened to Jim Elkin, so getting the aircraft to ground quickly and safely was the right thing to do."

The first thing I did was inspect the hydraulic fluid reservoir; it was empty. I called Captain MacDonald over as I opened the inspection panel below the transmission and discovered that the roll servo was leaking. I suggested to him that we get Captain Cook to radio our TOC and have a chopper bring Mike Worthen out with a gallon of hydraulic fluid.

"So, what's the plan Henry?"

There was that "Henry" again, and he put his hand on my shoulder.

"Well, sir, it's too late in the day to get a heavy-lift helicopter out from Phú Lợi. And we definitely don't want to destroy 097 to prevent her from getting into enemy hands, she's got more than a few good years left in her. Of course, we could leave the aero rifle platoon here to guard it overnight, but that's risky."

With frustration, Captain MacDonald said, "But what DO you suggest we do?"

"I'm thinking we refill the hydraulic reservoir, start her up, check the leak, and see if I can coax her back to Quần Lợi."

"Hold on Henry, that seems like a cockamamie plan if ever I heard one. Explain your reasoning."

"Well, sir, ever since Jim crashed Cobra 581, which had a cyclic and collective control problem, I've discussed the issue with Dave Tela and Ed Soliday on several occasions. The dual hydraulic lines in the Cobra run to the same servo from one hydraulic reservoir. The pistons in that servo are side by side and are in constant motion because of the stability control augmentation system . . . the autopilot. We came up with the theory that if, over time, one of the cylinder seals in the servo wears thin from the friction and bleeds fluid between the two cylinders it causes a fluid leak resulting in a loss of pressure."

I looked at him and he narrowed his eyes and said, "Okay, continue."

"Once hydraulic fluid gets here, and we've filled the reservoir, I should have enough airtime to get at least to Lộc Ninh, south of the border."

Captain MacDonald didn't look convinced, but after looking at his watch he said, "Okay, Henry, I'll tell Captain Cook what we're doing."

Thirty minutes later Mike arrived and refilled the hydraulic reservoir. Craig and his co-pilot got a ride in the Huey back to Quần Lợi. I started 097 and asked Mike to check the roll servo. The captain, standing on the ammo bay door, called to me, "Henry, it's still leaking." He sounded worried.

"Tell Mike to secure the inspection compartment and give me a thumbs-up when I'm clear to take off."

Once I got the all-clear, I checked the engine readings—they were all in the green. I felt my stomach tighten and the butterflies told me I had pre-performance anxiety. *What the heck was I doing?*"

I took off and immediately made a 180-degree turn and headed for Lộc Ninh, flying low. The flight controls were normal for a few moments, but then the cyclic stiffened. "Now to put my true theory to the test," I shouted *Don't fail me now, damnit*! The captain and Mike followed me in his OH-58. I imagined they thought I was crazy and that they'd be scraping bits of me off the Vietnam forest floor.

My anxiety levels were now off the Richter scale. I shifted the hydraulic switch from system one to system two. *Yes! The controls were normal again. Phew*! Relief flooded through my body, and I picked up my airspeed to shorten the flight time. Every time the controls began to stiffen, I switched from system one to system two. This tactic allowed me to land on a road south of the town of Lộc Ninh. Mac, h*eck if he was calling me Henry, I could call him Mac—maybe—*landed behind me and a couple of ARVN soldiers came over and offered their help. He and Mike jumped out of the OH-58 and came over. Mike opened the hydraulic reservoir inspection panel, checked it, and refilled it with hydraulic fluid.

Mac said, "Let's leave it here now with Lieutenant Kelly and his men, it'll be safe here."

I shook my head, "Let me fly it back to Quần Lợi, it's only a ten-minute flight. The hydraulic reservoir is full, and I know how to handle the problem now."

I wasn't sure whether Mac, who was now calling me Henry, was going to let me, but the eyebrow went up, so I took it as permission. Once again, after a few minutes the controls stiffened, and so did I, but the switching trick worked and I arrived at Quần Lợi. Not wanting to push my luck, I opted for a running landing instead of bringing the Cobra to a hover. Skidding on the ground to a stop, I realized I had been gripping the controls a whole lot tighter than was necessary. I sat in the cockpit for a while, trying to figure out if what I'd just done was insane, or just part of my job.

By the time Lieutenant Kelly and the Cobra platoon leader, Captain Hickman, landed and came over, I was cool, calm, and collected—at least on the surface. They both shook my hand and congratulated me on a job well done.

Later, over at the bunker I said, "Here's what I did flying 097 home. The roll servo was leaking, so system one gradually lost pressure and the collective stiffened. As soon as I felt that, I switched to system two, which brought the pressure back up and freed up the controls. Switching back and forth bought me some time, until, of course, the bird eventually ran out of hydraulic fluid, probably a few seconds after I landed." I said with a laugh.

A few more pilots had gathered around and congratulated me. I added, "It's too bad that we destroyed 581 back in June before the reason for the crash was evaluated." It was a good evening at the officers' club. I felt a sense of achievement, and silently thanked Dave and Ed for helping me solve the problem of landing a Cobra with stiff controls, instead of crashing it nose first into the ground.

Later, I suggested to Captain Hickman that perhaps the ACs should carry out a post-flight check of the hydraulic servos compartment after each mission, and especially after their last flight of the day. However, he didn't consider this necessary.

After we removed the servo the next day, Mike took it over to the work bench to clean it and check for cracks or stripped threads on the hydraulic lines connected to the servo. He found none, but I was still not satisfied. I told Captain MacDonald that I wanted to take the servo to Phu Loi and personally give it to the Bell Helicopter factory rep. He said he couldn't spare me as I was going to be immediately responsible for test flying both Hueys and Cobras because the new Huey test pilot's arrival had been delayed. Besides, he told me he'd write a note to the Bell rep and put it with the servo and get Lieutenant Devane to deliver it on the next ash-and-trash run.

Sometime later, I was in Phú Lợi and asked Captain Fight about the servo. He said that he had given it to the Bell Helicopter manufacturer's representative, but never heard back from him. I never did find out if any modifications were made to fix the problem, but for my part, I personally told all the Cobra ACs the trick of switching from system one to system two, should they encounter stiff control problems.

A couple of weeks later, Captain Hickman headed home, and Captain Albert Seidel became the new weapons platoon leader. When I met him for the first time, I told him about my hydraulic servo theory. He wrote down a note about it, and then he asked me if 636 was mission-ready. Thinking to myself that the word must have finally gotten out through the crew chiefs that 636 had been rebuilt, I said, "Yes sir, and you should take it out and see for yourself, because it is basically a new bird."

Captain Seidel did just that. In fact, he liked the ship so much he made it his own bird and had his crew chief paint his call sign, number 36, on the outside of the backseat door handle. All in all, the first month of fall had turned out pretty well.

*Al Seidel and Joe Jackson*

# CHAPTER 36

# ODDS 'N' ENDS AND R&R

Nineteen-seventy was coming to an end, and I was looking forward to my week's R&R with Ginger. We would be vacationing in Hawaii and would welcome in the new year on Oahu. Thoughts of Ginger, sea, sand, and a comfortable bed made it hard to focus. I was also still processing the loss of Tom Barnett and the horrific injuries that Dave Toms sustained. Any one of us could have fallen victim to either scenario, and while I refused to dwell on that inevitability, thoughts would creep through from time to time.

During the early hours of a mid-November morning, I was helping a couple of my guys fix a stubborn hydraulic leak when I heard a Huey coming in to land at the Special Forces camp at the end of the runway. I didn't think too much of it, even though it was a little odd. Those Special Forces guys were a covert lot and often undertook missions in the dead of night. I often wondered what Skip Newman was up to.

We were so focused on our work that we didn't hear anyone approach. I must have sensed someone was there because I looked up, and there was a two-star general standing on the ammo bay door of the Cobra. His name clearly stood out in the moonlight, "Putnam." His sergeant stood a few meters back and to one side.

I probably looked surprised that we were getting a visit from a general at 3:00 a.m. under the cover of darkness, but he didn't elaborate.

"Working late, aren't you, Chief?"

"Yes, sir. What can I do for you?"

He asked for directions to the major's hooch, and I offered to take him over. He shook his head, handed me a high-powered flashlight, and said, "Use this; point to it."

I did as instructed. He thanked me and marched off with his sergeant major. Thirty minutes later, they walked back down the flight line, past the Cobra I was sitting in, followed by our major, head down, duffle bag thrown over his shoulder. I thought, *this can't be good.*

I heard the general's Huey lift off no more than fifteen minutes later. Putting two and two together, I thought this appeared to be a stealthy way to relieve a troop commander of his command without embarrassing him in front of his staff.

It was dawn before we finished fixing the servo-hydraulic leak on 044, and my mechanics headed straight for bed. I went to the mess hall, excited to tell someone what I'd just witnessed. Two of my hooch mates, Mike Billow and Robby Hodge were grabbing an early breakfast, so I sat down with them.

Mike said, "You're up early!"

"Yep! I haven't been to bed yet. I've been up all night working on your leaky servo so you'll have something to fly today. But you won't believe what I saw at about 3:00 a.m."

As one, everybody stopped eating and looked at me with anticipation.

"A Huey landed at the end of the runway, and the 1st Aviation Brigade Commander asked me to direct him to the major's hooch. They've taken him away."

"What? They've done what?"

"You heard me; he followed them with all his stuff. I couldn't see his face clearly, but the way he was walking with his head low, he looked defeated."

The mess hall started getting busier, "Listen, you didn't hear this from me, right? I'm sure there will be an announcement later. Anyway, I can't stay, I'm off to test-fly 044, so Mike has his ride back."

The test flight went without a hitch, and I signed 044 back into service. I'd been up for twenty-two hours straight; I was dog-tired and hit the sack without talking to anyone.

It was noon before I woke and headed over to the maintenance tent. Mike Worthen was still sleeping, so I talked with Busto, his assistant, who told me the team was on track and everything that needed to be done was being handled. Confident that my team was in control of all our Cobra maintenance needs, I headed off to lunch.

A few minutes after I sat down at a table, Captain MacDonald came over and joined me.

"Morgan, the major has been relieved of his duties. His XO, Captain Grindstaff, has been put in charge of our troop temporarily."

I nodded and continued eating.

"You don't look surprised, Morgan."

"Sorry, sir, but I was working on 044 last night when General Putnam turned up and asked me to direct him to the major's hooch. I saw the major follow the general to his helicopter."

Captain MacDonald choked on his coffee and coughed uncontrollably; his eyes watered. It took him a while to calm down and catch his breath. When he could talk, his voice croaky, he said, "Talk about being in the wrong place at the wrong time, Henry; no one knows yet, so keep it to yourself until it's been announced."

I shrugged. *It's a little late now,* I thought, and smiled.

I didn't think anyone was going to be surprised. The major had lost everyone's respect at his first officers' meeting when he changed how units flew to the area of operation, increasing the risk to all pilots and crew. News of behavior such as that has a way of finding its way back to brigade headquarters. News of the major's departure was soon common knowledge, and, as no one cared for the man, it was a dead issue within days.

At the beginning of December, Captain Cook received intel from a captured Vietcong soldier that there was a possible NVA encampment in the Long Binh province. During his interrogation, he had given up the camp's coordinates. A stealth attack plan on the encampment was devised. Captain Cook presented the risky venture to Captain Grindstaff, who approved it for the early hours of Christmas Eve when there would be a full moon. A Scout and Cobra team, piloted by Tom White and Bill Yount, was formed. Yount's co-pilot was Lieutenant Joe Spence.

The team took off at 2:00 a.m. and climbed to 2,000 feet, traveling at ninety knots for the thirty-minute commute. Close to the target, the lieutenant instructed Tom to begin his descent. The moonlight, as promised, allowed him to go in low at 100 feet above the trees. Bill could see his rotating beacon flashing over the rear of the engine compartment and lost altitude to position himself for the attack. Joe, whose job it was to calculate time and distance, notified both pilots that they were close to the target. The second Tom began strafing the trees with his minigun, enemy automatic weapons tracer fire erupted from the trees. Taking evasive action, he exited the area to the left, and his observer dropped a WP grenade, marking the target for Bill.

In preparation, Bill, in the Cobra, had moved his rocket selector from two pairs of rockets to four pairs and unleashed a devasting barrage of firepower on the encampment. Tom felt confident they had destroyed the enemy location and continued to climb when Bill, who was also climbing, screamed over the radio, "Inbound!" Tom stopped his climb and turned the Scout to face the direction of fire. At that point, all communication with Bill ceased, as did the inbound tracers. Tom began circling the area and witnessed a massive explosion on the ground. He continued climbing, so he could report to our TOC that he had lost contact with Bill and suspected the Cobra had crashed into the contact site. A team revisited the site the following day, and Tom's suspicion was confirmed.

I looked over at Bill and Joe's bunks when I got dressed that morning. A sadness and weariness overwhelmed me. I couldn't assimilate the information. I didn't want to accept the loss of my friends and roommates. It was Christmas Day, for goodness sake. I wandered over to the mess hall, numb. Captain MacDonald was there, and I joined him for breakfast. In a war zone, it's always business as usual; emotions need to be contained, sectioned off, dealt with later, or never. I was heading out shortly to meet with Ginger in the warm Hawaiian sun. I was one of the lucky ones—so far. I thought of Bill and Joe and felt guilty.

I told the captain that eight of the nine Cobras were combat-ready, and with a bit of luck, there would still be four in that state when I got back in a week. For a second, I could imagine Bill's crashed Cobra and imagine my friend's final moments. I shook it off.

"Also, sir, I've talked to Bill Birdsell at 1st Cav Cobra Maintenance at Phú Lợi; he's agreed to come up and test-fly any Cobras that Mike Worthen has ready while I'm gone."

MacDonald changed the subject.

"So, are you excited about going on R&R and seeing your wife in Hawaii tomorrow?"

"You betcha! It's been eight months since I last saw her. I've been counting the days."

I returned to my hooch and tried not to dwell on the two empty bunks. All their stuff had already been removed. I would be on the early ash-and-trash flight in the morning. I doubted, however, that I would sleep well.

*Mike Cook holding rocket*

*Paul Bennett, Mike Billow, Tom White, and Dave Tela*

# CHAPTER 37

# OPERATION
# LAM SON 719

W hen I reluctantly returned to Vietnam, it was the New Year, 1971 and the war was dragging on. I arrived after dinner time, so after dropping my bags off at my hooch, I walked over to the Officers' Club. As soon as I opened the door, there were whoops and hollers. Mike Billow shouted, "How was the honeymoon, lover boy?" Some other guys followed this theme, adding their ribald and earthy comments. I took it all in good stead, and for a moment, it felt good to be back among my comrades in arms. I knew we all had each other's backs, which meant a lot.

They were thirsty for details, so I told them about the fabulous Ilikai Hotel, the bellman in the green tuxedo, and the Dom Perignon champagne, all courtesy of my Uncle Trigg. There were shouts of, *you lucky bugger,* and *tell us about the bedroom!* Of course, I left out all the steamy details of Ginger and our romantic reunion after eight months; I was sure they could put two and two together. I did, however, describe the view from our room's balcony, which spanned Diamond Head to Pearl Harbor, the huge bed, and the Jacuzzi tub. They salivated when I told them about eating fresh sea bass and a rack of lamb. When I told them about the New Year's Eve concert we attended and that I'd worn a tuxedo, someone said, "Wow! You in a penguin suit; I'd have paid money to see that!" Everyone laughed. There was great interest in my story about visiting Pearl Harbor and the U.S.S. Arizona; they wanted me to remember every detail. They didn't allow me to buy a drink all night; such was the value of hearing about home. It was a late night, and the camaraderie made me feel at home—at least in my second, very temporary home.

The following day in the mess hall, Mike Billow was with Rick Normand, my Cobra instructor from Vũng Tàu, and they called me over. They were discussing the shortage of experienced Cobra pilots since we lost Bill Yount and Joe Spence. We all agreed that we weren't getting replacements because of the ongoing pullback of American forces. Without giving it much thought, I said, "Ya know, I'd be willing to take an AC check ride and help out when I can." I knew that Scout pilot lives depended on our Cobras blasting the heck out of enemy targets within seconds of a Scout drawing fire.

As one, they sat back in their chairs, and Mike said, "Really, Morgan? That would help a lot. And I'd be happy to take you out and help bring your hunter/killer reaction times back up to snuff."

Rick said, "Then I can give you your AC check ride."

It was a huge responsibility, but now that my Cobra maintenance was functioning efficiently, I felt I could handle it. Mike and Rick were smiling widely, so I said, "Okay, gentlemen, I'm gonna go see what Captain MacDonald thinks about our plan. I'll be right back."

Mac was disinclined but said he would discuss it with Cobra platoon leader Captain Seidel. Within days, the A Troop Commander had given us his approval with the proviso that I would only be used as a backup and that Cobra maintenance was my priority. The following day, I began daily one-hour flying missions with Mike; by the end of the month, I was ready for my check ride with Rick, which I passed and became an AC. There's a saying, *put your money where your mouth is*, and I felt that I earned a new level of respect now that I was putting my life on the line as an AC, not just repairing their aircraft.

To further facilitate the withdrawal of American combat units from Vietnam, General Creighton Abrams and his staff at Military Assistance Command Vietnam had been planning to once again invade Cambodia and Laos: code name Lam Son 719.

The plan was to use American air power, including helicopters carrying ARVN soldiers in the ongoing Vietnamization of the war. The goal was to hand over all ground combat operations to the South Vietnamese Army. The top-secret reinvasion was to begin on February 8, 1971. We were notified of our part in the operation less than twelve hours before the invasion began.

By this time, we had a replacement commander for A Troop. His name was Major David Russell, and he was immediately respected by everyone. We were all pleased to have a professional back in charge. Major Russell briefed us on operation Lam Son 719. The new Huey test pilot, Lieutenant Tannyhill, and I got our specific briefing from Captain MacDonald.

By this time, due to the policy I had initiated, which allowed Cobra mechanics and crew chiefs to be involved in the maintenance decision process, and the easing of our parts problems with the help of Captain Fight, we had seven of our nine Cobra gunships mission ready.

Captain MacDonald told us that the 1st of the 9th Air Cavalry Squadron, from Phú Lợi, would be supporting the operation. The following morning, I was with Lieutenant Tannyhill and Captain MacDonald, watching two of our heavy hunter/killer teams, joined by two regular hunter/killer teams from the 1st of the 9th, depart for Cambodia. It was also easy for me to see that Captain MacDonald was proud that, over the previous several months, we had managed to iron out all the systemic maintenance bugs with our long-distance supplier and our primitive working conditions.

Walking back to our maintenance area, the 1st of the 9th Cobra platoon leader approached us and told us that one of his Cobras wouldn't start.

Captain MacDonald turned to me and said, "Morgan, this is Captain Jack Adams."

"Hi Sir, welcome to Quần Lợi, let's take a look at your Cobra." As I said this, I waved to Mike Worthen to join us.

Walking toward the Cobra, I could immediately see it was listing to the right. "Hold on Captain Adams, it appears from here that the aircraft has more than a starting problem, because it is leaning to the right. Here is Mike, my chief mechanic. Let's get him to take a look, with you, that way I won't have to Red-X it.

Adams looked furious, as if it was my fault the aircraft might be unflyable. I walked back to the maintenance tent and left Mike checking the chopper while Mac returned to his office. Thirty minutes later, Mike and Captain Adams came back looking grim, and shaking his head, "Mr. Miller the front landing gear mount is broken, and that's not all; the front transmission mount on the same side is cracked. This bird has some serious structural issues; it's unsafe."

Before the captain could express his feelings, I said, "Captain Adams, let's go and talk to my boss." He looked deflated but said, "Okay, and call me Jack, I see I'm going to need your help."

As I expected, Captain MacDonald was in his office doing what he regularly called *this bloody interminable paperwork*; we walked in, and he pushed aside a six-inch stack of papers. "What can I do for you, gentlemen?"

I explained the situation with the Cobra to Captain MacDonald, and he offered to fly Jack back to Lai Khe to pick up another Cobra. "Thanks, Captain, I'm a little embarrassed; it looks like the damaged chopper was placed on flight status by mistake."

I shook Jack's hand, excused myself, and headed back to work. Mike was there waiting for me. I told him what had been agreed to and that the structurally unsound Cobra would be sling-loaded out at some point and taken back to Lai Khe. The base was busy, and more hunter/killer teams were taking off.

It wasn't long before our first hunter/killer teams returned. Mike and I welcomed them back and I asked AC Curt Maunder and AC Bob Pogue, both second tour men, whether they'd experienced any mechanical problems. They smiled and said, "No, everything's good, but we need to be rearmed." Within minutes, the rearm team arrived with a trailer full of rockets, minigun ammo, and 40-millimeter grenade ammo. I joined Mike and we walked around both Cobras to check for any damage, leaks, or anything out of the ordinary. Both aircraft were clear; we couldn't even see any bullet holes—always a good sign.

Mike headed back to the maintenance area, and I walked up the flight line with the pilots and crew. I asked Curt, "How did it go out there?"

"The intelligence was spot on, Morgan. We caught the enemy encampment by surprise. It was devastating; we unloaded everything we had on them; then we saw fighter jets from the 35th Tactical Fighter Wing dropping bombs and napalm canisters."

He looked down at his boots and paused, before continuing, "I doubt there would have been many survivors—it was carnage. If there are any survivors, the hunter/killer teams that just took off will finish the job."

Bob Pogue cautiously jumped in, "Hey, sorry to change the subject, but I didn't have any breakfast, and I'm hungry. Do you guys want to see if the mess hall has anything left?"

While we all acknowledged the loss of life on some level, we had a job to do, and life went on. The image of fire and brimstone raining down on the enemy was replaced with the simple need for sustenance. I said, "Sure Bob, I didn't get a chance for breakfast either." War desensitized us—but only to a degree.

Everybody agreed they needed food. Curt, his Cobra co-pilot, Scout pilot "RatSo" Chodara and his observer followed us to the mess hall. Lam Son 719 was in full swing; the base was busy, so there were plenty of scrambled eggs, bacon, hot buttermilk biscuits, and gravy, and the coffee was hot and freshly brewed. The hunter/killer team members slumped rather than sat down at the table. The story of their last mission was imprinted on their faces like contours on a map. The topography featured fear, stress, exhaustion, and the ghosts of an unseen enemy engulfed in jellied gasoline.

Curt and I left the mess hall together. As soon as we stepped out into the 80-degree heat, the whine of the base siren began announcing a downed helicopter. We ran to the tactical operations center to find out who was down and how we could help. It was Robby Hodge in Cobra 075.

Mike Billow and Rick Normand in their Cobras, along with Paul Bennett in his Scout helicopter and our aero rifle platoon guys in three Hueys, were already taking off en route to the crash site. Curt and I were glued to the incoming radio communications. We could only pray that Robby and his co-pilot were not critically injured. Forty-five minutes later, we learned they had been medevacked to Long Binh hospital. That's all we knew; at least they were alive.

An hour later, Robby's Cobra arrived slung under a Chinook helicopter. Once it was safely on the ground, I checked it out. The first thing I noticed was that it had hit the ground hard, very hard, with its nose down—the damage under the front seat was extensive. I cringed; Dennis "Howdy Doody" Patterson would have been occupying that seat and probably took the brunt of the impact. As I continued my inspection, I counted seven bullet holes.

As I continued my initial inspection, I heard a Huey land; it was Al Fleenor returning from taking the two pilots to Long Binh. A few minutes later, he came over to look at 075, "That looks like it went down hard, nose first; I can't believe Dennis survived. Surprisingly he looked in a lot better condition than Robby."

"Robby's not good then?"

Al looked to the ground and shook his head, "No, he looked to be in a bad way."

Finally, the sun began to set on the first day of Lam Son 719. In the officers' club later, operations officer, Mike Cook, told us that the A Troop's mission as part of the greater operation had been a big success. I thought, *try telling that to Robby and Dennis.*

Mike Billow and I offered to fly the ash-and-trash Huey to Long Binh the following day so that we could visit Robby and Dennis in the hospital. The 93rd Evacuation Hospital was a sprawling complex of buildings. We had to ask several people for directions before arriving at Robby's bedside. He was in a body cast, reaching from his armpits to his butt. He was hooked up to more drips and monitors than I could count. I'm not sure what I expected, but I was shocked, and it showed on my face.

Mike stood beside him and gently placed his hand on his bare shoulder, "How are you doing, buddy?"

"What do you think? You shouldn't have come."

His tone was detached and distant; he was in a world of discomfort and pain. I felt concerned; I'd hoped he would be less injured and more positive. He was neither of these things.

Mike removed his hand, "Is there anything you need, or can we do anything for you?"

"You can pray for me and then leave me alone. Please just leave."

He was in a world of hurt, so we honored his wishes."

"Okay, Robby. Godspeed. We'll be back."

Outside the ward, we bumped into a nurse about to enter Robby's room. We asked her how he was doing and said that the body cast looked deathly serious. She told us that it was to immobilize him to prevent further damage to the crushed vertebrae in his lumbar spine.

I said, "He's very down; he asked us to leave. Will he be able to walk again?"

"Currently, he's paralyzed from the waist down, but the surgeon hopes the body cast will relieve the pressure on his lumbar nerves and, hopefully, he will regain feeling in his legs."

Suddenly, I felt nauseous. I turned away and bent over, thinking I was going to vomit. The thought of being paralyzed from the waist down was something I had difficulty contemplating.

I vaguely heard the nurse say, "Check back with us in a week. Hopefully, by then, the doctor will have a better idea of the next steps. Mr. Hodge might also feel a little more open to receiving visitors."

Mike asked, "Would you be able to direct us to Lt Dennis Patterson's ward?"

"Was he with Mr. Hodge?"

"Yes."

"Well, he's not here in the spinal cord injury ward. I suggest you check with admissions."

We discovered that Dennis was no longer at the hospital, but no one seemed to know where he'd gone. Mike and I did the ash-and-trash chores and errands for the rest of the day, mostly in silence. As a helicopter pilot in a war zone, thoughts of crashing or being shot down are never far from the surface. But seeing a close friend in a body cast brings it all home. *There but for the grace of God.*

When we arrived back at Quần Lợi, we immediately headed to the mess hall for dinner. Several exhausted pilots asked about Robby. We told them what we knew. His injuries were not life-threatening, his lower back was in traction, and he might require surgery in a few days.

Someone asked about Howdy Doody, and I told them that Dennis wasn't at the hospital, but we didn't know anything else. We hoped that was good news. We sure needed some.

*075 undergoing inspection and maintenance*

*Cobra Maintenance preparing a main rotor blade for reinstallation at Quần Lợi. Work is being done between the control tower and active runway outside the maintenance tent.*

*Tailboom of 202 with tail rotor ripped off*

*Rick Normand*

*"Pete" Gunn*

# CHAPTER 38

# CBS NEWS REPORT BY MORTON DEAN

M id-afternoon, on the sixth day of Operation Lam Son 719, the peace was shattered by the Quần Lợi siren. A helicopter was down. I stepped outside the maintenance tent and saw the clerk from the command bunker running toward me. Breathless, he said, "Mr. Miller, Cobra 202 has crashed in a small clearing ten miles north of Lộc Ninh."

My first thought was, *Shit, that's Rick Normand's Cobra, and he's over the border in Cambodia.* I followed the clerk back to the TOC, and as we ran, I could see Major Russell Spur 6, taking off in his command and control Huey. Three other Hueys were close behind, carrying our aero rifle platoon. As I reached the TOC, two Cobras took off and followed the four helicopters. Captain MacDonald walked in as I was following the situation on the radio. A slow twenty minutes passed before we heard, "202 went down in a small clearing. Both pilots are standing outside the bird, and they appear to be fine. Tell MacDonald and Miller to get out here."

Captain MacDonald looked at me; his eyebrows steady for the first time in a while. We turned and walked out to the OH-58 Scout helicopter without saying a word. Captain MacDonald cranked it up, and we were headed for enemy territory within minutes. The major briefed MacDonald and confirmed that the pilots were not injured. As we drew closer, I pointed to the circling Cobras and Huey's in the distance. Closer in, we flew over the crash site, searching for a place to land. The only spot close to Rick's chopper was tiny. MacDonald said, "Damn, that's going to be tight. Do you think there's enough room for us, Henry?"

"Yes, Sir. It'll be tight, but you can do it."

I'd registered the caution in his voice. He was going home in a little under two weeks; the last thing he wanted was to crash on the wrong side of the border—or crash at all, for that matter. He made a perfect approach, and as he was about to touch down, I could clearly see AC Rick Normand, the aero rifle platoon leader Lieutenant Kelly, and the downed Cobra. What surprised me was that 202 looked undamaged. We landed and I jumped out. On closer inspection, I was astounded—the tail rotor and ninety-degree gearbox were missing. I went over to Rick and shook his hand.

"Geez, man! You are one lucky S.O.B. How the heck did you get this machine on the ground? You have got to be the only Cobra pilot to have ever experienced this type of high-torque mechanical failure and survived!"

Rick just smiled. Cool as a cucumber.

I continued inspecting the Cobra. The drive shaft between the engine and transmission was undamaged, and there was no damage to the landing gear. I shook my head; *this is just crazy!*

MacDonald came up and said, "What do you think, Henry?"

"Sir, assuming we can locate a tail boom and tail rotor assembly, I could have this bird back in the air in about a week."

I could hear the circling helicopters high above us; it was reassuring. MacDonald updated the major, who said he'd arrange for a heavy-lift helicopter from the Black Cats, out of Phú Lợi to extract the Cobra and take it back to Quần Lợi. Shortly after, the major confirmed that a Black Cat Chinook helicopter was on its way.

We had six hours of daylight left, the weather was good, and the area was quiet, so we left the infantrymen to guard 202 and headed back to Quần Lợi with Rick and his co-pilot, Captain Pete Gunn. Two Cobras circled overhead, ensuring the men's safety.

On the flight back to base, I couldn't stop thinking about the miraculous landing Rick had pulled off. I felt sure that if it had been any other pilot, both men would have died in the crash. He was flying with our platoon because the army had closed the Cobra transition school at Vũng Tàu due to the U.S. pullback. He could have taken a safe job at squadron headquarters doing AC check rides, but he volunteered to fill a vacancy with us in A Troop. He'd need area-of-operation training, which took a month, but then he was promoted to aircraft commander. I said to myself, *Captain Pete Gunn, you were a lucky son of a gun to be flying with Rick today.*

I got to thinking about the Cobra's nickname—the *Widow Maker*. Ever since it arrived in service back in 1967, it had gained a poor reputation. A common problem was losing its tail rotor control while hovering in a quartering tailwind. Another was the stability control augmentation system or the autopilot. In the spring of 1970, Jim and Cal crashed because the controls seized up, and Craig Johnson had to put 097 down because of control problems. Although Chief Warrant Officer Yount and Lieutenant Spence were probably shot down, they could also have had control problems.

After landing back at Quần Lợi, we took Captain Gunn to the infirmary; the crash had shaken him badly. The medic said he'd be fine and prescribed a "stiff one" in the Officers' Club. So, we acted like pharmacists and marched him over to the Bunker, and after his third Scotch and water, he began to relax. The "medicine" was taking effect.

I asked him, "How long have you been in the country?"

"Almost a month."

He was still shaking a little, which wasn't surprising. He had just barely arrived in the country and had already survived what should have been a devastating crash in enemy territory.

Mac and I were eager to hear the whole story and asked Rick to fill us in.

"We had discovered no enemy activity in and around our target map coordinates, so the Scout pilot and I decided to give Captain Gunn some rocket target practice in case we did come upon the enemy. The Scout's observer dropped a smoke grenade into the jungle to give Captain Gunn a target.

While breaking away from his first rocket run and starting his climb to a higher altitude, he suddenly lost yaw and pitch control because he yanked in too much collective in an abrupt manner. At only 500 feet above the ground, I took over flying, entered auto-rotation to stop the spin, and, with full aft cyclic, guided the ship into the only clearing, which was right off our nose. Rick took a slug of his beer and was thinking of taking another when we urged him to continue.

"The fact that we landed at all was a miracle. If that clearing had not been off my nose, we would have gone down in the trees, and there would have been a very different result."

We continued to talk about Rick's coolness and his crazy skills. He told us that one of the emergency procedures he taught in flight school was landing without tail rotor control. Still, there was no procedure for landing without a tail rotor. He explained that the tail rotor assembly is about twenty-seven feet aft of the center of gravity and weighs approximately 90 pounds.

"So, losing the whole damned thing changed the longitudinal balance and anti-torque. I immediately knew we were in a life-threatening situation. It was a catastrophic mechanical failure."

I said, "What amazes me, Rick, is that not only did you land the helicopter, you did it from the front seat, which has only a quarter of the response rate of the controls in the rear seat. It was bad luck that it occurred when you were training a rookie pilot."

After a few more drinks and a lot of backslapping, we heard the heavy-lift Chinook arrive and went outside to watch it lower 202 to the ground. Once the Chinook left, I inspected the Cobra thoroughly. I shook my head. I still couldn't believe there was no damage other than the tail rotor was missing.

The following day, Bell Helicopter representatives—accompanied by 1st Aviation Brigade maintenance personnel—flew to the base to inspect 202. My estimate that the Cobra would be back in service in a week was thwarted when it was decided to transport the helicopter to Tan Son Nhut Air Force base in Saigon, in preparation for being shipped back to the U.S. and Bell Helicopter.

Over lunch, I had an opportunity to talk to the Bell rep, who told me that its engineers were aware of the continuing problems with the tail rotor of the Cobra at high-power settings. There were ongoing discussions about moving the tail rotor to the opposite side of the tail boom. Hence, it would rotate in the opposite direction. The aim was to reduce the strain on the tail boom in high-power situations. The tail fin and the ninety-degree housing would also be strengthened if this new retrofit went ahead.

Warming to his theme, he told me that Hughes Aircraft, who manufactured the OH-6 Scout helicopter, also had tail rotor problems under certain situations, such as a quick nose-low attitude to get away from enemy fire. This evasive maneuver caused the tail rotor to be instantly placed in clean air with no downwash from the main rotor, which dramatically increased the tail rotor's effectiveness and caused the helicopter's nose to drop even lower. If a Scout was close to the ground and this flight condition occurred, the pilot couldn't recover, resulting in a crash.

As I walked back to the maintenance area after lunch, I thought Rick's crash was a perfect example of how AH-1G Cobra pilots in Vietnam were technically test pilots; manufacturers counted on them to discover inherent design flaws. A significant Cobra deficiency was identified thanks to Rick Normand, and it saved many lives.

Operation Lam Son 719 ground on, and although we all remained in battle mode, everyday life at the base continued. On February 19, 1971, we held a going-away party at the Bunker for my boss and good friend, Captain MacDonald. He was heading home to Massachusetts the following day. The Bunker was busy. So while we waited for Lieutenant Tannyhill, Lieutenant Devane, and the other platoon leaders to arrive, my new boss, Captain Evans, Captain Cook, and I sat on empty rocket boxes drinking. I was a little down. MacDonald and I had become close friends, and while I was happy, he was going home to his family, things wouldn't be the same without him. Becoming friends as an adult is one thing. Becoming friends during a war, in life-or-death circumstances, is another thing altogether. Even if you rarely speak to one another, there's an unbreakable bond, a brotherhood that ties you together for life, whether you survive the war or not.

The evening progressed as these things do, with jokes and many stories about Captain MacDonald's exploits at the base. There was a bit of good-natured roasting, and a lot of alcohol was consumed. At some point, Captain Cook suddenly fell off his rocket box seat and landed on his face. *Thunk!* His nose was bleeding. This was not unusual at the Bunker, especially during a send-off. However, the officer would usually get up, grab an ice cube from his drink, wrap it in his handkerchief, and hold it to his nose to stop the bleeding. In this case, Captain Cook looked like a beached whale trying to get back to the ocean. He was still bleeding when he got upright and back on his box. With proper military etiquette gained from attending the Citadel military academy, Captain Seidel offered a clean handkerchief to the stunned but alert Captain Cook. The rest of us continued drinking—nothing to see here.

Once Captain Cook regained his composure, he rejoined the conversation with an announcement. A CBS News team, including correspondent Morton Dean, would be coming to Quần Lợi. I suppose we should have been more interested, but the alcohol and the celebratory nature of the evening resulted in a somewhat ho-hum response.

The evening eventually wound up, and some of us walked back to our hooches under a cloudless and starry sky while others staggered to bed. Early next morning, we said a final farewell to Captain MacDonald. The platoon leaders, now fully briefed, went to brief their platoons about the impending arrival of a CBS television crew. Within less than an hour, the base was buzzing with excitement, especially when the men learned that Morton Dean—one of the most respected news correspondents in the world—would be leading the CBS team.

With only a few days until their arrival, the base was in full clean-up mode. Helicopter crew chiefs set about cleaning and polishing their respective birds. Maintenance officers, including yours truly, got their mechanics to clear their individual areas of clutter and reorganize equipment in a more orderly fashion. The mess hall and Orderly Room were also given the spit-and-polish routine.

At precisely 9:00 a.m. two days later, the CBS News team arrived. Two Military Assistance Command Vietnam helicopters, led by our squadron Huey carrying our commander, landed. Most of the base watched with excitement. I saw our squadron commander get out of the lead helicopter, followed by Morton Dean. His producer, cameramen, and others got out of the other two helicopters. They headed for the mess hall, where Major Russell, Captain Cook, and the Weapons, Lift, and Scout platoon leaders were waiting to meet them and go over the plan for the filming of a live hunter/killer mission.

I was surprised that in the television world, things happened very fast. After the briefing, Morton Dean and his cameraman got into one of our Hueys and headed out to our area-of-operation. Their job was to film Captain Al Seidel in his Cobra 636, protecting his Scout on the mission. Cobra 636 was the helicopter I had gotten rebuilt; the helicopter no one initially wanted to fly was now a TV "celebrity."

While they were gone, another camera crew remained at the base to get some "background." They filmed our troop area and carried out interviews. One focus was on the rockets we carried in our Cobra gunships. The CBS interviewer was most interested in the rockets, which were packed with over 2,000 Flechettes, small pointed metal darts with vanes. He was surprised to learn that we were using antipersonnel rockets that would kill anyone unlucky enough to get in their way. According to the CBS interviewer, one rocket carried enough nails to build a three-bedroom home with a garage, which was a total exaggeration.

A week later, the film clip appeared on the *CBS Evening News with Walter Cronkite*. To his credit, Morton Dean gave the CBS viewers their first accurate glimpse of the sights and sounds of a real-life hunter/killer mission in Cambodia during Operation Lam Son 719.

*Spur Cobra and Kiowa departing Quản Lợi on February 8, 1971, for a hunter-killer mission in support of Operation Lam Son 719*

# CHAPTER 39

# SHOULD WE FLY TO QUAN LOI AT NIGHT?

B y the morning of February 24th, I began to feel that Operation Lam Son 719 was having its desired effect on the NVA in Cambodia; we'd had little to no enemy contact for several days.

While things were quiet, I decided to fly Cobra 155 to the 605 Maintenance Depot so they could replace the two intervalometer cables that ran from the selector switch on the instrument panel and cyclic stick to both the outside and inside rocket pods. This cable allowed the pilot to select how many pairs of rockets he wanted to fire and when to fire them. However, because of the rain and humidity, sometimes the rockets didn't fire at all or fired intermittently. Obviously, random reliability put lives at risk. I remembered, as a Cobra co-pilot, flying with, Dave Toms a time when we rolled in on a target and our rockets failed to fire. Dave said, "Jesus Christ, all we have here is a two-man transport helicopter!"

I planned to drop off 155 and head straight back with Cobra 730, which had been there to have the middle cockpit plexiglass replaced. I asked Mike Worthen if he needed any parts from the 605 tech supply before I left, but he said he was okay.

When I arrived in Phú Lợi, my first stop was to check in with Captain Fight. He told me that his team could replace the intervalometers and have the Cobra ready that afternoon. This good news posed a challenge; how would I fly two helicopters back to Quần Lợi later that afternoon? Using the captain's radio, I made contact with our TOC at Quần Lợi and asked if any qualified Cobra pilots were heading to Dĩ An who could fly the second Cobra back. He said he'd get back to me.

I borrowed the Captain's Jeep and drove to my home base, Dĩ An. Once there, I went to the orderly room and asked the clerk whether there were any pilots around. He said, "You're in luck, sir; we have a new Cobra pilot here waiting for a ride to Quần Lợi. His name is Mr. Barr. He just had his proficiency ride with Mr. Neal."

"Do you know where they are at the moment?"

"I saw Mr. Barr heading toward the Red Horse Inn, and I imagine Mr. Neal is completing his check-ride paperwork in his office."

I walked over to the club, and there was a young guy at the bar, looking a little out of place. My immediate thought was, FNG— *fucking new guy*. I walked up to him, and his name tag confirmed he was Barr.

"Hi, I'm Morgan Miller; the clerk told me I'd find you here. Welcome to the madness. How are you adjusting now that you've arrived in the combat zone?

"I'm fine, but I'm looking forward to getting to Quần Lợi as soon as possible. And please, call me Chuck."

"Well, Chuck, you're just the man I'm looking for! I need a Cobra pilot. I need to get two Cobras back to Quần Lợi tonight, and I can't fly both. How would you feel about flying one of them? I realize I'm throwing you in the deep end, but that's the army for you."

"Okay, but I'd need to follow someone."

He sounded hesitant, and although I needed a pilot, I didn't want to put too much pressure on him.

"Well, Chuck, you could always ride with me to Quần Lợi, and I can come back and pick the other Cobra up tomorrow. And by the way, call me Morgan."

"No, it's okay, Morgan; I'll be fine. It's what I'm here for, to fly helicopters. It's just that I wasn't expecting it to happen within hours of arriving in Vietnam."

I asked him whether he'd like to join me in a drive to the PX at Biên Hòa Air Force Base. "That would be good; I need some toiletries and stuff."

"Well, we'd better drop into the orderly room and check with the First Sergeant as to how safe the drive is today."

It was a pleasant surprise when the sergeant suggested we take the XO's Huey instead of driving. The XO was away in meetings with the squadron commander for the rest of the day.

"Thanks, that's great; it'll be safer and give me a chance to give Chuck an aerial tour of the area."

The sergeant looked over at Chuck and noticed he didn't have a sidearm.

"Mr. Barr, you don't have a sidearm?"

"No, after my welcome chat with the XO, it somehow got lost in the mix."

"Well, we better rectify that immediately. Colt 45 or Smith and Wesson 38?"

Chuck looked down at my hip, saw that I carried a 38, and said he'd take the Colt 45. After completing the paperwork, we headed over to the armory, where Chuck was issued his weapon and a box of ammunition.

On the ride to Biên Hòa, Chuck was quiet. I remembered the feeling of being handed a gun for the first time. It made everything come into focus; it was real; you were in a combat zone. The enemy was everywhere.

Once we landed, Chuck asked if we should leave our weapons in the Huey before heading to the PX.

"No way! You wear your sidearm from the minute you get up in the morning until you lay your head on your pillow at night."

It was always good to visit the PX; there was a semblance of normalcy to shopping, and I got a haircut on this occasion. On the flight back, Chuck's voice came over the intercom, "Where exactly is Quần Lợi, and what's it like?"

I gave him the *Reader's Digest* version. "It's seventy miles north of Dĩ An and has a 3,500-foot hard surface runway right down the middle of the base. Other than a Special Forces A-Team, twelve guys, and an ARVN Infantry company that provides base security, we're the only American unit there.

"Even so, that sounds a little spooky."

I shrugged, "It can be when I'm working late at night with my guys in Cobra maintenance, trying to get a Cobra ready for the next day's mission."

Chuck was silent for a while, digesting this information.

"Does the base have radar or an ADF?"

"No."

"Well, if the sun goes down before we reach the base; how will you find it at night?"

I sensed that he was second-guessing his decision to fly the Cobra back to our base. Flying at night can be scary, especially without radar or an ADF (Automatic Direction Finding) aid to help guide you. Finding the base and the runway is one thing, but if you have an engine or systems failure, putting the bird down, possibly in enemy territory, when you can't see the ground, is terrifyingly dangerous. Squadron Operation Procedures (SOPs) usually required Aircraft Commanders, (ACs) to have a minimum of 300 hours total time in the country and 100 hours at night, plus they needed an AC to back their promotion.

I chose my words carefully.

"I've been in and out of that base many times at night, and as long as there are no thunderstorms or low clouds to obstruct visibility, I can find it."

"Impressive," he muttered.

Back in Dĩ An, I discovered from the First Sergeant that the ash-and-trash flight back to Quần Lợi that evening, piloted by AC Tom Bennett, would be transporting five passengers, helicopter parts, and the mail. It was mid-afternoon, so I said to the First Sergeant, "Mr. Barr and I are driving back to Phú Lợi. Would you tell AC Tom Bennett that we'll wait for his arrival there?"

Driving to the gate at Dĩ An, Chuck asked how safe the ride was to Phu Loi. I smiled; there was that FNG nervousness.

"We should be fine. It's a heavily traveled road, part of Highway 13, and goes to Snoul in Cambodia. Some stretches are even paved. However, I suggest you keep your hand on your 45, just in case."

"What sort of problems could occur?"

"Mines, mortars, snipers, but it's usually okay."

I pulled up at the gate, and the MP sergeant stepped out.

"Hi, sergeant, how's the road? Should we expect any problems?"

"No sir, it's been quiet; you should be fine."

Chuck exhaled slowly as he loaded his gun.

Thirty minutes later, we pulled into the base at Phú Lợi, safe and sound. I checked my watch; it was 4:00 p.m. I parked at the 605 Maintenance Depot and went in to see Captain Fight. He told me 155 was ready to go. I signed the work orders for the Cobras, and Chuck and I headed to the flight line. When we approached the Cobras, Chuck immediately noticed that 155 was a 20-millimeter ship.

"How do you like it?" he asked.

"Love it."

"That's interesting because some Cobra school instructors didn't like how it shook the aircraft when firing the gun."

"Yeah, they're right, but you get used to it. While we're waiting for the ash-and-trash Huey, can you pre-flight 730, and I'll do the same to 155."

Chuck had told me that before deployment, he had been on a thirty-day leave. Although he'd just done a check-ride in Dĩ An, I wanted to see how confidently he handled a Cobra, so I suggested we take 730 up for a quick flight around the area. I had Chuck climb into the back seat while I got in the front seat. Once we had donned our helmets, I told him to start the bird. Once the engine and main rotor got into the correct operating range, I made the radio call to Phú Lợi tower, told them our intentions, and took off. After leaving the Phú Lợi traffic pattern, I said, "It's your aircraft, Chuck."

Once I felt Chuck had control, I released my hands.

"Chuck, climb to 3,000 feet on this heading. It will take us right over Dĩ An."

"Roger that."

Ten minutes later, I said, "Okay, we are approaching Dĩ An. Make a shallow 180-degree turn to the left."

While Chuck was in the turn, I could see our ash-and-trash Huey below at Dĩ An with a deuce-and-a-half truck parked nearby.

"Chuck, it looks like they are loading up our Huey. Dĩ An is only six miles from Phú Lợi, and that's Phú Lợi right off your nose. Descend to 1,000 feet and set yourself up for a right traffic landing to the south."

"Roger that."

"Phu Loi tower, this is Spur 37, five miles south for landing at the 605."

"Roger, Spur 37, enter right traffic. You are number two behind a Chinook entering downwind."

"Roger, Phú Lợi, have the Chinook in sight. Understand we are number two." Then, I added, "Nice job Chuck. I am going to let you make the approach and landing."

"Roger that," he replied. After flying downwind, he made a base leg turn and a turn to final.

I asked, "Can you see the Cobra down the runway on the right?"

"Roger that."

"Land at the pad next to that Cobra."

After landing and shutting the Cobra down, Chuck said, "I feel much better now about the flight to Quần Lợi."

"Glad to hear that."

Fifteen minutes later, Chuck and I watched the Huey arrive from Dĩ An. We had to turn our backs on it to avoid the debris from the rotor wash as the helicopter landed on the pad next to us. After its rotor blades stopped turning, WO Tom Bennett and WO Steve Goelz got out and came over to join Chuck and me.

By now, the sun was starting to go down. The Huey was later than usual because it carried four FNGs, who all had to be checked in and issued firearms. We always tried to do ash-and-trash runs in daylight whenever possible.

I introduced them to Chuck and turned to AC Bennett.

"Have you landed at night at Quần Lợi?"

He shook his head.

"No, I have always made it back before dark, but I have flown the route many times."

Chuck listened intently and said, "Why don't we just get going? The more daylight, the better."

As the most experienced pilot, I took control of the situation.

"Okay, gentlemen, this flight is no different than the nighttime cross-countries we made back at Fort Wolters during primary flight training, remember?"

The three pilots nodded. The cross-countries I referred to were daisy chains of helicopters following each other around checkpoints in Mineral Wells, Texas.

"However, if you feel uncomfortable, we can spend the night here."

Bennett asked, "Where?"

I said, "I have a good relationship with Captain Fight, and I am sure he'll be able to find us bunks for the night. The choice is yours."

The Huey pilots looked at each other, and Goelz said, "The sun is about down; let's get going."

"Okay. This is what's going to happen. I will lead the formation out of here, followed by Chuck, who will be followed by Mr. Bennett and Mr. Goelz. Chuck, as the new guy, will be in the middle. Goelz, you'll be able to advise him on his spacing if necessary. When we leave here, we'll climb to 3,000 feet, and fly north right up Highway 13 to our first checkpoint, Lai Khê, which you will still be able to see in the twilight. During that first leg of the flight, I will call our tactical operation center at Quần Lợi to get a weather update and inform them that we are en route. After Lai Khê, we will continue to fly north, following Highway 13, to An Lộc, and then proceed east-northeast for about two miles to Quần Lợi. Because Quần Lợi has no landing lights, I'll land first and use my landing light to illuminate the runway. Chuck, you will fly right over me and land. Goelz, Bennett, you will fly right over Chuck and land. Any questions?"

Without hesitation, the three pilots confirmed that they understood the plan. We headed for our helicopters. After buckling in, I made radio contact with the other two pilots, who were on our unit frequency, asking them to let me know when they were ready for departure. Minutes later, they each responded in turn. I contacted the Phú Lợi Control Tower.

"Phú Lợi, this is Spur 37, flight of three, at the 605-helo pad ready for takeoff."

"Roger, Spur 37, you are clear for takeoff."

We departed the Phú Lợi Fire Support Base and, as the sun was setting, headed north up Highway 13. I contacted our TOC and told them we were on the way. Twenty minutes later we flew over Lai Khê; the perimeter of the FSB was still visible, even though the sun had dropped below the horizon. The next checkpoint, twenty minutes further north, was the village of An Lộc. A few lights were visible. When I saw them, I called the others and asked if they also had a visual of An Lộc's village lights. They answered in the affirmative. When I was over An Lộc, I began my turn east to Quần Lợi; I could see the two helicopters behind me and to the right.

"Do you see me turning south?" I asked, and again, they answered in the affirmative.

As I approached the middle of the Quần Lợi airfield, I saw a couple of lights from the company area on the east side of the runway and began to set up for my landing. A minute later, I turned left ninety degrees from a south heading, I saw the two helicopters again off to my left, approaching the airfield. As I turned left again, on a final heading of 310 degrees, I could see the two helicopters off to my left. On the final approach, I turned on my landing light and could see the other two helicopters at altitude parallel to the Quần Lợi airfield. On my short final approach, I saw the French Rubber Plantation house. I began to slow down further and landed. Five minutes later, Chuck flew over me and landed.

Another five minutes passed, and WO Goelz and WO Bennett were nowhere to be seen. I was worried; *where the heck were they*? I lifted my Cobra to a hover and turned 90 degrees to the west to look for them but found no one. *WTF*? Over the radio, I asked Chuck if he had seen them. He said he hadn't. I told him to stay put while I went to look for them. Climbing out, I looked for the Huey's red and green running lights. Nothing.

As I made a 360-degree turn, I called our tactical operation center to see if they had heard from the Huey. Negative. I made a second 360 turn, this time looking toward the ground. *There*! On the northwest side of Quần Lợi, flames. With dread, I called our TOC again and told them that the Huey had crashed. I gave them the location and told them to immediately get a rescue team over there. The radio operator informed me that they were aware of the crash and were on it. *Oh no! Damn*!

On my way back, I informed Chuck on the radio about what had just happened. There was no response. I landed and parked my Cobra in a revetment. Then, I walked over and got in the front seat of 730—Chuck was still sitting in the back seat; I thought he might be in shock. I parked the helicopter in the revetment behind 155.

I told him to get out, and we ran up the dark, quiet flight line to the tactical operation center to find out what had happened. There was no news. The TOC was small, so we waited outside. Chuck asked, "Do you think they were shot down?"

"Highly unlikely. They didn't make a radio call, which tells me it was probably a mechanical problem."

As we waited, word of the crash got out, and other pilots and troopers joined us. Besides an occasional "Any news?" from a newcomer, an eerie silence descended on the scene outside the TOC. We all knew that a crash from high altitude usually resulted in no survivors. A little over an hour later, Lieutenant Kelly returned with his rescue team. He looked somber. He walked up to our group, which had grown to thirty or more; he didn't say a word, just waved his hand palm down, from left to right. All hope lost, the men disbursed in silence.

Lieutenant Kelly headed down into the TOC to brief our troop commander, and I told Chuck to follow me, "There's an empty bunk in our hooch."

"My stuff is still in the front seat of 730; I need to fetch it first."

"Okay, stay here. I'll go and get it for you." On my way back, I dropped his duffel bag onto the spare bunk in our hooch and then walked back to find him talking to Mike Billow.

"I see you've met Mike. Are you hungry?"

"I was on the flight here, but now the crash has made me feel nauseous. I just want to lie down and rest."

He looked deathly pale.

"So, how many fatalities have you had here?"

I put my hand on his shoulder.

"Chuck, I know it's tough. This is your first day in Quần Lợi, and we lost two veteran pilots, four new pilots, and another good man in a single crash, and we don't yet know why. It's a tragic day, but to put it into perspective, we've lost seven pilots and crew in the ten months I've been here. Today's crash represents the largest number of fatalities we've suffered in one day."

"Mike, could you direct Chuck to our hooch while I go and get something to eat? There probably won't be much left at this hour, but I'll grab whatever's available. Chuck, can I get you anything at all? You should eat something."

I wasn't sure he had heard me. He was far away, dealing with who knew what? Then, he registered that I had spoken.

"Thanks, Morgan, okay, perhaps a glass of milk and some peanut butter on bread?"

"Okay, will do. By the way, I've left your duffel bag on an empty bunk."

The mess hall was empty. I walked through the chow line; there were slim pickings. I absent-mindedly grabbed whatever I could and sat down at a table. *What had happened? Why did we lose seven men?* Scenarios ran through my mind. *What catastrophic mechanical failure could have caused the Huey to go down so dramatically?*

When I got back to my hooch, I found Chuck sitting on his bunk unpacking.

"Sorry, man, there was no peanut butter, but I brought you some Spam and bread with your milk."

He went to work on his make-do supper. Hunger ruled, despite the situation.

"I'll be back, Chuck; I'm going to hit the showers."

The warm water began to work its magic as I massaged away the knots and the stress from my neck. When I returned to my bunk, I saw Chuck resting quietly, so I said nothing. I laid on my bed thinking—again—about the crash. I felt guilty. *Was there anything I could have done differently? Could I have prevented the horrific accident? Was the Huey overloaded?*

My sleep was restless, haunted by the loss of so many young men. The following morning, I went to the orderly room and re-

298 • MORGAN MILLER

viewed the list of men lost on Huey 038. Tom Bennett, Steven Goelz
. . . I was shocked to see among those listed Captain MacDonald's
"Silver Bullet Mechanic," Craig Jakel; "Silver Bullet" was a name
we gave mechanics that could do anything and everything. They
were prized. Jakel had been scheduled to be released from his duties in Vietnam. He was only on the doomed flight because he'd
gone to Dĩ An to sign up for another six months, which would
allow him to get out of his army enlistment early.

The next day, Lieutenant Tannyhill invited me to visit the crash
site with our troop commander, Major Russell, but after seeing the
names of the dead listed in black and white, I couldn't face it. Not
this time.

He later told me that on initial inspection, the main rotor blade
had been intact and lying across what was left of the helicopter's
body, indicating the aircraft had suffered a catastrophic transmission failure. If the main rotor had been turning on impact, it would
have disintegrated when the Huey hit the ground.

The bodies of seven men were brought back to the base. Several days later, I attended the memorial service in Dĩ An. It wasn't
my first, but I hoped now I was coming to the end of my tour, it
would be the last. It was awful losing men to enemy action, but as a
maintenance chief, losing men to mechanical failure was alarming.
It was a Huey this time, but how would I deal with it when it was
one of my Cobras that lived up to its nickname, The Widowmaker?

# CHAPTER 40

# OUT WITH THE OLD, IN WITH THE NEW

My time in Vietnam was drawing to a close, thank goodness. Operation Lam Son 719 was winding down, and things were less stressful. During the final weeks of March 1971, Captain Evans introduced me to my replacement, CW2 Ron Ray. He was my age and height but a little heavier set. He'd just arrived on the ash-and-trash helicopter from Dĩ An. One poor soul arrives, and another ships out—the cycle of life, or at least that's how it was in the army.

I looked at my watch, "It's chow time; would you like to join me for dinner?"

As we shuffled our way along the chow line, I took a deep breath—*I'm going to survive this place; I get to go home to Ginger and my parents. At last.*

We got our food and sat down to eat. It was early, and we had the place almost to ourselves; it made it easier to talk. Ron told me that he'd decided to make the army his career because there were limited job opportunities in his hometown of Fresno, California. He was a second-tour pilot and had recently graduated from Cobra school and the Army Maintenance Officers Course. Before the AMOC, he was a primary helicopter flight instructor at Fort Wolters.

We fell into easy conversation and discussed our backgrounds and where we came from—I liked him. I said, "It's about time the army got a properly-trained test pilot over here; my predecessor, Ed Soliday, and I were trained on the job."

"Really?"

"Yep, we learned on the job. I assume no one's had a chance to allocate you a bunk yet?"

I told him there was an empty bunk in our hooch, so we picked up his stuff and walked over. On the way, I showed him the latrines and showers. He looked around, "Boy, some things don't change."

"When was your last tour?"

"June of '67 until June of '68. I was with the 173rd Assault Helicopter Company out of Lai Khê; we regularly flew in and out of Quần Lợi."

I sat on my bunk while he unpacked and got settled, and I replied to a letter from my grandmother. When he was finished, I asked, "Would you like to go to the O-Club, otherwise known as The Bunker, for a cocktail?"

His broad smile was all the answer I needed.

At the club, we ordered a couple of drinks and waited for our eyes to adjust to the darkness. I saw Cobra pilots LT Patterson and WO Barr, and Mike Billow, who had just been promoted to CW2, seated at a table. Once we got our drinks, we walked over, and I introduced Ron, who got the usual new-guy harassment. He took it all in good humor. He was going to fit right in. I was pleased.

At the Cobra maintenance tent the following day, Ron jokingly commented on our primitive maintenance operation. Laughing, he said, "At AMOC, we were told that all maintenance should be done in a windless hanger or in as close to pristine conditions as possible to eliminate dust and dirt contamination. I wonder how many instructors have visited a frontline base such as Quần Lợi?"

I continued the tour, and Ron asked many insightful questions and talked to several of my mechanics. Once again, I could tell he was being received well by my team. It felt good to be handing over things to such a competent replacement.

Leaving him with my crew, I went to see Captain Seidel for an update on the day's hunter/killer missions. Things were quiet, and there had been no enemy contact, but we both knew that could change in a heartbeat.

"I'll be here all day training our new maintenance officer; if you need backup, I am available."

"Thanks, Morgan, but I'm in good shape as far as pilots are concerned. Thanks for checking in, though."

We had two Cobras in for their 100-hour inspections but none for repair. It was the perfect day for me to be training the new guy. Later, Ron and I had dinner then went to The Bunker. I'd seen him all day using a black notebook. Now he asked question after question, interspersed with observations. I did my best to provide as many answers as I could. He was a serious professional; he'd do an excellent job keeping our pilots safe.

We discussed the importance of the parts supply chain, and he asked, "Where is your parts facility located?"

"Phú Lợi. Tomorrow, we'll fly the ash-and-trash helicopter there, and I'll introduce you to Captain Fight at the 605 and his men in tech supply. He's an interesting guy—loves his cocktails."

The following day, I changed my plan and took a Cobra to Phú Lợi instead. It didn't make sense to be away all day. We arrived mid-morning, and I gave him the tour; we visited the hangar and went next door to where we picked up our parts. After a pleasant lunch with the captain, we returned to Quần Lợi.

I stepped back for the next few days to let him get used to his new job. Occasionally, he'd find me and ask a question or two, but he quickly picked it up. On his sixth day, Mike Worthen announced that Cobra 847 was ready for its test flight. I asked Ron whether he wanted to do it before or after lunch. "Let's do it now," he said; I wasn't surprised that the professional would put work before pleasure.

I showed him how I had been trained to do a test flight. He liked the idea of carrying out hovering auto-rotations first, shutting the bird down, getting out, and rechecking everything. We'd only had Cobra 847 for about three months, so, not surprisingly, it passed the test flight with flying colors.

As March drew to an end, my crew planned a surprise going-away party for me with the Cobra crew chiefs and pilots. Of course, keeping a secret in such a close-knit environment is almost impossible. However, they did a good job, and it wasn't until the day of the party that I stumbled upon their preparations. I walked over to the Cobra tent and saw the legs of something sticking out from under a tarp. I pulled it back, and lo and behold, there was a waist-high five-foot-long barbecue. I quietly recovered it and left the tent.

At about 10:00 a.m. the following morning, I was with Ron looking for Mike Worthen. Not only could we not locate him, but SPC Busto and SPC Cooper were missing too. I eventually found them in the mess hall kitchen, and the game was up; they were all busily preparing food. Mike was making his mom's modified Hasselback potatoes. He carefully cut each potato into slices, but not all the way through, added garlic, salt, pepper, and stuffed butter between each slice. He then placed them in aluminum foil and topped them with sliced onions and more butter before wrapping them entirely in the foil.

I asked Mike, "So, what time is the party?"

"I told Captain Pogue a few days ago to invite all the Cobra pilots to arrive at noon."

Mike took the potato parcels out to the Cobra tent and gave them to SPC Cooper, who was manning the barbecue, along with a gallon can of Campbell's pork and beans. When Mike returned, he began seasoning the steaks with salt, pepper, and garlic powder telling me he wanted them to come to room temperature before hitting the grill. I was impressed; I had no idea he could cook. It was going to be quite the feast.

Come noon, the party was already in full swing. The Beach Boys were playing loudly, and Captain Seidel, Mike Billow, Curt Maunder, Rick Normand, Bob Pogue, Chuck Barr, new Cobra AC Patterson, Captain Evans, Lieutenant Tannyhill and Ron Ray along with my mechanics and a few crew chiefs had all arrived. Mike announced the food was ready and started to serve the potatoes, steaks, and beans. While my friends lined up to be served, I walked up, shook their hands, and thanked them for coming.

Once everyone had been fed, Captain Seidel asked for quiet. Once he had everyone's attention, he said, "Morgan, I never went to bed at night wondering if you and the Cobra team would be able to meet the daily mission readiness commitment of four flyable Cobras. In fact, you and your team usually had five or six mission-ready Cobras. My counterpart with the 1st of the 9th could never believe how you managed it."

He walked up and shook my hand, "Here is a plaque from the weapons platoon, with your call sign, Spur 37, engraved on it. And thanks again for volunteering to be a Cobra backup AC. Best of luck with your next duty assignment."

Everyone applauded. Mike Worthen stood up.

"Mr. Miller, thanks for leading our Cobra maintenance operation and for breaking Army protocol by allowing me and my team to work with the Cobra crew chiefs to make decisions."

He then handed me another plaque. This one featured his name along with the other eight team members. Everyone stood and cheered. I was touched. After looking at the plaque and shaking Mike's hand, I said, "Gentlemen, let's stand and raise our drinks to toast our weapons platoon leader, Captain Al Seidel, our new maintenance platoon leader Captain Evans, and my replacement Ron Ray. I would also like to toast Mike Worthen, Tom Lehman, Jim Cooper, Ned Zaglow, and James Boyd, who were here when I took over from Ed. You men did a great job and put in a lot of long hours under difficult circumstances, especially when we had to move up here at short notice. Damn, I am proud of you, men! Oh, and thank you for this party!"

When the applause died down, I continued, "Gentlemen, this has been the most worthwhile thing I have ever done. Flying in the Gun Platoon, and being the Cobra maintenance officer, has been tremendously rewarding. It is with sadness that our professional bond with each other here in Vietnam has been forged in a world that only we, who have served here, can understand. After the war, I fear these relationships will fade when we no longer work side-by-side every day. I truly hope not, but the unique respect we share with each other here at this moment in history is rare; it only thrives in combat conditions. Again, thank you all for your support and friendship. I can't tell you how much I appreciate and value you all. Please enjoy the rest of this amazing farewell party."

Lying in bed that night, I knew I would miss these guys and my role in Cobra maintenance. I'd even miss being a backup Cobra aircraft AC. I tried to summarize, to myself, what I felt about my year in Vietnam. The one thing I knew for sure was that being in the army accelerates maturity at warp speed.

Honestly, I didn't know who Morgan Miller was until I flew AC Johnson's Cobra 097 out of the area of operation in November. Flying that helicopter back to base while continually shifting the hydraulic switch between systems to keep the damn thing airborne was a catalyst. I had put duty and my fellow troopers' safety before my own without a thought.

I enjoyed my time in Cobra maintenance, even though it meant dealing with constant crises. And although there were too many sad and tragic moments and little joy, there was great satisfaction in keeping those Cobras flying. Before I dozed off, I remembered Captain MacDonald commenting that our mission here was like watching sand pass through an hourglass. Now, for me, the sand was almost all at the bottom. Would I turn the hourglass over?

# CHAPTER 41

# MY LAST DAY IN VIETNAM

T he army loves its paperwork, so on the day I was scheduled to leave Vietnam, I went to the orderly room and signed the necessary "DEROS," or "Date of Expected Return from Overseas" paperwork. Major Russell saw me and invited me into his office. After a few pleasantries, he thanked me for the work I had done as maintenance chief and for volunteering as a backup AC. He passed my personnel file over and said, "Mr. Miller, I have placed a letter of recommendation in your file requesting you be sent to Army Maintenance Officers' Course."

"Thank you, sir. It's been an honor to have been a member of A Troop. I've learned a lot of skills and even more about myself. It has been a life-changing experience working for you and your platoon leaders here at Quần Lợi."

He stood, we shook hands, and he walked me out of his office. My next stop was to the TOC to say goodbye to Captain Cook and thank him for his strong leadership. I'd already said my goodbyes to everyone else, so I headed for the flight line to ride the ash-and-trash Huey to Dĩ An. On the way, I saw Henry Harris in the cargo bay sporting his signature broad grin. He was on his way home too. I hoisted my duffel bag and suitcase into the cargo bay and smiled back—his grin was infectious. AC Al Fleenor was our pilot. I walked up to him and asked, "Al, can I be co-pilot?"

"Sure, Morgan. Bert, can you hop in the back for this first leg?"

Bert Graybeal was Al's co-pilot and seemed happy to take the back seat. While the bird was winding up, I told Al over the intercom, "I can't believe it—I am going home!"

He replied, "I'm only thirty days behind you, Morgan, and I can't wait."

It was a beautiful April morning. After reaching a hover, we took off to the southeast, because of the wind, which felt very different—I wouldn't be coming back. As we left the FSB traffic pattern and turned due south, I looked down at Quần Lợi for the last time. I had mixed emotions; I had only been in Vietnam for twelve months, but I was returning home a different person. It felt like I'd been away from my old life for several years.

Once on the ground, we headed to A Troop headquarters. I told Henry that we should meet for dinner at 5:00 p.m. That brought the grin back big time. The rest of the day was spent preparing for my departure. At dinner, Henry and I talked about Ginger, his girlfriend, Molly, and what we were going to do when we got home. He said he would be attending college in the fall. All in all, it was an upbeat and positive conversation about family, one that reinforced the fact that we were, indeed, going home.

After dinner, I went to the Officers' Club to meet Charlie Neal for a drink. The club was quiet, as B and C Troops had moved out of Dĩ An's area of operation. Half a dozen officers were hanging out; new guys waiting for assignments to either A, B, or C Troops of the 3/17 Air Cavalry Regiment.

While I waited for Charlie, I watched four of the FNGs playing pool and drinking cocktails. One of the new warrant officers walked over, "Are you headed home?"

"Yes."

"How bad was it?"

I stared at him for a few seconds before answering. *Was I this green when I arrived one year ago?* I said, "I found it to be the most rewarding thing I've done in my life. You will work with some of the bravest and most honorable men you have ever met. You will experience things that will touch you to your core. What you see, live through, and experience, will shape your character. You will reach a whole new level of maturity."

By the time Charlie arrived, I had attracted an audience of newbies, all listening to the "old" guy, the veteran. He'd caught the tail end of my conversation with the FNGs. He said, "Hey Morg, don't sugarcoat it to the new guys, tell them the truth. What are you drinking?"

I laughed, "Well, that made me feel ancient. Rum and Coke please."

When he returned with the drinks, the conversation became more animated. Charlie was a funny guy. It was good to be the center of attention, but after a while boredom set in and I decided to head to my hooch. Coincidentally, it was the same bunk where I had spent my first night, 365 days earlier.

The following morning, Henry Harris and I met at the squadron orderly room. A ride was organized, and we flew to the 90th Replacement Battalion to complete our out-of-country processing. Everything is by-the-book in the army, so we had our blood and urine tested for who knew what—probably for an STD. We were told that if all our paperwork checked out, we'd be on a flight out mid-morning the following day. We had our blood drawn, went for lunch, and then, to kill some time, we headed to the PX to see if they had something to buy that we didn't need.

The day dragged on. Late afternoon, Henry and I went to the lab to get our results. We both got negative results—the last rubber stamp required to leave the following day. We looked at each other, smiled, and in unison said, "We're heading home!"

• • • • •

It was still early evening, but I felt exhausted, so I told Henry I was going to find a bunk and take a nap. The next thing I knew it was 6:00 a.m. and I was starving. I'd slept for about twelve hours. Sleeping in a safe zone, not a combat zone, is very different.

I quickly showered and shaved and donned my fire-resistant Army Nomex flight suit. Looking and feeling great, but hungry, I headed to the officer's mess. Once again, there were a lot of FNG officers in civilian clothes hanging about. I talked to a few of them, and some had just arrived, while others said they had had difficulty sleeping since they arrived.

It's funny how like attracts like. Once I got my food, I sat with other officers who were heading home. It was easy to tell the difference between newbies and those hardened individuals heading home after a tour of duty. It wasn't just their flight suits or fatigues, it was their demeanor, their hardened faces, the looks in their eyes. Never be fooled; war changes a person.

I shook hands with the officers next to me and acknowledged the FNG officers across the room. A unique camaraderie exists between strangers who have served that can only be earned. I began to chow down on my last meal in Vietnam—the food had never tasted so good.

Reaching for my coffee, I looked around and saw some of the new guys were looking over at our table. There were questions in their eyes, but no one approached us. As I walked out, I could imagine what the FNGs were thinking because I'd been them exactly one year earlier. *How bad is it going to be? What am I getting myself into? Will I survive?*

I headed to the DEROS departure counter where the clerk handed me my World Airways boarding pass and took my suitcase and duffle bag. I kissed the boarding pass and saw that my departure gate was number 9. It was 7:45 a.m. Strangely, there were only a handful of departing vets there. Then I read the departure board; my flight wasn't leaving until 5:30 p.m. I should've read the pass, not just kissed it! A wave of disappointment came over me; almost ten more hours stuck in this damned country. *Aargh!*

I stuffed my boarding pass inside my T-shirt, set the alarm on my watch for noon, and headed back to the billet area to lie down and relax. When the alarm woke me, I headed for the mess hall, where I got my Vietnam Special, hamburger, fries, and a Coke. I was feeling well rested, but I freshened up my face in the restroom and headed back to the terminal. When I arrived at Gate 9 the waiting area was half full, so I picked a seat, put my Class A uniform on it, ready to change into when I reached San Diego. At the newsstand. I selected a Snickers bar, a *Time* magazine, a *U.S. News and World Report*, and picked up a free issue of *Stars and Stripes*. It was still only 1:30. I opened my copy of *U.S. News and World Report* and scanned the table of contents. The first article was *The Pentagon Papers*, which described a top-secret study about how Presidents Eisenhower, Kennedy, and Johnson got us into the Vietnam War. Other articles in the magazine covered the congressional debates about lowering the voting age to eighteen and passing a law making it illegal to advertise cigarettes for sale.

After a while, I stood up and stretched. As I did, I saw Henry walking into the waiting area. I waved and he headed in my direction.

"So, Henry, what have you been doing to keep yourself out of trouble?"

"Sleeping mostly," he replied. "Speaking of sleeping, why do you think we're so doggone tired?"

"Sleeping at Quần Lợi wasn't really sound sleep at all; it's what I call watchful sleep. We're like dogs, sleeping with one eye open. In the back of our minds, we always knew an incoming rocket attack could happen at any time, and we'd need to be under our bunks in an instant. Also, now that we know we are heading home, our minds and bodies are in "relax" mode."

"Yeah," he said, "that makes sense. What time did you arrive at the gate?"

"Well, I was here early this morning before I looked at the board and discovered that the flight didn't leave until late afternoon. So I went for lunch and yet another nap."

"Mr. Miller, the departure time was on your boarding pass."

I got it out, "Yep, so it is!" I felt a little foolish so change the subject.

"Have you heard of *The Pentagon Papers*?"

I handed him my magazine and suggested he read the article. I dozed off, only to be woken by a loud broadcast from the gate attendant: "World Airways flight 26 to Travis Air Force Base in California will be boarding in fifteen minutes."

We looked at each other, stood up, smiled, and headed for the gate. In what seemed like an instant, we were seated and belted in, and prepared for our long flight home.

*Myself, our Quần Lợi hooch maid Thu (pronounced "too")*
*and Mike Billow*

# CHAPTER 42

# CALIFORNIA OR BUST!

After the push back from the loading ramp and the taxi for departure, the DC-8's 200-plus veterans cheered the moment the airplane left the ground. After a moment, I looked out the window, we would soon be leaving Vietnamese airspace. *Why was I feeling conflicted about what I did in this country?*

Once we reached cruising altitude, Henry and I began to chat. I told him, after receiving letters of recommendation from Captain MacDonald and Major Russell encouraging me to attend the Army Maintenance Officers' Course, I was considering it.

He smiled, and said, "I'm hoping to get out of my army commitment early because I was captured. Major Russell told me that that might be the case."

"That would be great, Henry, you've done more than enough for your country. It's time to look after yourself and your loved ones."

"I'm really looking forward to seeing my girlfriend and Mom and Dad. Beyond that, I've not given much thought to the future. It'll be time for the spring cattle roundup very soon, and I'm looking forward to helping Dad. Then it'll be calving time. I love seeing all the new life on the ranch."

"Didn't you mention that you were planning on going to college in the fall?"

"Yeah, I did say that, Mr. Miller, but the next semester is five months away, so I have plenty of time to take care of that. I haven't even gotten home yet."

I took his last comment as a sign he wanted to change the subject. I reclined my seat and fell into a deep sleep as the airplane headed toward Japan. When I awoke, there was a new person sitting next to me on the plane. Apparently, I'd slept through our brief stopover in Japan, when most people deplaned and took an opportunity to stretch their legs and grab some non-airline food. I was surprised the flight attendant hadn't awakened me. I stood up and looked around. Henry was sitting in the row behind and waved. *What the heck was with all this sleep? Enough's enough!*

I was stiff, so I walked to the front of the plane and back, stretching my arms overhead, arching my back, and doing a few knee bends. Back at my seat, the soldier sitting next to Henry agreed to trade seats and we resumed reminiscing about our time in Vietnam, and all the things we were looking forward to doing once we were stateside again.

Six hours after refueling in Anchorage, the plane landed at Travis Air Force Base in California. Henry and I deplaned, headed over to baggage claim, and then reported to the army processing center, a short cab ride from the terminal. As we left the base, we passed a small group of protestors.

Henry and I were in separate lines, one for officers and one for enlisted men. This made me feel uncomfortable—like my "brother" was less important than I was. I shuffled along the line and was eventually greeted by a Captain Armbruster. He informed me that, basically, I had two choices. I could either get out of the army today, or I could extend my enlistment to an indefinite status.

Okay, there's that term indefinite again, whatever that means. I looked at the captain, and asked, "What happened to the five-year contract I signed when I graduated from flight school?"

"It has been rescinded because of the Vietnam pullback."

I was shocked. Part of me wanted to dance with joy, and the Morgan from a year ago would have undoubtedly signed on the dotted line quicker than the captain could say "sign here." Instead, I said, "Wow. This is a big decision! Is there any chance that I could be placed on a two-week leave, so I could discuss this with my wife?"

Captain Armbruster said, "No problem," and gave me the requested leave.

I was perplexed. I sat down and waited for Henry. Fifteen minutes later, he came over and said, "Let's get out of here."

We walked outside, flagged down a cab and told the driver to take us to San Francisco International Airport. We were both transfixed by the beautiful scenery; it was our first car ride in a year. I cracked a window and could smell the fresh sea air. In the terminal, I offered to buy Henry dinner.

"That sounds really nice, Mr. Miller, but my first priority is to try to get a flight to Salt Lake City as soon as possible."

"Yes, of course, Henry, I completely understand."

I looked long and hard at my wartime brother. A flood of mixed emotions overtook me. "Well, my friend, I guess this is it." I placed my hands on his shoulders and held him at arm's length. You are a fine young man, Henry, and I wish you the very best. I know you will do well in life and make something of yourself." He gave that charming grin again and we shook hands.

"Thank you, Mr. Miller. I'm sure glad we got to know each other. It seems like you were always there for me when I needed a friend. I'll never forget you."

We hugged and shook hands again, and then Henry turned and headed for the information kiosk. It was only later that I realized we'd never gotten around to exchanging contact information. I never saw him again.

I went to the Pacific Southwest Airline ticket booth and bought a one-way ticket to San Diego. There was a two-hour wait before the PSA jet was to depart, so I headed for the terminal bar. The bar was busy, but there was a single seat at the bar. I sat and ordered a margarita. As I was absent-mindedly watching the bartender mix my drink, there was a tap on my shoulder. I turned and came face-to-face with Brad Paulson.

"Holy shit!" I said, shaking his hand. "How are you doing?"

"I'm good, sir. You?"

"Good. Ever run into that sergeant?" I asked.

Sporting an ear-to-ear grin he said, "No, but I wish I had. Please join me and some army buddies for a drink."

He told his friends that we had gone to Basic and Advanced Infantry Training together at Fort Ord. I told the story of Brad flooring the abusive drill sergeant and their raucous laughter made everyone in the bar turn to look at us.

For the next hour, Brad and I shared stories about our tours. Then I said, "So, what are you doing here?"

He smiled. "Going back to Vietnam."

He told me that he had arrived in Vietnam on January 9, 1969, as planned, and was assigned as an infantryman to a company in the 25th Division at Cu Chi. He was wounded in the abdomen in April while his platoon was in the jungle in the Parrot's Beak area. I told him that I had flown hunter/killer missions over that area a year later. After initial treatment at Biên Hòa Hospital, he was sent to Letterman Army Hospital in San Francisco for additional surgery, followed by extensive rehabilitation. After four months of recuperation, he went home on two-week leave and then went to Fort Benning, Georgia, and enrolled in parachute school. He graduated top in his class, got his jump wings, and was offered a reenlistment bonus and promotion to Sergeant E5. He accepted, which extended his army obligation for five years.

While at Fort Benning, he got orders to the 101st Airborne Division located at Fort Campbell, Kentucky.

"Morgan, I've decided to make the army my career. I used the cash bonus to put a down payment on a home in Hopkinsville, Kentucky, near Fort Campbell. I like the army—the way of life, and its code. I find it more rewarding than being a cowboy; the workdays are shorter, the food is much better, and so is the pay. And I get to sleep in a bed most nights. Plus, after twenty years, I can retire with a pension."

He looked happy and less intense than I remembered.

"Are you going to stay in the army, Morgan?"

"I haven't decided. I'm heading home on leave, and I'll be talking it over with my wife."

I looked down at my watch, I'd have to get moving soon. "What about Oakley and Ault?"

"Yes! I ran into them at the Fort Ord bowling alley a week before I left for Vietnam. They were waiting for their orders to helicopter flight school.

"Ah, that's great!" I said. Then added, "Boy! Brad it was sure good seeing you again, and I wish you the best of luck on your return to Vietnam. They need people with your leadership qualities and experience over there."

We shook hands, and I said goodbye to his buddies who had been laughing and joking about who knows what while Brad and I were catching up. On the way to my gate, I headed for the restroom, where I washed, shaved, and changed into my clean dress uniform for the last leg of my journey home.

# CHAPTER 43

# HOME AT LAST!

After taking one final look in the bathroom mirror to ensure my CW2 warrant officer rank was in the proper position on my collar and my medals were secure on the left side of my khaki shirt, I walked to the gate. I sat in an empty row toward the front of the waiting area.

The boarding area started filling, but no one sat near me. As I looked around, some civilian passengers looked at me with frowns. I got a distinct feeling of disapproval. Perhaps because I proudly wore my army uniform. I knew a faction of the public disagreed with our government's position on Vietnam, but I was just a draftee. *I didn't start the damned war.*

I squirmed in my seat; the pride I'd felt walking from the restroom to the gate had evaporated. The waiting area became increasingly busy, but still, no one sat near me. I looked around and saw a marine captain standing by the window, so I went over and joined him, and we soon fell into conversation.

Soon, the gate agent announced that our flight was ready to board.

It was almost as if she was trying to make a point when she announced, "Out of respect for our military personnel on this flight, we are pleased to invite them to board first."

The marine and I looked at each other and headed to the airplane. There was a ripple of applause from a few passengers. When we entered the plane, the captain greeted us and shook our hands welcoming us aboard.

The stewardess showed the marine and I to first-class seats and I said, "Sir, did you get a negative feeling from the passengers at the gate about us, or was it just me?"

"Maybe a little, some people aren't satisfied with blaming the government for our involvement in the war; they feel the need to take it out on military personnel, many of whom were drafted and had no choice but to go to Vietnam. I blame the media for stirring things up."

I felt a lot better after talking to the captain, who had turned a negative experience into a positive one. Once we reached cruising altitude, the stewardess told us the captain wanted to buy us drinks. Things were looking up! I followed the marine's lead and ordered a Jack and Coke. During the hour-long flight to San Diego, the marine and I discussed our different roles in Vietnam. He had been an infantry platoon leader in Quảng Trị province.

As we entered the arrivals lounge, his wife and family mobbed him. Seeing it was heartening and made me look forward even more to my family reunion. He asked if I needed a ride. I thanked him but told him I was a day earlier than planned and would take a cab and surprise my wife at the hospital where she worked. We shook hands and wished each other luck. Once again, I felt a strong bond with a fellow brother-in-arms.

Outside the terminal, I flagged down a cab. As I got in, the cabbie said, "Welcome back from Vietnam, sir. Where to?"

"Grossmont Hospital in La Mesa, please."

"I know right where that is, sir! Is that where your wife works?"

"Yes, she's a nurse there."

"I noticed the wings on your shirt above your medals. What did you fly?"

"Cobra gunships."

"My son, Dave, is a door gunner with 101 Airborne over there."

We arrived at the hospital; I paid Dave's dad and stood outside the entrance for a minute or two and took a few deep breaths. Once inside, the receptionist greeted me with a big smile. It was as if she recognized me, but I didn't recall ever meeting her. She stood up and shook my hand. I thought about the people at the airport. She walked me to the elevator and pushed the button for the outpatient surgery ward. When I exited the elevator, a woman greeted me, "Hi, Morgan; I'm Ginger's boss, Marcia. Come with me." It was becoming apparent that the receptionist had been waiting for me. Me being a day early wasn't fooling anyone.

Marcia showed me into her office and said, "Make yourself comfortable. Ginger will be back in a jiffy."

I laughed, "I assume she knows I'm here, then?"

"Oh yes, we've had the receptionist on alert in case you came home early. Ginger is a big asset to me; I couldn't run the outpatient surgery department without her. She'll be here in a second. Morgan, thank you so much for your service, and welcome home."

Finally, Ginger appeared. We hugged and kissed for the first time since R&R in December. Seeing her, feeling her in my arms, and absorbing her energy was a tonic.

Everything became clear; Vietnam was officially behind us.

"Come on. Let's get out of here!" she said as she grabbed her purse. "But first, I want you to meet the wonderful team of people I work with." We went to the break room, and she proudly introduced me to everyone. It was a little overwhelming; they all stood and clapped. Then, one by one, they hugged me and shook my hand, thanking me for my service. I was overwhelmed.

We took the elevator to the underground parking garage, which allowed us to make out a little. By the time the doors opened at parking level two, we were both more than eager to go straight home.

Ginger tried to hand me the keys to our car, "You drive."

"No, no, Mrs. Miller. The only thing I've driven in a year is a Jeep, and then only occasionally. I'll need to get used to city traffic gradually."

Pulling out of the parking garage, I shuffled across the bench seat and kissed her cheek. My hand was on her leg. The sexual tension was palpable.

After six blocks, she pulled into a Holiday Inn.

"What are you doing?" I asked.

"Well, I wasn't sure whether you'd want to go straight home, so I have a backup plan. I booked us a room. Apparently, I was right."

We checked-in; the man at the front desk just said, "Welcome, Mr. and Mrs. Miller. And thank you, sir, for your service." But his smile—that spoke volumes.

Our room was on the eighth floor. It was a typical Holiday Inn room, but to me, it was paradise. I walked out onto the balcony and took in the view of downtown La Mesa.

"This is nice."

Ginger held out her hand and pulled me back into the room. From her bag, she pulled a bottle of Dom Perignon wrapped in a plastic bag with melting ice, two champagne flutes that I recognized from our wedding, and some cheese and crackers.

"Wow!" I said. "I'm impressed; you certainly know how to welcome a guy home."

I grabbed an ice bucket and went in search of ice. When I returned, Ginger had moved our little feast to the balcony. We sat and toasted our future. She sat on my lap, nestled her face into my neck, and we sat silently. We didn't need words.

After a while, I told her how proud I was of her, how glad I was to be home, and that I was so thankful to have her in my life. I said that her audio tapes and cards were a lifeline to home and that my time in Vietnam would have been very lonely without them.

I took her hand and kissed it. "Thank you, thank you, my love."

The king-size bed beckoned, and we spent the rest of the afternoon in each other's arms.

As the sun got low in the sky, I said, "I'm starved."

She held me tight. "Let's meet our parents in El Cajon for dinner."

"Great idea."

She called both sets of parents with the same message, "I have him, and we will meet you at the Hungry Hunter."

We got dressed, me still in my army dress uniform. As we left the hotel, the manager smiled at me and winked.

Our parents were at the restaurant when we arrived. The first thing I did was hug my mom and kiss her on the cheek. It had been a tough year for her; she worried about me. "I made it, Mom!"

Our parents led the way into the restaurant, and heads turned. Maybe it was the warm smiles, the positive energy—or my dress uniform. As we sat, I said, "I can't tell you how wonderful it is to be home." Ginger laid her hand on my arm and gently squeezed it. A simple gesture, but it felt like I was finally safe.

The waitress came and took our drinks order. I asked for a Jack and Coke, my new favorite. Everyone's attention turned to the menus, and once again, I felt uneasy. "Are those people looking at me disapprovingly?" I asked my dad if he had noticed it.

"Son, don't let them bother you. The local media perpetuates anti-war rhetoric because we have the Navy's and Marine's basic training facility here."

"I felt the same thing at San Francisco Airport. What's with these people?"

"It's a minority, son. They're not bright enough to know that it's the government they should be targeting, not draftees like you."

I took his advice and focused on ordering my food. I didn't need to look at the menu; I wanted the prime rib. The waitress returned with a basket containing hot, black bread and took our orders. The first bite of black bread brought my senses home. Dad held his martini glass aloft, and I clinked it with my highball cocktail. His smile said it all—he had his son home and was happy.

I'd ordered a Caesar salad, and when it arrived, I thought of the difference between army food and what was sitting in front of me—no contest! The romaine lettuce was crisp; the dressing perfectly balanced with a subtle hint of anchovy. I savored every bite. I'd missed this restaurant, I'd missed home, and I'd missed my wife and family.

The conversation around me buzzed with excitement. We were lucky; both sets of parents got along famously. I looked at Ginger and winked; her smile melted my heart. A new waiter brought my medium-rare prime rib, with a baked potato, topped with butter, sour cream, and chives. Lightly steamed green beans, bright green against the white plate, completed the meal. I cut into my perfectly cooked prime rib. The first mouthful was heaven on earth; I closed my eyes, shook my head from side to side, and said, "Unbelievable."

I noticed that the conversation around the table had stopped. When I opened my eyes, everyone had been watching me savor that first bite. They all laughed and then started on their own food. During dinner, we didn't talk about Vietnam; the conversation drifted into a discussion about retirement, which was only a couple of years away for all four parents.

Hungry Hunters' famous cheesecake followed the main course, with a cup of delicious organic coffee. As the evening wore down, my dad asked for the bill. The waitress smiled and said, "The couple behind you took care of it, sir."

I was stunned, and as Dad got up to thank them, I joined him. The man said it was his honor; he had lost a grandson in Vietnam and wanted to thank me for my service. He stood, turned to face me, and clapped. It was as if the restaurant was collectively holding its breath. Then, several other diners stood and clapped, followed by more. I was humbled and grateful; it immediately made me smile. I had no time for those small-minded people who remained seated. Blame the government for taking us into war, but don't take it out on those that serve their country. I saluted the diners and then took a bow.

Afterward, the Good Samaritan came over to our table and told us he was a World War II Navy veteran, just like my father-in-law. Ginger's dad, Bill Palmer, and our new friend got into a conversation while the rest of us headed out to the parking lot.

I hugged my mom again and remembered to thank her for the stencil she created for our unit—crossed sabers with 3/17 in the center and the word GUNS below. I told her that our crew chiefs had used them to paint our unit insignia on each Cobra helicopter's pylon just below the main rotor. It meant a lot to us, I assured her.

I hugged my wonderful mother-in-law, kissed her on the cheek, and told her she was a classy lady. Finally, my father-in-law came out. There was another round of hugging before we said our final goodnights and drove off. In the car, I moved closer to Ginger, and she drove me home.

Once I had returned home, I expected life to resume its familiar rhythm, to seamlessly pick up where I had left off. However, Vietnam had left an indelible mark on my mind. Thoughts of the Cobra helicopters, their tail rotors, and hydraulic problems haunted me relentlessly. I couldn't shake the question of whether the mechanical faults that took the lives of so many brave men had been rectified.

In an effort to reintegrate, my parents threw a coming-home party for me, reuniting me with my aunt, uncle, grandmother, and cousin Robert. Yet, the gathering felt strange and distant. Conversations with old neighbors and close friends lacked their former familiarity. To my surprise, no one mentioned Vietnam, as if it were a subject forbidden, too painful to broach. I had anticipated being bombarded with questions, but the eerie silence was disconcerting. Ginger, ever perceptive, suggested they might fear stirring up traumatic memories, but I couldn't help but wonder if there was more to it.

Determined to pursue my dream of flying for a national airline, I visited Breise and Johnston Flying Services at Gillespie Field. Pat Hill, the school's chief pilot, informed me that Pacific Southwest Airlines required a minimum of 1,500 hours of airplane flight time, and I only had a meager 190 hours. He advised me to obtain my multi-engine, instrument, and airplane flight instructor ratings. The latter, he explained, would allow me to earn money while teaching others to fly and, in turn, accumulate the necessary flight hours. Seizing the opportunity, I utilized Food Basket's returning veteran policy of not having to return to work for sixty days. During those two months, I diligently acquired my instrument and multi-engine ratings. The flight instructor rating, however, would have to wait as economic realities compelled me to return to my job.

As the days passed, I came to realize that being a meat cutter no longer satisfied my aspirations. My heart yearned for the skies. I began to co-pilot with Pat, regularly ferrying bank checks and receipts from San Diego to Federal Reserve banks in the company's twin-engine Navajo. Yet, the more I delved into this flying life, the stronger my passion for aviation grew.

Years later, still working at Food Basket and now promoted to the head of the meat department, fate threw me a potential lifeline. An old high-school friend, Walt Kephart, informed me of a job in the Gulf of Alaska, transporting men and equipment to oil rigs. Flying Huey helicopters out of Merrill Field in Anchorage, I considered the prospect and, as luck would have it, Ginger's brother resided there. Taking a month's vacation, we ventured to Anchorage to explore the opportunity.

Maritime Aviation, the helicopter contractor, had a unique ten-days-on, ten-days-off rotation, allowing its pilots ample time to return home between shifts. But the job proved perilous, with hazardous flights over the Cook Inlet, landing on minuscule helicopter pads. After two rotations, I decided it was an unsustainable way to make a living. With Ginger by my side, we returned to our Southern California home and settled into our more conventional lifestyle.

My dreams of becoming a commercial airline pilot faced numerous setbacks, as the economy plunged into a tailspin. Airlines halted hiring, and Braniff Airlines shut down due to soaring fuel costs. Moreover, Boeing's adoption of computerization in their new aircraft rendered the flight engineer's role obsolete.

By 1982, my once-vibrant dream seemed out of reach. Turning to business studies, Ginger and I took a bold step and purchased a liquor store. The transition from pilot to retailer happened swiftly, and I found genuine satisfaction in this new venture. With enthusiasm, I expanded our inventory to include convenient food items, established a Deli, and introduced a check-cashing service, which bolstered sales and profitability. Joining the local chamber of commerce, I relished my involvement in the economic council. Retailing had become my new life challenge, a path I trod for the next two decades until we eventually sold our thriving business and retired.

In 2010, during our customary Christmas call, Captain Mac-Donald suggested that we meet at the A-Troop reunion in San Antonio, Texas. The event proved grand, with esteemed guests like Joe Galloway, the former Associated Press Correspondent who spoke eloquently of his experiences in L-Z Xray. Among the attendees were Dave Toms, Dave Bonello, and Mike Carothers. As the night wore on, Dave Toms and I delved deep into our memories of the Cobra Nighthawk missions we flew out of Quần Lợi in 1970. The bond forged in Vietnam, though four decades old, felt as strong as ever, as if those moments were but yesterday.

Still, I find myself grappling with the question of whether the loss of American lives in Vietnam was truly worth it. And perhaps even more importantly, will our country remain worthy of the sacrifices made by the 58,220 men who gave their lives? As I reflect on my journey from pilot to retailer, these ponderings linger, and I remain without a definitive answer.

**Henry Morgan Miller** (May 2023)

*Mike Billow and myself at the 1994 Vietnam Helicopter Pilots
Association reunion in Reno, Nevada.*

*My wife, Ginger and me.*

# ACKNOWLEDGMENTS

My book might have crumbled long ago were it not for my wife, Ginger, who served as my unwavering support while I embarked on the journey of reliving my experiences as a helicopter pilot in Vietnam. Through my recorded tapes, I delved into the intricacies of my life in Vietnam, a process that turned out to be far more challenging than I had anticipated but also astonishingly therapeutic, offering me profound psychological relief.

Furthermore, I owe a tremendous debt of gratitude to Judy Campbell, Mike Cook, Harry MacDonald, Dave Tela, Dave Toms, Mike Billow, Ed Marzola and Decker A. Decker for their input and my publisher, JuLee Brand. Without their invaluable assistance, this book would never have seen the light of day.

# AUTHOR BIO

**MORGAN MILLER** is a military veteran and retired liquor store owner from San Diego, California. He lives with his wife, Ginger, a retired nurse, in the serene desert community of Borrego Springs. In 2002, to escape the scorching summer heat, they drove their motorhome to Alaska. It was the first of many annual road trips crisscrossing America. During these leisurely cross-country vacations, Morgan listened to his much younger self recounting details of his year in Vietnam on a collection of fifty-two vintage Craig Reel-to-Reel tapes. Over several years, Morgan transcribed his audio letters to Ginger, containing the story of his wartime combat experiences, into a draft manuscript.

A decade later, with Ginger's support, a memoir took shape. However, the rigors of getting it ready for publication meant the draft manuscript languished in the backwater of his computer until 2022, when Ginger once again encouraged him to dust it off and find a professional to help take the promising memoir to the next level.

Typing "ghostwriter" into Google, thousands of results immediately appeared. However, one name stood out from the masses: an experienced ghostwriter living in Canada. It only took one phone call for a bond to form between the two men. As the co-author of an award-winning military memoir, *Fire from the Sky: A Diary Over Japan*, this writer possessed the perfect qualifications to skillfully transform Morgan's factual yet mundane narrative into an exhilarating and gripping memoir.

Made in United States
Orlando, FL
27 August 2024

50804400R10205